Trekking in the
Nepal Himalaya

Trekking in the Nepal Himalaya
4th edition

Published by
Lonely Planet Publications
PO Box 88, South Yarra, Victoria 3141, Australia
PO Box 2001A, Berkeley, California 94703, USA

Printed by
Colorcraft, Hong Kong

This edition
October 1985

Photographs by
colour photos by Stan Armington & Kalyan Singh
black & white photos by Stan Armington, except pg 71 by Marcus Brooke and pg 159 by Singh Photo, Kathmandu

National Library of Australia
Cataloguing in Publication Data

Armington, Stan
Trekking in the Nepal Himalaya

4th ed.
Bibliography.
Includes index.
ISBN 0 908086 66 0.

1. Nepal — Description and travel — Guide-books. 2. Himalaya mountains — Description and travel — Guide-books. I. Title

915.49'604

Copyright © Stan Armington, 1985

Stan Armington has been organising and leading treks in Nepal since 1971. A graduate engineer, he has also worked for the US National Park Service in the Yellowstone and Olympic parks, as well as serving as a guide on Mt Hood in Oregon. Stan is a fellow of the Royal Geographical Society, a member of the American Alpine Club, the Explorers' Club, and the Alpine Stomach Club. He lives in Kathmandu where he runs a trekking company.

A word of thanks to the many people who encouraged and assisted me with writing this material. Lewis Underwood, Bob Gibbons, Bob Pierce, Chuck McDougal, Charles Gay, Bill Jones, Dana Keil, Anoop Rana, Harka Gurung and Tek Pokharel provided information about recent changes, places I have not been or things I did not understand and checked many facts for accuracy. Hundred of trekkers have helped me by asking questions that I would never have otherwise thought of; I have tried to answer most of them here.

A trekking book could never be written without the help of many Sherpas who led me up and down hills and patiently answered all my foolish questions about what we were seeing. Tsering Ongchu, Ang Tsering, Pemba, Tsering Ongdi and Ila Tsering helped with this edition. Prins Bharati typed the entire book and Utpal Sengupta assisted with some of the passages. Chris Kolisch and Kalyan Singh supplemented my photo collection with their professional work and David Shlim's medical chapter provides a first class analysis of the medical problems of a trek. Most of all, thanks to Tony Wheeler who pushed me to tackle this project and who continues to provide suggestions on how to improve it.

Despite the common plural usage, the Himalaya are singular – as you will find them throughout the text and, at last, on the cover.

Thanks to Cambridge University Press for permission to quote four lines from *Nepal Himalaya* by H W Tilman.

Corrections or suggestions can be sent to Stan Armington at Himalayan Journeys, PO Box 989, Kathmandu, Nepal.

Contents

Contents

Preface

To travel in the remote areas of Nepal today offers much more than superb mountain scenery. It provides an opportunity to step back in time and meet people who, like our ancestors many centuries ago, lived free of complications, social, economic and political, which beset the developed countries. To the Nepal peasant, his life revolves around his homestead, his fields and, above all, his family and neighbours in the little village perched high on a Himalayan mountainside. Here we can see the meaning of community, free of the drive of competition. We see human happiness despite – or because of – the absence of amenities furnished by our modern civilisation.

Change will come to the Nepalese way of life, but it behoves travellers from the modernised countries to understand and respect the values and virtues of life today in rural Nepal. They have much to teach us about how to live.

John Hunt

Lord Hunt was the leader of the 1953 Mt Everest expedition when the peak was first scaled by Sir Edmund Hillary and Tenzing Norgay Sherpa.

Introduction

The Himalaya, the 'abode of snows', extends from Assam in eastern India west to Afghanistan. It is a chain of the highest and youngest mountains on earth, and it encompasses a region of deep religious and cultural traditions and an amazing diversity of people. Nowhere is this diversity more apparent and the culture more varied and interesting than in Nepal. This book concentrates on trekking in Nepal. Treks in the Himalaya of India, Pakistan and China, while the traditions may be similar to those described here, are not quite the same sort of experience as a trek in Nepal.

This book is designed to help you prepare for a trek. The first section provides some background information about Nepal and trekking, and describes some alternative methods by which you may trek. The second part provides detailed information about how to prepare yourself and your gear and cope with the details of arranging a trek, and the third section describes the important trekking regions of Nepal and gives day-to-day descriptions of the best routes through these regions.

A trek in Nepal is a special and rewarding mountain holiday; do not lose sight of this fact as you read about the possible problems you may encounter and formalities you must observe in order to trek. They sound worse here than they really are. If you trek on your own, remember that during a trek you will be pretty far from western civilization (and that includes medical care, communication facilities and any transport except your own two feet) no matter how many local hotels or other facilities may exist. It is only prudent to take the same precautions during a trek in Nepal that you would take on a major hiking or climbing trip at home.

Nepal has attracted trekkers, tourists and mountaineers ever since she opened her borders for the first time in 1950. It was a hippy mecca in the '50s and the early '60s because of the availability of high quality marijuana and hashish. These are now illegal in Nepal, but the remnants of that crowd still hang around Kathmandu and patronise a few black market dope dealers. Kathmandu's 'Freak Street' has become as much a tourist attraction as the temples of Durbar Square. A particularly important element of living this life style is an attempt to live as cheaply as possible. This, coupled with the tradition of 'getting back to the land', has resulted in many westerners trekking through Nepal on an extremely limited budget.

Tourism is Nepal's major industry, and one of the largest sources of the foreign exchange necessary for the continued economic development of the kingdom. Tourists are encouraged to visit Nepal because they spend money. While it is important that you spend this money wisely and in places where it may have a useful economic impact, it is important to Nepal's tourist industry that you do spend some money there. Even the poorest porter in the hills buys an occasional cup of tea from local inns and purchases rice from villagers. The people in the hills expect to gain a bit of income from every traveller. This book makes some suggestions on how you can arrange a trek in a manner that is economically beneficial to both you and Nepal with a minimum of hassles no matter what style of trekking you choose.

The information here is based on my own experiences in trekking, leading and organising treks, and living in Nepal since 1970. Based on these experiences, I have included a lot of material that is my own opinion, particularly concerning equipment. If you have done a lot of hiking you will

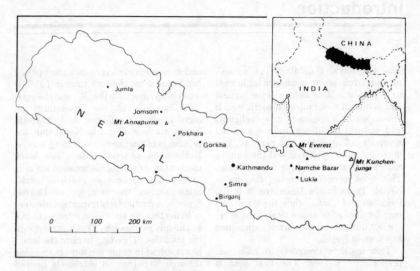

have certainly developed your own preferences in equipment and technique. Since my opinions are the distillation of my own experiences on a particular type of outdoor trip, they may easily differ from yours. Read my suggestions about equipment – then make your own decisions.

I have tried to present an unbiased picture of the alternative styles of trekking that are possible in Nepal. There has been a tremendous increase and improvement in hotel facilities in the hills since the last edition of this book. This has made trekking much more comfortable on the main routes, though some of the so-called hotels are pretty rough. Remember that these new facilities exist primarily on the routes that are used by lots of trekkers; in remote regions and on unusual routes, the local inns are still primitive by any standards. Remember too, that you will be far from western medical care and assistance; you must be self-sufficient in this regard. Dr Shlim's medical chapter can assist you here. There will often be nobody but your own companions to help you if you are sick or injured.

This book is used by people of various means and temperaments. As you read it,

be aware that others are not like you and that there are many ways to approach a trek. If you have booked a group trek, you may be amazed that there is any need to discuss the relative merits of carrying a sleeping bag. If you are a budget trekker, you may find this discussion useful, but will find it preposterous that anyone would consider paying from US$50 upwards per person, per day to trek. There is room for both of these attitudes (and a lot in between) in Nepal and you will certainly meet 'the other half' during your trek. This book is your introduction to these diverse opinions and styles.

I have tried to avoid preaching throughout the text about how to behave on a trek. Obviously, you should pay for what you eat and drink, bury your faeces, minimise the amount of firewood that you consume, respect local customs and attitudes and try to interact gently with Nepal. Some trekkers do not do this, and it is unlikely that anything said here will change that. If you are overcharged, abused, refused food or accommodation, insulted or disgusted by filthy hotels, campsites and latrines, it is because someone (probably the person who spent last night there) contributed to the problem. You have the choice of continuing to escalate the mess or doing your own small part to make Nepal more pleasant for those who follow you.

A note on trekking that may help you understand it better at the outset: a trek in Nepal is many days long. A 'long' trek is four or more weeks; a 'short' trek is at least a week or 10 days. These terms conflict with our preconceptions of backpacking or hiking where a short hike may only be for a few hours and a long hike is a three-day weekend.

What is a Trek?

WHY TREK IN NEPAL?

Just as New York is not representative of the United States, so Kathmandu is not representative of Nepal. If you can take the time and have the energy to trek, you should not miss the opportunity to leave Kathmandu and observe the spectacular beauty and the unique culture of Nepal. Fortunately for the visitor to Nepal there are still only a few roads extending deeply into the hills, so the kingdom must be visited in the slowest and most intimate manner – by walking. The time and effort required for this mode of transportation certainly is greater than other ways, but then the rewards are correspondingly greater. Instead of zipping down a freeway, racing to the next 'point of interest', each step provides new and intriguing viewpoints, and you will perceive your day as an entity, rather than a few highlights strung together by a ribbon of concrete. For the romanticist, each step is a step in the footsteps of Hillary, Tenzing, Herzog and other Himalayan explorers. If you have neither the patience nor the physical stamina to visit the hills of Nepal on foot, aircraft and helicopters are available, providing an expensive and unsatisfactory substitute.

Trekking in Nepal will take you through a country that has captured the imagination of mountaineers and explorers for over a hundred years. You will encounter people in remote mountain villages whose lifestyle has not changed in generations, yet they will convey a trust of foreigners that is made possible by their secure position as one of only a handful of countries in the world that has never been ruled by a foreign power.

A trek also provides a glimpse into the ancient culture of Tibet. This culture has all but disappeared in its homeland, and is now rapidly being altered in Nepal by the influx of tourism and foreign aid.

On a trek you will see great diversity throughout Nepal. Villages embrace many ethnic groups and cultures, and the terrain changes from tropical jungles to high glaciated peaks in only 150 km. From the start, the towering peaks of the Himalaya provide one of the highlights of a trek. Appearing first as many clouds on the horizon as your plane approaches Kathmandu, they become more definable and reach to seemingly impossible heights as you finally land at Kathmandu's Tribhuvan airport. During a trek the Himalaya disappears behind Nepal's continual hills, but dominates the northern skyline at each pass – Annapurna, Langtang, Gauri Shankar and Everest. Finally, after weeks of walking, you will arrive at the foot of the mountains themselves – astonishing heights from which gigantic avalanches tumble earthwards in apparent slow motion, dwarfed by their surroundings. Your conception of the Himalaya alters as you turn from peaks famed only for their height to gaze on far more picturesque summits that you have never before heard of: Kantega, Ama Dablam, Machhapuchhare and Kumbhakarna.

A TREK IS NOT A WILDERNESS EXPERIENCE

The landscape of Nepal is almost continually inhabited. The majority of Nepal's population live, not in the cities, but in tiny villages that seemingly blanket the hills. Even in the high mountains, small settlements of stone houses and yak pastures dot every possible flat space. Much of the fascination of a trek is derived from the opportunity to observe life in these villages, where people truly live off the land, using only a few manufactured items such as soap, kerosene, paper and matches, all of which are imported in bamboo baskets carried by barefoot porters.

It is difficult for most westerners to comprehend this aspect of Nepal until they actually visit the kingdom. Our preconception of a roadless area is strongly influenced by the places we backpack or hike at home – true wilderness, usually protected as a national park or forest. In the roadless areas of Nepal, there is little wilderness up to an elevation of 4000 metres. The average population density in Nepal is more than 98 people per square km, and if this statistic is altered to eliminate all the mountainous places, the average rises to an incredible 525 or more persons per square km of cultivated land. The size and type of rural settlements varies widely, but most villages have from 15 to 75 houses, a population of 200 to 1000, and are spread out over an area of several square km.

Many of the values associated with a hiking trip at home do not have the same importance during a trek in Nepal. It is impossible to get completely away from people, except for short times or at extremely high elevations, though isolation is traditionally a crucial element of any wilderness experience. The concept of ecology must be expanded to include the effects of conservation measures on rural people and the economic effects of tourism on indigenous populations. Even National Park management must be modified because there are significant population centres within Sagarmatha (Mt Everest) and Langtang National Parks.

Rather than detract from the enjoyment of a trek, the hill people, particularly their traditional hospitality and fascinating culture, make a trek in Nepal a special kind of mountain holiday unlike any other in the world.

A TREK IS NOT A CLIMBING TRIP

Whether you begin your trek at a roadhead or fly into a remote mountain airstrip, a large part of your trek will be in the middle hills region at elevations between 500 and 3000 metres. In this region, there are always well-developed trails through villages and across mountain passes. Even at high altitudes there are intermittent settlements used in the summer by herders, so the trails, though often indistinct, are always there. All trails are easily traversed without the aid of ropes or any mountaineering skill. There are rare occasions when snow is encountered, and on some high passes it might be necessary to place a safety line for your companions or porters if there is deep snow, but alpine techniques are almost never used on a traditional trek. Anyone who has walked extensively in the mountains has all the skills necessary for an extended trek in Nepal.

Though some treks venture near glaciers, and even cross the foot of them, most treks do not allow the fulfillment of any Himalayan mountaineering ambitions. Nepal's complicated mountaineering regulations allow trekkers to climb 18 specified peaks with a minimum of formality, but a few advance arrangements must still be made for such climbs. Many agents offer 'climbing treks' which include the ascent of one of these peaks as a feature of a trek and there are a few peaks that, under ideal conditions, are within the resources of individual trekkers. A climb can be arranged in Kathmandu if conditions are right, but for more difficult peaks it should be planned well in advance. This is discussed in greater detail in the section on climbing, later in this book.

The beauty and attraction of the Nepal Himalaya emanates not only from the mountains themselves, but also in their surroundings: friendly people, picturesque villages and a great variety of cultures and traditions that seem to exemplify many of the attributes we have lost in our headlong rush for development and progress in the west. While the ascent of a Himalayan peak may be an attraction for some, it is not necessary to have such a goal to enjoy a trek. Throughout this book, trekking always refers to walking on trails.

A TREK REQUIRES PHYSICAL EFFORT

A trek is physically demanding because of its length and the almost unbelievable changes in elevation. During the 300 km trek to and from the Everest base camp, for example, over 9000 metres of elevation are gained and lost during many steep ascents and descents. On most treks, the daily gain is less than 800 metres in about 15 km, though ascents of as much as 1200 metres are typical of some days. You can always take plenty of time during the day to cover this distance, so the physical exertion, though quite strenuous at times, is not sustained. You can always take plenty of time for rest. Probably the only physical problem that may make a trek impossible is a history of knee problems on descents. In Nepal the descents are long, steep and unrelenting. There is hardly a level stretch of trail in the entire kingdom. You should be in the best possible physical condition before beginning a trek. If you are an experienced walker and often hike 15 km a day with a pack, a trek should prove no difficulty. You will be pleasantly surprised at how easy the hiking can be if you only carry a light rucksack and do not have to worry about meal preparation.

Previous experience in hiking and living outdoors is, however, helpful as you make plans for your trek. The first night of a month-long trip is too late to discover that you do not like to sleep in a sleeping bag. Mountaineering experience is not necessary, but you must enjoy walking.

The Hill Country of Nepal

GEOGRAPHY

Nepal is a small landlocked country 800 km long and 200 km wide. In the longitudinal 200 km, the terrain changes from the glaciers along the Tibetan border to the flat jungles of the *terai* on the Indian border, barely 150 metres above sea level. The country does not ascend gradually from the plains; instead it rises in several chains of hills that lie in an east-west direction, finally terminating in the highest hills in the world – the Himalaya. Beyond the Himalaya is the 5000-metre-high plateau of Tibet. The Himalaya is not a continental divide; a number of rivers flow from Tibet through the mountains and hills of Nepal to join the Ganges in India. These are joined en route by many other rivers flowing southward from the glaciers of the Nepal Himalaya itself. The country, then, is scarred by great gorges in both the north-south and east-west directions, resulting in a continual series of hills, some incredibly steep.

Kathmandu lies in the largest valley of the kingdom – according to legend it was once a huge lake. This valley is connected to the outside world by narrow mountain roads running north to China and south to India. Nepal is undergoing a major roadbuilding programme and extensive construction is underway everywhere. There is a new East-West Highway that runs near the Indian border and the old Tribhuvan Rajpath has been made almost redundant by the new road along the Narayani River from Mugling to Narayanghat. There are many new roads that wind their way into the hills, but once these end all travel is on a system of trails that climb the steep hills of Nepal as no road possibly can.

The southernmost region includes the *terai*, the flat plain which was, until 1950, a malarial jungle inhabited primarily by rhinoceros, tiger, leopard, wild boar and deer. Now, with malaria controlled, a large number of farming and industrial communities cover the *terai*. The southern region also includes the first major east-west chain of hills: the Siwalik hills and the Mahabharat range. In some parts of Nepal these hills are inhabited only by farmers, but in others they are the sites of large and well-developed villages.

The midlands or middle hills, a band only 60 km wide, is the most populated region. This is the home of the ancient Nepalese people. The cities of Kathmandu, Patan, Bhaktapur, Pokhara, the ancient town of Gorkha (from which the word 'Gurkha' – a name given to the Nepalese who enlisted in the British and Indian Armies – was derived) and Jumla, in the far west of Nepal, are all within this region. Other than the Kathmandu and Pokhara valleys, the midland region is hilly and steep. Extensive farming takes place on thousands of ancient terraces carved into the hills.

The Himalayan foothills and the Himalaya itself comprise only a small portion of the kingdom along the northern border. This inhospitable region is the least inhabited part of Nepal. Most of the villages sit between 3000 and 4000 metres elevation, although there are summer settlements as high as 5000 metres. Winters here are cold, but the warm sun makes most days comfortable. Because of the short growing season, crops are few and usually small, consisting mostly of potatoes, barley and a few vegetables. The primary means of support is trading and the herding of sheep, cattle and yaks. Part of this region, Solu-Khumbu, is inhabited by Sherpas; much of the economy of this area is influenced by mountaineering expeditions and trekking.

From east to west the kingdom is divided into regions that are less clearly defined, although the political division is

GANESH HIMAL MANASLU ANNAPURNA DHAULAGIRI 23750 FT. 7246 M. | LANGTANG-LIRUNG 26150 FT. 8013 M. | GOSAINTHAN 22870 FT. 6975 M. | DORJE-LAKPA 21840 FT. 6660 M. | PHURBI-GHYACHU 19550 FT. 5970 M. | CHHOBA-BHAMARE 19550 FT. 5970 M. | GAURI-SHANKAR 23442 FT. 7145 M. | MELUNGTSE 23560 FT. 7181 M. | CHUGIMAGO 20660 FT. 6297 M.

KATHMANDU 4423 FT. 1350 M.

KODARI 5800 FT. 1770 M. ROAD TO LHASSA

east to west, not from north to south. The primary difference between eastern and western Nepal is that the influence of the monsoon is less in the west. In the east the climate is damp and ideal for tea growing, the conditions being similar to Darjeeling in India. In the far west the climate is quite dry, even during the monsoon season. Another influence on the east-west division is the large rivers that flow southward in deep canyons, often limiting travel as they wash away bridges during monsoon. For this reason the major trade routes are south to north, allowing manufactured goods from India to be carried via the shortest route to hill villages.

PEOPLE OF THE HILLS

Nepal has a population of more than 16 million, but only 800,000 live in the Kathmandu Valley. The rest of the people live in the flat *terai* or in the hills and except for a few manufacturing centres, their economy is dominated by agriculture. In the hill regions, every possible piece of land is cultivated except where the hillsides are too steep or rocky to carve out even the smallest terrace. Pressure from the increasing population is forcing people to bring even the most marginal land into cultivation; this is resulting in erosion, flooding and landslides. Extensive systems of trenches and canals provide the irrigation necessary for food production. Houses are built near a family's fields, so a typical Nepalese village extends over a large area and may have an elevation differential of several hundred metres or

more between the highest and lowest homes.

Most Nepalese families are self-sufficient in their food supply, raising all of it themselves and selling the excess in the few places, such as Kathmandu, Pokhara, Biratnagar, Janakpur and Birganj, that do not have a strictly agricultural economy. In return, the villagers purchase the items that they are not able to raise or produce themselves: sugar, soap, cigarettes, tea, salt, cloth and jewellery. This exchange of goods creates a significant amount of traffic between remote villages and the larger population and manufacturing centres throughout Nepal. In the roadless hill areas, goods are transported by porters carrying bamboo baskets with a tumpline across their foreheads. During the many days they travel, porters either camp alongside the trail and eat food that they have carried with them from home, or purchase food and shelter from homes along the trail. There are occasional tea shops, called *bhattis*, but porters rarely patronise them for more than an occasional cup of tea, because prices in *bhattis* are much higher than sharing an already-prepared meal with a family. Often porters travel in groups and take turns cooking food that they carry themselves, thus securing a substantial saving in the cost of travel.

The most typical meal for hill porters is a thick paste called *dhindo*, made from coarse ground corn or millet, often mixed with a few hot chillis. In the northern regions this is replaced by *tsampa*,

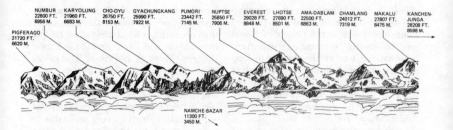

roasted and ground barley which is mixed with buttered and salted Tibetan tea. The most common meal in Nepal is *daal bhaat*; rice (*bhaat*) with a soup made of lentils (*daal*) poured over it, but this is more expensive than *tsampa*. Rarely is meat or an egg included in the local diet; protein is gained from *daal*. Unleavened bread (*roti* or *chappati*) is another frequent addition to a meal, often substituting for rice. Other items may supplement a meal, usually a curry made from potatoes or whatever vegetables are available locally.

Second to the transportation of goods is the flow of people between the warmer climates of the *terai* and the colder Himalayan regions, including both people on seasonal migrations and people moving permanently because of the pressures of increasing population in the hills. People also travel extensively in connection with weddings, funerals, festivals, school, and government or military business. Several of the hundreds of festivals that occur annually in Nepal require that people visit the homes of their relatives. Of particular importance is the *Dasain* festival in October, during which thousands of people travel from urban centres to hill villages. Those who travel during these times are from a wide variety of economic backgrounds, so their mode of travel may range from trailside camps similar to those of porters to service by an entire household staff. It is certainly rare, but not impossible, to see a woman being carried by a porter in a sedan chair or basket. Men who were born in hill villages

and served in a Gurkha regiment in the British or Indian army often return home on leave, or upon retirement, with a huge retinue of porters carrying items they have collected during their assignments in Singapore, Hong Kong, Brunei or England.

Therefore, a wide variety of modes of travel exists on the trails of Nepal, influenced almost exclusively by one's economic and social position. Whatever his means of travel and whatever his economic status, a traveller makes a direct contribution to the economy of most villages through which he travels. In some cases, it is the purchase of food; in others it is the sale of necessary goods or services; and in others it is the hire of local people to serve as porters for a few days. The inhabitants of villages situated along major trails have come to expect and depend on this economic contribution – in much the same way as our cafes, road-houses, motels and petrol stations rely on travellers of all sorts to provide their income.

Another phenomenon that occurs in the hills is people coming into continual personal contact. There are no trail signs, few hotel signs and no maps available locally. No matter how shy a person may be, he must continually ask for directions, help in finding food and other items, and information about places to stay, how far it is to the next village, and so on. This is a habit that many of us have lost in the west. We rely on the isolation of our car to insulate us from strangers; we rarely need to ask directions because of the abundance of road signs and maps; we can easily shop in a supermarket without speaking a word to anyone. Because the people of Nepal are constantly exchanging important information, it often develops into long exchanges of pure conversation or useless information ('what time is it?' 'What are you carrying in that basket?'); a traveller may spend an hour or two discussing trail conditions, where he has been, politics, the weather, crop conditions, the price of rice in a neighbouring village, who is married (and who isn't, but should be), who died recently, or hundreds of other topics with a complete stranger whom he may never meet again. This is an important part of life in the hills. There are no telephones, no newspapers, no televisions and few radios. Most of the news comes from travellers. It certainly is more interesting to hear firsthand experiences than the radio news broadcast. Once the crops are planted for the season there isn't much to do, beyond the day-to-day activities of housecleaning, cooking and taking care of children, until harvest time. Besides their economic importance, travellers are valued as a diversion, a source of information and a glimpse into a new and different world.

HOTELS IN THE HILLS

Local inns or *bhattis* have existed for centuries in the hills. A *bhatti* usually has a simple mud stove with a pot of milk and another pot of hot water to make tea and caters mostly to local porters as they pass by. There is usually a jug or two of alcoholic *chhang* or *rakshi* in the back room to provide a bit of diversion for the village elders and the few overnight guests who happen along. As trekking increased and as Nepali travelers began to have a bit more money, these inns expanded into the extensive system of hotels that now exists on the major trekking routes.

The primary incentive that people have for operating a hotel is to turn locally produced food, labour and firewood into cash. The hills of Nepal are increasingly

becoming a cash-oriented society, and there are few ways to earn this cash, other than operating a hotel, that allow people to remain at home and tend to the house, children, livestock and crops. The prices in most hotels in the hills are artificially cheap for this reason. Intense competition and the lack of an alternative way to secure cash keeps prices ridiculously low – it certainly cannot be very profitable to sell a cup of tea with sugar for 50 paisa (about 3 cents) when sugar is Rs 8 per kg, tea is 18 rupees per ¼ kg packet and it takes a full day to fetch a load of firewood.

With few exceptions, hotels in the hills are family-run affairs that started in the living room. Some, as you can read in the in the trekking route reports, have expanded into separate quarters, or even separate buildings, but most are still living-room affairs in which the family that operates the inn eats and sleeps in the same room that is offered to guests. Only since the mid-1970s have trekkers become an important source of income for hotels in the hills. Most of the hotels that cater to trekkers were started after 1979 or 1980; some of these have obtained government loans and have become quite grand. These establishments are well known and all have English language signboards. A *bhatti*, (small local inn), is also easy to recognise – it is usually a wooden or even bamboo building as close to the trail as possible, with the large house of the owners situated some distance away.

Hotels are often operated by wives and children, and when the man of the house is away trading or working as a porter or trekking guide, the family usually lives in the hotel, not in their own larger house. Sometimes hotels are left in the care of children; some pretty wierd meals and service can result when a six or eight-year old tries to deal with customers! Some hotels offer a separate place to sleep, but in many only the communal living space is available. In remote areas that are not frequented by trekkers, the 'hotel' may exist only in the mind of the proprietor and will consist of sharing the eating and living accommodation with a family.

A NEPALESE VIEW OF FOREIGNERS

Although Nepal has been accessible to foreigners only since 1950, there are few places in the kingdom that have not been visited by either trekkers, photographers, expeditions or foreign aid representatives. Foreigners, particularly light-skinned westerners, stand out readily in Nepal, and are viewed by the Nepalese according to the stereotype created by those who have preceded them. They too will contribute to the image of the next westerners who happen to come along.

Unfortunately, the image which has predominated is one of great wealth and a superior culture which westerners wish to share with the Nepalese. Such traditions as passing out balloons, candy and pens to kids contribute to this view, but it is on a far grander level that the real image has been developed. Mountaineering expeditions have spent seemingly limitless sums of money for porters, sherpas and equipment, including much fine gear for the high altitude sherpas. At the conclusion of an expedition, the excess food and gear is usually given away – this being cheaper than repacking and shipping it home. This type of extravagance, even though it is often supported by foundations and other large organisations, not by the expedition members themselves, leads many Nepalese to believe, justifiably, that westerners have a huge amount of money and will simply pass it out to whomever makes the most noise. An interesting by-product of this phenomenon is that all sorts of used mountaineering gear in Kathmandu was once sold at ridiculously low prices – because nobody in Nepal ever had to pay for it. A Nepalese received it as a gift, or bought it for a very cheap price and then sold it for whatever he could get. Now, however, prices are the same – or higher – than in the west because shopkeepers have seen equipment catalogues and

charge according to the retail prices for new items.

The sherpas and other Nepalis who dealt with trekkers and expeditions quickly discovered that the airfare to Nepal from America, Europe or Australia is more than US$1000, which is an astronomical amount of money. No matter how small a trekker's budget may be, he was still able to get to Nepal. The Nepalis know this and are generally unable to accept a plea of poverty from someone who, according to their standards, has already spent the equivalent of about two years wages, or enough money to build three large houses. It is impossible to explain the difference in our relative economic positions to a Nepali in the hills. We ourselves find it difficult to comprehend that a dollar buys the equivalent of more than 10 dollars in Nepal.

Many trekkers and expedition members in the past have given huge tips to sherpas. Reports of US$100 tips are not unheard of; one group tipped each of three sherpas US$40 for a six-day trek (for which their total salary was only US$10). This type of extravagance not only forces up wages, resulting in higher demands on the next trekker or expedition, but also contributes to an unhealthy view of westerners as rich, lavish and foolish. It makes it difficult for an individual on a tight budget to convince Nepalese people that he cannot afford outrageous salaries, tips or huge amounts of food during a trek.

Well-intentioned trekkers often over-react to the needs of porters and sherpas on treks and provide an exorbitant amount of free equipment to their staff. This is certainly kind and generous, and porters do need to be equipped with warm shoes, clothing and goggles when they are travelling into the mountains. Many trekkers overdo this, however, and it is becoming increasingly common for porters to demand fancy new equipment which they then sell (and in order to keep the gear in pristine condition, they pack it away and use their own old blankets to keep warm). Porters need protection and attention, but many trekkers have gone far beyond what is necessary and are creating unreasonable expectations in the minds of many porters and making it difficult and expensive to hire them, especially in the Annapurna region.

A number of schools, hospitals, roads, and electric and water projects have been built in Nepal. These facilities are largely supported by contributions from organisations of the western world, although a great effort has been made to require contributions of local labour and money. These unquestionably perform a great service and are sorely needed, but this method of financing does help to sustain the preconception of a westerner as a person with a huge amount of money with which he will readily part if he is approached with sufficient cleverness. Many trekkers, feeling a strong affinity for villagers or sherpas they have met, have supported the education of children or even provided free overseas trips for them. This practice is certainly worthwhile and kind, but it does encourage Nepalese people to actively seek such favours in their dealings with westerners.

Nor is the problem confined to the hills and the efforts of some thoughtless individuals. Many nations, eager to have a foothold in what they feel is a strategic part of the world, contribute vast sums of money to aid programmes in Nepal. Such programmes might not contribute further to an unhealthy view of westerners (and would undoubtedly do more good) if they did not also support the westerners who work for them in lavish style. Many foreigners live in Kathmandu and other places in Nepal in conditions similar to their western homes, eating food flown from home at their own government's expense and being served by more servants than they could conceive of at home.

Most foreigners carry with them an astonishing array of camera gear, tape recorders and other gadgetry. It's obvious that these things are expensive, even by western standards. Yet a surprisingly large number of people seem to have no care for this wealth and leave cameras behind on rocks or give their watches away at the conclusion of a trek. Not only can we afford to buy such expensive things, but we don't even take care of them. Compare this attitude to that of the porter carrying a double load of 60 kg to make more money or the sherpa kitchen boy with patched and repatched jeans, shoes and rucksack.

This is the westerner with whom the Nepali is familiar. They may also recognise the qualities of sincerity, happiness or fun, but the primary quality they see is wealth. Many Nepalese consider it their personal obligation to separate a share of a westerner's money from him by calling on his sense of fair play, through trickery or blackmail (a porter's strike in a remote location), through shrewdness or even outright thievery. Westerners are stuck with this image, no matter what they do personally to dispel it, and an appreciation of this situation is very helpful in developing an understanding of local attitudes during a trek in Nepal.

A NOTE ABOUT SHERPAS

There are a great number of ethnic groups in Nepal. Although the Sherpas are the most famous of these groups, they form only a tiny part of the total population and live in a small and inhospitable region of the kingdom. Sherpas first came into prominence when a number of them were hired for the 1921 reconnaissance of Mt Everest from the Tibetan side. The expedition started from Darjeeling, India, where a number of Sherpas were living, so it was not necessary to travel into then forbidden Nepal to hire them. Later expeditions, impressed by the performance of Sherpas at high altitudes and their selfless devotion to their jobs, continued the tradition of hiring Sherpas as high altitude porters. Most of the hiring was done in Darjeeling or by messages sent

Tenzing Norgay Sherpa

into the Solu Khumbu region of Nepal (where most Sherpas live) through friends and relatives.

The practice continues to the present day with a number of trekking organisations hiring Sherpas as permanent employees, and others hiring them on a per-trek basis. The emphasis has been shifted from Darjeeling to Kathmandu and to the Solu Khumbu region itself as these areas have become accessible to foreigners.

It is confusing to discuss the roles of sherpas on an expedition or a trek. The word 'sherpa' can refer both to an ethnic group and to a function or job on a trek. The job of 'sherpa' implies someone who is reasonably experienced in dealing and communicating with westerners, and who often speaks some English. A sherpa has a good knowledge of his job: either cook, kitchen boy (a job increasingly performed by Sherpa women, but the job title has not been desexed in Nepal), sardar (head sherpa on a trek, who is responsible for all purchases and for hiring porters), guide or high altitude porter. The term also implies a knowledge of the region a trek will visit. A sherpa acts as as guide in the lowlands, asking directions from the locals, if necessary, to find the best trail to a destination.

The term sherpa does not, however, imply any technical mountaineering skill. Sherpas, although they live near the high Himalayan peaks, never set foot on them, except to cross high passes on trade routes, until the British began to introduce the sport of mountaineering. Many trekking sherpas have served as high-altitude porters on mountaineering expeditions, carrying loads along routes already established by technically proficient mountaineers, but it is only in the past few years that sophisticated mountaineering training has been made available to Nepalese at the Nepal Mountaineering Association school in Manang.

The term 'Sherpa' with a capital 'S' refers to members of that ethnic group.

On a trek or expedition, the role of 'sherpa' (without that capital 'S') is generally fulfilled by a Sherpa, but there are many exceptions from this tradition. Sambhu Tamang, who reached the summit of Everest with the Italian expedition in 1973, was the first non-Sherpa Nepalese to reach the summit of a major Himalayan peak. In this book the words sherpa and guide are used interchangably, while 'Sherpa' always refers to members of that ethnic group.

A porter is a person who carries loads and whose job is completed once camp is reached. The job of a sherpa, on the contrary, is just beginning once the group is in camp. A porter may be a member of any ethnic group. Many Rais, Tamangs and Magars spend almost their entire lives on the trail serving as porters, not only for trekkers, but also bringing supplies to remote hill villages. On an expedition the term 'high-altitude porter' is often used interchangeably with 'sherpa' to denote those who are carrying loads to high camps on the mountain.

On the subject of nomenclature: a western (or Japanese) man is a *sahib* (pronounced 'sob'), a western woman is *memsahib*, and a porter is a *coolie*. These terms no longer hold the derogatory implications that they did during the British Raj. In a peculiar turnabout, a trekker on his own is called by the locals a 'tourist', and someone with a trekking group is called a 'member'.

Sherpas are frequently named after the day of the week on which they were born. Sunday is Nima, and the following days are Dawa, Mingma, Lakpa, Phurba, Passang and Pemba. Often the prefix Ang is added to the name; this is similar to the English suffix – son or Jr. Ang Nima would be called 'Nima' for short, never 'Ang'.

Because the Sherpa economy has become highly dependent on tourism, and many Sherpas have developed western-style tastes and values, wages and other costs are often higher – and non-negotiable – in areas of Sherpa influence. This has given Sherpas the reputation amongst many independent trekkers for being rather grasping and difficult to deal with. Once you agree to fees and conditions, or if you have a trekking agent or trekking shop to do the negotiating for you, you will generally find them charming and helpful. In Sherpa-run hotels the prices are usually fixed and not subject to bargaining.

Styles of Trekking

There are hundreds of alternatives to bushwalking or hiking in the west – from the 'go light' backpacker who carries but five kilograms for a weekend trip, through the surplus store backpacker who hauls an axe and a cast iron skillet, to the technical climber who carries 25 kilograms of climbing hardware, but neglects to bring a cooking pot. In Nepal there are all these options, plus a considerable number of other alternatives as a result of the availability of inexpensive (by our standards) non-professional and professional labour and the large population that inhabits most trekking areas.

The only similarity between the hill regions of Nepal below 4000 metres and the places you may have hiked or climbed in the west is that both are accessible only by trail. Even this similarity is misleading, because trails in the west are usually constructed by National Park and Forest services and tend to switchback and follow established standards for maximum gradient. But Nepalese trails take the most direct route up a ridge or through a valley, diverting only to visit a village or to avoid trampling a field of rice or millet. It is extrordinary to see some of the steep climbs that trails make in order to avoid walking an extra km or two.

With this background in mind, consider the major ways in which you can outfit yourself for a trek, and how various approaches to trekking may result in a wide variety of experiences. The primary result (other than the obvious economic differences) of the trekking style you choose will be the way in which you interact with people in the hills. You will encounter so many people – both western and Nepali – that this interaction becomes important. No matter what trekking style you choose, the mountain views will still be spectacular, but this is only one aspect of a trek in Nepal.

For simplicity I have condensed the infinite possibilities for trekking into four approaches: backpacking, village inn treks, self-arranged treks and treks with a trekking agency. There is a lot of overlap between these four styles; many aspects of each trekking style spill over into the next one. A backpacking trek that stays a few nights in hotels has many of the attributes of a village inn trek, and a village inn trek with porters starts to become a self-arranged trek. A self-arranged trek that uses the services of a trekking company in Nepal is similar to the trekking agency approach.

BACKPACKING

In the west you would prepare for a hiking trip by loading a pack with a stove, freeze-dried food and a light tent, and set off for the trail. An ideal campsite will have a stream, some trees to sleep under and a spectacular view. In Nepal, however, running water means a village, or at least a house, nearby; most trees have had most of their lower limbs cut off for firewood; and dogs bark and radios are played at high volume late into the night. All the fancy backpacking equipment, most of which is unavailable in Nepal, becomes the centre of attention, a situation that may be difficult to deal with after a full day on the trail. It is enough trouble to light a stove, follow the instructions on the food packet, try to get some clean water to cook in, and set up camp without continually having to chase kids, dogs and goats away from camp.

The backpacker should be aware of the two cardinal rules for travellers in Nepal: they should contribute to the economy, and he should entertain villagers. So much food is available in the hills that it doesn't make much sense to try to be totally self-sufficient while trekking, except perhaps in the far west, where food is scarce.

At higher altitudes, however, the backpacking approach may be useful. Depending on the terrain and local weather conditions, villages extend up to 4000 metres and there are summer settlements as high as 5000 metres. Many of these high villages are deserted from autumn to early spring, and it is in these regions that you may wish to alter your trekking style and utilise a backpacking or mountaineering approach to reach high passes or the foot of remote glaciers. It is difficult to arrange for porters who have the proper clothing and footgear for travelling in cold and snow. Often the best solution is to leave much of your gear behind at a temporary 'base camp' in the care of a hotel or trustworthy sherpa and spend a few days carrying your own food and equipment. This will provide you with the best of both worlds: an enriching cultural experience which conforms to the standards and traditions of the country in the lowlands, and a wilderness or mountaineering experience in the high mountains.

VILLAGE INN TREKS

Most trekkers visit Nepal armed with a pack containing only clothing and bedding, and spend from one to three weeks trekking in either the Annapurna or Everest region. Some trekkers, either at the beginning, or as their packs become too burdensome, hire a porter to carry their extra gear. A large number of people operate with a bare minimum of equipment and rely on hotels along the major trekking routes for food and shelter and (on the Jomsom trek) use the bedding available in hotels. In this manner, you can operate for US$2 to US$5 a day depending on where you are (it's more expensive at high altitude and in very remote areas) and on how simply you are prepared to live and eat.

By arranging your food and accommodation locally you can move at your own pace, set up your own schedule, move faster or slower than others, and make side trips not possible with a large group.

You can spend a day photographing mountains, flowers, or people – or you can simply lie around for a day. You will come into contact with other trekkers from throughout the world in a unique situation where both of you are out of place. Bonds can develop that would not be possible in either his or her home or yours. Often you will discover that you're travelling at much the same schedule as several others and you can share experiences, expenses and information. You are free (within the limits imposed by your trekking permit) to alter your route as you learn about other interesting places in the vicinity, or to join up with other trekkers and head off in their direction. You will have a good opportunity to see how the people in the hills of Nepal live, work and eat and to develop at least a rudimentary knowledge of the Nepali language.

Below are some of the important aspects of this kind of trekking.

Food

Although there are some hotels in the hills that can conjure up fantastic meals, the standard hotel diet is *daal bhaat* in the lowlands and potatoes at higher elevations. *Daal bhaat* twice a day for a month presents a pretty boring prospect to the western palate. (Forget about *tsampa* – it's really terrible, especially as a steady diet.) Hotels on the major trek routes vary in standard from primitive to luxurious. Several inns on the Jomsom trek even have sidewalk cafes where you can enjoy a meal in the sun! Beer, coke and other soft drinks are available everywhere (at high prices), and the menus are often attractive and extensive. Too often, however, the menu represents the innkeeper's fantasy of what he would like to serve, not what's available, so the choice almost always comes back to rice, *daal*, potatoes and pancakes.

Thirty years ago, Tilman observed that one can live off the country in a sombre fashion, but Nepal is no place in which to make a gastronomic tour. It hasn't changed.

It takes a considerable amount of imagination to provide the variety in diet that westerners are used to in Kathmandu, where a considerable amount of imported food is available. It is almost impossible to provide this variety in remote regions unless you've brought the food with you. Most people can adapt to a Nepalese diet, but try it for a few days at home – boiled rice with a thick split pea soup poured over it is the closest approximation – so you know what you are getting into. It might help convince you to fill the remote corners of your rucksack with spices, trail snacks and other goodies.

In many places, even where there are reasonably sophisticated hotels, you may have to wait two hours or more for a meal, something you will already be used to if you have spent any time in Kathmandu, or other parts of Asia. This means that many breakfasts and lunches will be tea and biscuits unless you are willing to keep your itinerary flexible and wait until the innkeeper gets around to preparing food or walk on to another place in the hopes of finding food already cooked. The alternative is to carry some food and cooking pots with you.

Hotel Accommodation

The standard of hotels along the trails of Nepal vary widely – as you will find from reading the day-by-day route descriptions. Some are quite comfortable, some extremely basic, but overall trekkers find them quite acceptable. Most inns have dormitories; some even have private rooms separate from the family living quarters, and most of these rooms have beds. Most Thakali inns (along the Pokhara-Jomsom route) have bedding available – usually a cotton-filled quilt. Sometimes the bedding has the added attraction of lice and other interesting bed companions, so it isn't a bad idea to bring along your own sheet and/or sleeping bag.

The accommodation available in some places, however, may be a dirty, generally smoky, home. Chimneys are rare, and a room on the second floor of a house can turn into an intolerable smokehouse as soon as the cooking fire is lit in the kitchen below. Often it is possible to sleep on porches of houses, but your gear is then less secure. The most common complaint among trekkers who rely on local facilities is about smoky accommodation. At higher elevations there are rarely private rooms and the dormitory has several huge beds that sleep 10 or 20 people – sometimes in two tiers. High altitudes can make people uncomfortable, sleepless, crabby and strange, so there is a lot of thrashing about and opening and closing of doors throughout the night. If you choose this type of travel and value sleep and privacy, reconsider again the advantages of bringing your own tent.

The thrashing-about problem is not limited to your fellow trekkers. Since a hotel doubles as a home, whether it has a sign that says 'hotel' or not, you may have a difficult time sleeping until the entire household has retired. Trekkers who walk and exert themselves all day require more sleep than they normally do at home; often you will sleep 10 or 11 hours each night. But the village people, who are not exerting themselves during the day, can get by with six to eight hours. This presents an immediate conflict in lifestyles and sleep requirements, particularly when the inevitable booze and card party erupts in the next room, or worse yet in your bedroom itself. Another universal deterrent to sleep is the ubiquitous Radio Nepal, which must always be listened to at high volume, and which does not stop broadcasting until 11 pm.

One solution to this problem is a tent, pitched a few hundred metres from the nearest house, but the tent is extra weight and may require a porter to carry it. On the bonus side, living with the family, even for a short while, gives you a unique insight into Nepalese family life. After dinner conversations between your host and trekkers from other countries can prove interesting and enlightening to everyone involved.

Routes

One problem with this kind of trekking is you are dependent on facilities located, for the most part, in villages, so you must trek only in inhabited localities. Because you need to know where and if you can eat, you will usually have to stick to the better-known routes. Your schedule may often be altered in order to reach a certain place for lunch or dinner time. You can miss lunch, or even dinner, if a hotel does not exist at a convenient time for stopping or the hotel you are counting on is closed (a few packets of biscuits in your rucksack is good insurance against these rough spots). Most of the major routes are well documented, but are also well travelled. A hotel can be out of food if there are a number of other trekkers there, or if you are late. Your destination for the day can also get severely altered when you discover that the lunch you ordered at an inn will take a very long time to prepare. You will usually discover this only after you have waited an hour or so already. It is wise to be aware of these kinds of problems and to be prepared to deal with them.

Accommodation is most readily available in the Khumbu (Everest region) and the entire trek around Annapurna. Elsewhere you should be more prepared to fend for yourself at least occasionally. If, however, you carry food, cooking pots and a tent to use even one night, you have escalated beyond the village inn approach into a more complex form of trekking with different problems.

Safety

Despite the caution advised by the US Embassy that is reprinted in the section on Health & Safety, most people in the hills of Nepal are friendly, helpful and honest. It is, however, essential that you travel with a well-chosen companion – either another westerner or a guide – for reasons of personal safety. The chance of theft is still remote, but a sprained ankle, debilitating illness or other misfortune can occur at any time. It is only common sense, applicable to a hiking trip anywhere, that you should not travel alone in the mountains.

Guides & Porters

On the Everest, Langtang and Annapurna treks the routes are so well-known by everyone that you do not necessarily need a guide – although a good guide should make things easier (and often cheaper) by negotiating on your behalf and will hopefully show you places of interest and trail junctions that you might have otherwise overlooked. There are, of course, poor guides who will do nothing but complicate everything throughout the trek and make considerable money at your expense. In Khumbu, there is the additional benefit of being invited (almost always) to the house of your guide where you can become familiar with the Sherpa culture, and where your guide – and you – will (almost always) get drunk. On other routes, where there are fewer signs that say 'hotel', accommodation and food is found by asking from house to house. A guide can be indispensable in such situations.

Tradition dictates that guides receive a salary (US$2.50 to US$3 a day in 1985) plus accommodation and food. If you are staying at inns, you will be amazed at how much your tiny guide can eat and drink at your expense. It may be worthwhile to set a limit on the guides' food bill before you set out. If you are really watching your pennies you could always carry a small amount of food and cook it yourself if you have a guide. This leads, however, to hiring a porter to carry the food and cooking pots; tradition also dictates that a guide does not carry a load. Suddenly your trek is transmogrified into a 'do it yourself' trek with all its attendant bureaucratic hassles. The answer may be to hire a porter in the first place. Although he may not be a guide in the true sense of the word, he can always ask directions for you and check routes with the local people, which may be all you really require. He isn't going to let you become completely lost.

An important consideration when you decide to trek with a guide or porters is that you place yourself in the role of an employer. This means that you may have to deal with personnel problems including medical care, insurance, strikes, requests for time off, salary increases and all the other aspects of being a boss. Be as thorough as you can when hiring people and make it clear from the beginning what the requirements and limitations are, after that be prepared to put up with some haggling – it's almost impossible to protect against it.

MAKING YOUR OWN ARRANGEMENTS

A third style of trekking is to gather sherpas, porters, food and equipment and take off on a trek with all the comforts and facilities of a trek arranged by an agent in your own country. The size of the party for such a trek may range from one or two persons on to an almost impossible size – 20 or more. For many, this is a satisfactory solution and trekkers who opt for this approach, particularly with a small group of friends, are often rewarded with an enriching and enjoyable trip.

It is possible to wander through Kathmandu and pick up a sherpa or two, have him hire porters, visit shops and purchase food, then set off on your trek. The biggest drawback to this method is that you have no way of knowing the organizational ability and honesty of the individuals you may hire, other than the letters they produce from their past (always satisfied) customers. Since those you hire obviously know the market prices and can bargain better than you, there is a significant opportunity to charge you much more for many goods and services – with the surplus making its way back to your employee. This is more a conformity to tradition (remember, you are wealthy)

than dishonesty; every tour guide in Asia, for example, receives a commission on whatever you buy from the shops to which he guides you.

October, November, March and April are very busy trekking seasons, and any sherpa who does not have a job during these months may be of questionable reliability. During other months, it is often possible to find excellent staff with the help of a trekking agency or trekking equipment shop in Kathmandu. You will find them more willing to help you if you offer them a fee for their assistance or hire some equipment from them. Many restaurants and hotels, particularly in the Thamel area of Kathmandu and in Pokhara have bulletin boards that have messages from trekkers who are looking for trekking companions or are recommending a reliable guide.

It is also possible to hire sherpas and porters on the spot in Lukla and sometimes in Pokhara, except during October and early November, so you might be successful if you fly to these places and try to arrange a trek without a lot of advance preparations. There are no sherpas or porters available at Jomsom or Langtang, however. It is becoming imperative to be cautious when you hire either sherpas or porters. Hotels, trekking agencies or other trekkers should be consulted before you employ anyone whom you do not know.

There are a host of regulations that govern trekking, although the degree of enforcement varies. Trekking agencies charge what they do because they are always subject to these rules, and compliance with them adds considerably to the cost of a trek. You should be aware that any regulation might be strictly enforced at any time; your trek may be curtailed, and you could be fined, if you do not follow them. A trekking permit is always required, and national park fees are conscientiously collected, but other regulations are generally ignored if you are alone and are relying on local accommodation. If you have porters and sherpas you may be required to comply with the regulations that relate to fuel and to insurance. There are also regulations governing filming; if you plan to make a 16 mm movie, you will certainly need the assistance of a trekking agent in Nepal – 8 mm movies and videos are not subject to any restrictions.

Fuel

The current National Park rules (see Day 13 of the Everest trek) prohibit the use of firewood in Sagarmatha, Langtang and Rara National Parks. But it is difficult to purchase paraffin (kerosene) in these regions, and the Indian pressure stoves are troublesome and inefficient, especially at high altitudes. You could be stopped at the park entrance if you are not self-sufficient in fuel. Note that this means that your whole party, including the porters, is supposed to cook on stoves.

Insurance

Theoretically you are supposed to provide insurance for porters, but this is complicated to obtain and there is no system for checking on whether you do this, though you will certainly have a major row if there is an accident and no insurance certificate can be produced. If you are climbing one of the trekking peaks, you must insure any Nepali who is going beyond base camp; there is a system for checking on insurance in this situation.

Using a Nepal Trekking Agency

You can use the services of a trekking agency in Kathmandu to make some, or all, of the arrangements. The list of Nepal trekking companies in the appendix indicates those that offer equipment for hire, those that will arrange a single sherpa or porter, and those that will undertake only the entire arrangements for a trek.

If you want to have things organised in advance, you can contact a Nepal trekking company by mail and ask them to make arrangements for your trek. There are more than 30 trekking companies in Kathmandu that will organise treks for a fee and provide all sherpas, porters and, if necessary, equipment. Communication to Nepal is slow, however, and the volume of correspondence required to provide you with the information you require, to determine your specific needs, to define your precise route and itinerary, to fit you into an already overcrowded schedule and to negotiate a price that both parties understand, can consume months, and even as long as a year. Mail takes up to three weeks each way to and from Australia, America or Europe.

One solution is to just go to Nepal and sort out the details in an hour or two of face to face negotiations with a trekking company. You should be prepared to spend a week or so (less, if you are lucky) in Kathmandu settling these details. An alternative to endless correspondence with Nepal is to use the services of the overseas agent of a Nepal trekking company. These agents should have someone who can give you the information you require, and they should have a better system, such as telex, for communication with Nepal. Dealing with an agent usually involves paying them a fee to make all the arrangements and then becomes the 'complete arrangements' approach that is described in the next section.

Setting the Ground Rules

Once you begin a trek you are entirely in the hands of your sherpa sardar, and his resources are limited to the food, equipment, money and instructions provided by either you or the trekking company. No matter how scrupulous the arrangements and how experienced your sherpa staff, there are bound to be complications. A trek is organised according to a pre-arranged itinerary and the sherpas expect to arrive at certain points on schedule. If you are sick or slow, and do not communicate this to the sherpas, you may discover that camp and dinner are waiting for you far ahead. Be sure to communicate such problems and other desires to the staff.

In most cases, the sherpas are true professionals and will make every possible effort to accommodate a trekker if they understand what he wants. They have a daily routine similar to the one described a little later in this book. If you do not wish to follow this routine it is important to decide this early in the trek. A routine, once established with the sherpas, is difficult to change later. You should be sure that you and your sardar or trekking company understands exactly who is expected to provide what equipment. It is most embarrassing to discover that there are no sleeping bags on the first night.

TREKKING WITH A GROUP

There are companies specialising in trekking that organise both individual and group treks from the United States, Germany, Britain, Japan, Switzerland, France, Australia, New Zealand and Scandinavia. The overseas trekking agents work through one of the established trekking companies in Nepal. Some agents have agreements for the exclusive representation of a Nepalese company in their own country. Names and addresses of some of the major trekking agencies are listed in the Further Information chapter.

A condition of a trek through a trekking agent is that the group must usually stick to its prearranged route and, within limits, must meet a specific schedule. This means that an interesting side trip may have to be foregone, and if you are sick you will probably have to keep moving with the rest of the group. You may not agree with a leader's decisions if a schedule must be adjusted because of weather, health, political or logistical considerations.

You will be trekking with a number of people you have not met before, and although some strong relationships may develop, there may be those in the party you would much rather not have met. For some people, this prospect alone rules out their participation in a group trek, however

the major drawback will probably be the cost. Organised treks generally start at around US$50 per person, per day of the trek. On the positive side, by fixing the destination and schedule in advance, all members of the group may be prepared for the trip and have proper equipment and a clear understanding of the schedule and terrain. Reservations for flights and hotels can be made well in advance and there is someone in Kathmandu to reconfirm them while you are out of communication on the trail.

Minimising Impact

A group trek is large enough to carry all its own food and fuel for cooking. This means that trekkers are not competing with the locals for food. They make a positive economic contribution when they hire local porters to carry their loads. Trekking organisations in Nepal are working together to further decrease their impact on the land. Such problems as waste disposal, rescue insurance, wages and benefits to porters and sherpas are all of concern.

Food & Accommodation

Because the group carries its own food for the entire trek a greater variety is possible. This may include canned goods from Kathmandu and imported food purchased from expeditions or other exotic sources. A skilled cook can prepare an abundant variety of tasty western-style food. The meals a good sherpa cook can prepare in an hour over an open fire would put many western cafes to shame.

A group trek carries tents for the trekkers. This gives you a place to spread out your gear without fear that someone will pick it up, and usually you will have a quiet night. A tent also gives you the freedom to go to bed when you choose – to retire immediately after dinner to read or sleep, or to sit up and watch the moon rise as you discuss the day's outing. Because you have tents, sherpas, a kitchen crew and all the visible trappings of an arranged

trek, villagers will know that a sardar will pay all bills and that the porters will probably purchase some food from the village. You are trekking according to Nepal's union standard and will be accepted and treated well along the way, particularly if your route takes you through the home villages of your sherpas or porters.

Money and staff hassles are almost eliminated on an arranged trek. The sardar is responsible for whatever minor purchases are needed along the way and for ensuring a full complement of porters every day. Unless you are particularly interested, or quite watchful, you may never be aware that these negotiations are taking place.

Your Fellow Trekkers
Since trekkers are generally recruited through outdoor-oriented stores, organisations and magazines, the group will usually have quite an interest in the great outdoors as a unifying factor, but will usually be quite diverse otherwise. It is not unusual to find people as different as a stockbroker and a steelworker becoming friends – an opportunity for an exchange of views which might never have been possible without the matchmaking of the trek. Read the brochures and other material prepared by the agent; see if it seems likely to attract the type of people you'd get along with.

Most prearranged treks cater to people to whom time is more important (within limits) than money. For many, the most difficult part of planning a trek is getting time off from work. These people are willing to pay more to avoid wasting a week of their limited vacation sitting around in Kathmandu making arrangements or waiting along the way for available space on a plane. A trekking agent usually tries to cram as many days in the hills as is possible into a given time span.

Emergencies

Trekking agents either partially subsidise a physician or provide a leader who has sufficient medical knowledge to cope with whatever problems may occur. You, therefore, have reasonable medical care. If you have an established organisation with all of its contacts behind you, you will have more help in case of emergency. Messages from home (heaven forbid) can be passed along to you through an agent in Kathmandu. If you become sick or unable to travel, a rescue helicopter or charter flight from a remote airstrip can only be arranged if you have some definite proof that it can be paid for. It now costs US$1500 for a helicopter evacuation from 4000 metres near Mt Everest and several whose lives were saved by such flights left Nepal without paying their bill. The Royal Army, which operates the service, refuse to send a chopper unless they have cash in hand. All trek organisers have an agreement in Kathmandu that guarantees the payment, although you will be billed later for the service.

Tradition

By participating in a prearranged trek, you conform to a tradition and routine that has been developed and refined for more than 50 years. You will have the opportunity to travel in much the same manner as the approach marches described in *Annapurna*, *The Ascent of Everest* and *Americans on Everest*, a feature not possible with other approaches. If your interest in the Himalaya was kindled through such books, you still have the opportunity to experience this delightful way to travel. There are a great number of reasons why these expeditions went to all the trouble and expense to travel as they did. It is an altogether refreshing experience to have all the camp and logistics problems removed from your responsibility so you are free to fully enjoy the land and the people which have attracted mountaineers for a century. A group of seven or more is desirable in order to fully appreciate this tradition.

Preparing for a Trek – At Home

Once you decide to go on a trek you can save time and hassles later by spending time at home preparing yourself physically, gathering the personal equipment necessary to make the trip comfortable, and dealing with the bureaucracy of international travel.

I have used the term 'trekking agent' to define the company, travel agent or individual that is organising the trek. If you are trekking on your own, you are the trekking agent and you can skip many of these preparations and deal with them after you arrive in Kathmandu.

If you are trekking through a trekking agent, be aware that the equipment supplied by various organisers of treks differs. You should read over the material provided by your trekking agent to assure yourself that they are not providing some of the equipment or services I suggest you arrange yourself. In addition, be sure that you are not expected to provide something that I do not include in my list.

TRAVEL INSURANCE
Trekking and travel agents can offer a travellers' insurance policy. Coverage will vary from policy to policy, but will probably include loss of baggage, sickness and accidental injury or death. Most policies also cover the reimbursement of cancellation fees and other non-recoverable costs, including losses due to advance-purchase plane tickets, if you are forced to cancel your trip because of accident or illness of yourself, or illness or death of a family member. It's probably worth purchasing this inexpensive protection.

Such a policy can often cover helicopter evacuation and other emergency services in Nepal. Be sure that the policy does not exclude 'mountaineering' or 'alpinism' or you may have a difficult time settling a claim. Although you will not be engaged in such activities, you may never be able to convince a flatlander insurance company of this fact. It would be prudent to check the policy specifically to be sure that helicopter evacuation is covered.

If you purchase insurance and have a loss, you must submit proof of this loss in order to make an insurance claim. If you have a medical problem, you should save all your bills and get a physician's certificate stating that you were sick. If you lose something covered by insurance, you must file a police report and get a copy to send to the insurance company, no matter how remote the location. No insurance claim is considered without such documentation. Read your policy carefully and be sure you understand all its conditions.

MONEY
You can carry either cash or travellers' cheques for your expenses in Nepal (American Express is the only travellers' cheques that can be refunded in Kathmandu). US dollars are the most acceptable, but Australian dollars and most European currencies are also welcomed, though Scandanavian money is difficult to change.

Bring enough money to buy whatever souvenirs, incredible bargains, or art objects you may find. In Kathmandu there are Tibetan carpets (US$90 to US$150), wool sweaters and jackets (US$5 to US$25), some genuine Tibetan art pieces (US$20+) and semi-precious stones (US$15 to US$25). On the trek you may have the opportunity to purchase things from Tibet (prayer wheels, *thankas*, butter lamps and bells) or Sherpa household articles (*chhang* bottles, boots, aprons, carpets and cups) at prices anywhere from US$1 to more than US$100.

If you plan to make a major purchase in Nepal, first visit a local importer and find out what is available at what price. Especially note the quality so that you will have a basis for comparison in Nepal. Many pieces exported from India and Nepal may be available in your locale at prices lower than in retail shops in Kathmandu because of large volume discounts. Tibetan carpets made in Nepal are for sale in San Francisco, for example, for less than it would cost to buy one in Nepal and ship it home.

VISA FOR NEPAL
When getting photographs for your passport get about 10 extra for your Nepal visa and trekking permit. It is a good idea to carry a few photos along in case some new regulation or restriction along the way requires them.

You can obtain a one month visa for Nepal in advance; it can be extended in Nepal for the full period of your visit, up to three months. You can easily enter Nepal without a visa, but it takes yet another form and a bit of time when you arrive at Kathmandu airport. The initial validity of an airport visa is seven days, but it can be extended for free for another three weeks. If you are arriving by road it would save time if you had a visa in advance, but it is not absolutely necessary. A Nepal visa is valid only within three months of the date of issue; do not apply too soon or it will not be valid when you arrive in Kathmandu.

Addresses of some of the Nepalese embassies and consulates abroad are:

Australia
1 The Strand, 870 Military Rd, Mosman, NSW 2088 (tel 960-3565)
Flat No 6, 204 The Avenue, Parkville, Vic 3051
66 High St, Toowong, Brisbane, Qld 4066
Hong Kong
Prince of Wales Building (in the gate of HMS Tamar) (tel 5 289-3255)
India
Barakhamba Rd, New Delhi 110001 (tel 38 1484)
19 Woodlands, Sterndale Rd, Alipore, Calcutta 700027 (tel 45 2024 and 45 2493)

Thailand
189 soi 71, Sukhumvit Road, Bangkok (tel 391-7240 and 392-4741)
UK
12A Kensington Palace Gardens, London W8 (tel 229-6231 and 229-1594)
USA
2131 Leroy Place, Washington DC 20008 (tel (202) 667-4550)
711 Third Ave, Room 1806, New York, NY 10017 (tel (212) 986-1989)

EQUIPMENT
I place considerable emphasis on the selection of equipment for a trek, but in fact you can get by with almost nothing, especially if you do not plan to go above 4000 metres. The task of selecting proper gear can almost overpower some people, but it is not a complex or difficult undertaking. Preparing for a trek is not much more complicated than equipping yourself for a weekend backpacking trip; in some ways it is simpler. There is no food to worry about, no eating utensils or cooking pots to organise, no tents to stow, and less overall concern with weight and bulk.

If you follow these suggestions, you can have many happy hours – planning the trek, sorting gear, packing and repacking. It is a great way to spend boring evenings and will impress your friends when they find down jackets strewn over your living room floor in mid-summer. On the other hand, if you don't have the time, you can probably gather most of the items you need in a single visit to an outdoor equipment shop.

It is helpful to have the proper equipment – particularly shoes and socks – before you leave home, because these can be difficult to find in Kathmandu. Some very good used equipment is available in Nepal (sometimes at lower prices than elsewhere), but you cannot depend on getting the proper size of boots and running shoes, and socks are hard to find. If you are on a prearranged trek it is better to have your entire kit organised in advance, rather than to spend the night before the trek begins scouring all over Kathmandu for an item of gear. If you are arranging your own trek, you can find everything you need in a day or two. Remember that all shops require a deposit to ensure that you return the equipment. This can cause complications if you don't want to change money to pay the deposit because the other options are to leave signed travellers checks or a passport with the shop, and this isn't a good idea. Cash dollars can solve the problem so they are a very useful thing to carry if you plan to rent equipment. Be sure to check the bill and receipt carefully before you leave the rental shop.

The equipment listed on the preceding page has been tested by many trekkers. Everything on the list is useful – most of it necessary – for any trek that exceeds three weeks in duration and ascends to above 4000 metres. Many things may be omitted if you do not exceed this elevation. Note that all of this gear (except the sleeping bag) will pack into a duffle bag and weighs less than 15 kg.

Some of this equipment will not be necessary on a given trek. You might be lucky enough to trek during a warm spell and never need a down jacket, or it might be so cold and rainy that you never wear short pants. As you read the suggestions which follow, be sure to evaluate for yourself whether you feel that you need a particular item of equipment. Do not rush out to an equipment shop and purchase everything on this list; what follows is what works for me and has worked for many other trekkers, but you may decide that many items in this list are unnecessary for you.

Selection & Use

You will probably have most of the equipment needed for the trek if you do much hiking in cold weather. A trek is a good place to finally destroy clothing that is nearly worn out or outstyled. A long trek, five weeks or so, is just about the maximum useful life for some clothing

items – be sure that used gear has enough life left to finish the trek. Repairs can be made at tailor shops at occasional points along the trail – they use hand-operated sewing machines.

Boots or Running Shoes

Proper footgear is the most important item you will bring. Your choice of footgear will depend on the length of the trek and whether you will be walking in snow or not. Many trekkers have found that tennis or running shoes are good trekking footgear, even for long treks, if snow is not encountered. However, boots provide ankle protection and have stiffer soles. If you have done most of your hiking in boots, you may experience some discomfort in lighter and softer footgear. There are several lightweight trekking shoes patterned after running shoes that have stiffer lug soles; these are available in both low and high-top models. You should try out the shoes you plan to wear on the trek during several hikes (up and down hills) before you come to Nepal. Whenever there is snow (possible anywhere above 4000 metres), boots are an absolute necessity. If you are travelling with porters, you have the luxury of carrying both and switching your shoes from time to time. If you are carrying everything yourself you will probably have to settle for one or the other.

Boots should be medium weight, 15 cm high, rugged enough to last, waterproof, well broken-in and must fit well. Be sure your boots provide enough room for your toes. There are many long and steep descents during which short boots can painfully jam your toes (causing the loss of toenails). The trails are often rocky and rough. If your soles are thin and soft, your feet will soon be bruised and walking will be painful. Soft rubber soles wear out very rapidly. Ensure that your boots have hard lug (Vibram) soles.

Camp Shoes

A pair of tennis shoes are comfortable to

change into for the evening and can serve as trail shoes in an emergency. A pair of rubber 'thongs' or shower shoes make a comfortable change at camp during warm weather. These may be purchased in Kathmandu. I always carry a pair of these in my rucksack and remove my boots or tennis shoes at lunch and in camp and put my shoes and socks in the sun to dry. I think this has saved me a lot of foot troubles.

Socks

Thermal ski socks – a nylon/wool combination – are probably the best. You will wash your socks several times during a long trek and pure wool socks dry slowly. Nylon/wool socks dry in a few hours in the sun – often during a single lunch stop. They are marketed as ski socks 'designed for plastic boots' and come in a variety of colours, a useful feature since coloured socks hide stains. Most people can wear these without a cotton liner, but a thin cotton liner sock is usually necessary with heavy woollen rag socks. Try on a pair on your next local hike and see whether you need an inner sock. Three pairs should be enough unless you are a real procrastinator about washing clothes. If you bring plus-fours, you will need a pair of high wool socks and two pairs of cotton or nylon inner socks. Most treks do not spend enough time at high altitudes to require carrying more than one pair of high wool socks. Good socks are at a premium in Kathmandu, so you should bring them with you. There are some heavy scratchy Tibetan wool socks available in Kathmandu and Namche.

Down-filled or Fiber-filled Jacket

Down clothing has the advantage of being light and compressible. It will stuff into a small space when packed, yet bulk up when you wear it. You should bring a good jacket on a trek. Most ski jackets are not warm enough and most 'expedition parkas' are too heavy and bulky. The secret is to choose one that will be warm enough even at the coldest expected temperatures, but also usable when it is warmer. Don't bring both a heavy and light down jacket; choose one that will serve both purposes. If your jacket has a hood, you can dispense with a wool hat.

Your down jacket can serve many functions on the trek. It will become a pillow at night, protect fragile items in your rucksack or duffle bag, and if you are extremely cold at high altitude, wear it to bed inside your sleeping bag. You probably will not wear down gear to walk in; it rarely gets that cold even at 5000 metres. Most trekkers leave their down clothing in their duffle bag at lower elevations and only use it during the evening. At higher elevations, carry your jacket and put it on at rest or lunch stops. Artificial fiber jackets, filled with Polargard, Thinsulate or Fiberfill are a good substitute for down – and much less expensive. Jackets rent in Kathmandu for Rs 8 to 10 per day and are available in Namche at about the same rate.

Wool Shirt, Sweater or Acrylic Pile Jacket

With clothing, two light layers are better than a single heavy layer. One or two light sweaters or shirts are superior to a heavy wool jacket. Most of the time you will need only a single light garment in the morning and will shed it almost as soon as you start walking. A long-sleeved shirt or sweater will suffice. An advantage of a shirt is that you can open the front for ventilation without stopping to remove the entire garment. Wool is warm, even when wet, so make yours wool, not cotton. Tibetan wool sweaters are for sale in Kathmandu, but they are pretty scratchy.

Acrylic-pile jackets and sweaters such as those made by Helly Hansen in Norway and Great Pacific Iron Works in California come in a variety of styles and thicknesses. They are light, warm (even when wet) and easy to clean. They are a little cheaper, are much lighter, and dry much faster than wool garments. Pile jackets can usually be rented in Kathmandu.

Hiking Shorts for Men, Skirts for Women

The weather will often be hot and humid, the trails steep and the wind calm. Long pants tend to pull at the knees and are hot. For hiking at the lower elevations, the sherpas usually switch to shorts. It's a good procedure. Either 'cutoffs' or fancy hiking shorts with big pockets are fine.

Women should consider a skirt as an alternative. Many who have worn them on treks are enthusiastic about them; the most obvious reason being the ease in relieving oneself along the trail. There are long stretches where there is little chance to drop out of sight and a skirt solves the problem. Skirts are also useful when the only place to wash is in a stream crowded with trekkers, villagers and porters. A wrap-around skirt is easy to put on and take off in a tent. Villagers can be a bit shocked at a woman in shorts; a skirt is also a useful way of looking a bit prudish and avoiding hassles from would-be cassanovas in the hills. Long 'granny' skirts are not good; you will be walking through too much mud to make them practical.

Poncho or Umbrella

There is really no way to keep dry while hiking in the rain, but a poncho, a large, often hooded, tarp with a hole in the centre for your head, is a good solution. The weather is likely to be warm, even while raining, and a poncho has good air circulation. The condensation inside a waterproof jacket can make you even wetter than standing out in the rain. An inexpensive plastic poncho is better than the more expensive coated nylon gear. The plastic one is completely waterproof at a fraction of the cost.

The most practical way of keeping dry is an umbrella. This is an excellent substitute for a poncho (except on windy days). An umbrella can serve as a sunshade, a walking stick, and an emergency toilet shelter. Umbrellas with bamboo handles are available in Kathmandu for about US$2, but they are bulky and tend to leak black dye over you when they get wet. Collapsible umbrellas are an excellent compromise, although they cannot serve as walking sticks. Imported collapsible umbrellas are available in shops on New Road and in the supermarket in Kathmandu. An umbrella is necessary in October, April and May and optional for treks in other months.

Sun Hat

A hat to keep the sun off your head is an important item, but its design is not critical. Obviously, a hat with a wide brim affords greater protection. If the hat you choose does not have a strap to fit under your chin put one on so that your hat does not blow away in a wind gust. The Nepal Cap House in Asan Tole has an amazing assortment of hats to choose from.

Bathing Suit

Almost nobody older than eight goes without clothing in Nepal or India. You will probably upset sherpas, porters and an entire village if you skinny-dip in a river, stream or hot spring, even to wash. There are numerous places to swim, although most are ridiculously cold – except along the Arun River in eastern Nepal where there are some great swimming holes; there are hot springs in Manang and in Tatopani on the Jomsom trek. Either bring along a suit, or plan to swim in shorts and then wear them till they dry.

Rucksack

Select a rucksack that fits comfortably. Try to find one that has a light inside frame to stiffen the bag, and a waistband to keep it from bouncing around and also to take some weight off your shoulders. A small day pack has many advantages on a trek: its small size prevents you from carrying too much during the day; it is a good 'carry-on' piece of luggage on flights; it will fit inside your tent at night without crowding you; and it is not overly cumbersome for you when going through low doorways into houses and temples. If you don't plan to take a porter, you will need a larger pack, either a frame (Kelty-type) pack or a large expedition rucksack. A soft pack is more versatile; if you do eventually hand your pack over to a porter, he will certainly put it on a *doko* (bamboo basket) and carry it with a tumpline. A frame pack can be cumbersome for a porter to carry; they will not use the shoulder straps. Be sure that your pack has a padded waist band to take the weight off your shoulders. There is a wide assortment of day packs and large rucksacks available for rent in Kathmandu.

Sleeping Bag

This is one item that you might consider bringing from home. Sleeping bags are readily available for rent in Kathmandu, but the dry cleaning facilities in Nepal are pretty strange and bags tend to lose their loft quickly during the process. The choice is usually between a clean (but old and worn) bag, a dirty (but warm) one or a new (and expensive) sleeping bag. Almost all sleeping bags available in Kathmandu are mummy-style expedition bags and rent for less than US$1 a day. It is cold from November to March even in the lowlands, so a warm sleeping bag is important at these times, and is a must at altitudes over 3300 metres.

Water Bottle

Bring a one-litre plastic water bottle that does not leak. Since all water must be boiled or treated, your bottle provides the only completely safe source of cold water to drink. Each night, fill your water bottle with boiled water. If the bottle does not leak, take it to bed with you as a hot water bottle on cold nights – very luxurious. By morning the water will be cool for your use during the day. Many people require two litres of water during the day. If you are one of those, consider a second water bottle. Good water bottles are sometimes hard to find in Kathmandu, but you can always find (leaky) plastic Indian bottles that will do in a pinch.

Sun Cream

Since most treks are in the winter season when the sun is low in the sky, except for the hazards of snow glare at high altitude, sunburn is not a problem for most people. You can use a commercial suntan lotion; those with more sensitive skin need a total sun screen such as zinc oxide cream. During spring treks, sunburn can be a problem. Sun cream is hard to find in Nepal.

Torch (Flashlight)

Almost any torch will do, a headlight is not necessary. You can get spare batteries almost anywhere in the hills of Nepal if you have a torch that uses 'D' cells. Larger batteries also perform better in the cold than small penlight AA' cells, but of course they are heavier. New Indian and Chinese torches and also exotic torches left over from expeditions are available in Nepal.

Insulated Pants

Most stores do not carry down-filled pants, but they are a real asset on a trek that goes above 4000 metres. You do not hike in down pants. Put them on when you stop for the night, over your hiking shorts or under a skirt. Some down pants have snaps or a zipper down the inseam of each leg, a design that allows them to be used as a half-bag for bivouacs. This design also lets you put them on without taking off your boots. When made into a half-bag, they give additional insulation in your sleeping bag when the nights get particularly cold.

Often you will arrive at your camp or hotel at 3 pm and not dine until 6 pm. Unless you elect to do some exploring, there will be about three hours before and an hour after dinner of physical inactivity and there is rarely a chance to sit by a fire to keep warm, even in hotels. In cold weather, down pants make these times much more comfortable. Ski warm-up pants are a good substitute, are much cheaper, and are available at all ski shops.

Down pants, and sometimes ski warm-up pants, are available in trekking shops in Kathmandu and Namche.

Nylon Windbreaker

Strong winds are rare in the places visited by most treks, but a windbreaker is helpful even in light winds and light rain and drizzles, at a time when a poncho is really not necessary. Be sure that your windbreaker 'breathes' – otherwise perspiration cannot evaporate and you will become soaked. A windbreaker is more in the line of emergency gear. If there is a strong wind, you must have it; otherwise it is seldom used.

Nylon Wind Pants

Many people use these frequently. The temperature will often be approaching 30°C and people prefer to hike in shorts. Early in the morning when it is cool, a pair of long pants is more comfortable. Wind pants provide the best of both worlds. Wear them over your shorts in the morning, then remove them to hike in shorts during the day. Most wind pants have special cuffs and can be removed over your boots.

Ski warm-up pants, or even cotton jogging pants, can be substituted for both wind pants and down-filled pants at a substantially lower cost with not much sacrifice in versatility or comfort.

Plus-fours ('Knickers')

These are a classic example of the prime rule of selecting equipment for any hiking trip: make each piece of gear serve at least two purposes. The great advantage of plus-fours is that, combined with long wool socks, they provide both short and long pants – simply by rolling the socks up or down.

During the several days which some treks spend at high elevations, you will truly be 'in the mountains' – where the weather can change quickly and sometimes dramatically. Although it will often be warm, it can cloud up and become cold and windy very fast – a disaster if you happen to be wearing shorts. You can wear the socks up on cold mornings before the sun comes up (which, since you are surrounded by high peaks, is often about 10 am). As exercise and the heat of the sun warms you up, roll the socks down to your ankles. Because of this versatility, plus-fours are better than long pants. Plus fours may be available in Kathmandu, but are usually for sale, not for rent.

Long Underwear

'Longjohns' are a useful addition to your equipment. A complete set makes a good warm pair of pyjamas and is also useful during late night emergency trips outside of your tent or hotel. Unless the weather is especially horrible, you will not need them to walk in during the day. You can bring only the bottoms and use a wool shirt for a pyjama top. Cotton underwear is okay, though wool is much warmer. If wool is too scratchy, duo-fold underwear (wool lined with cotton) is an excellent compromise.

Wool Hat or Balaclava

A balaclava is ideal because it can serve as a warm hat or be rolled down to cover most of your face and – most important – your neck. You may even need to wear it to bed on some nights. Much of your body heat is lost through your head, so a warm hat helps keep your entire body warmer.

Gloves

Warm ski gloves are suitable for a trek. You might consider taking along a pair of woollen mittens in addition – just in case your gloves get wet.

Down Booties

Many people consider these excess baggage, but they are great to have and not very heavy. If they have a thick sole, preferably with ensolite insulation, they can serve as camp shoes at high elevations. Down booties do make a cold night a little warmer since somehow your feet seem to feel the cold when everything else is warm.

They are good for midnight trips outside into the cold.

Gaiters

If your trek visits high elevations, there is a possibility of snow and also an opportunity to do some scrambling off the trails. A pair of high gaiters will help to keep your boots and socks cleaner and drier in such situations.

Stuff Bags

It is unlikely that you will be able to find a completely waterproof duffle bag or rucksack. Using coated nylon stuff bags helps you to separate your gear – thereby lending an element of organisation to the daily chaos in your tent or hotel – and also provides additional protection in case of rain. If you get stuff bags with drawstrings, the addition of spring-loaded clamps will save a lot of frustration trying to untie knots you tied in too much haste in the morning. Plastic bags can be used, but they are much more fragile; a plastic bag inside each stuff sack is a good bet during the rainy season.

Sunglasses or Goggles

The sun reflects brilliantly off snow making good goggles or sunglasses with side protection essential. At high altitude, they are so essential that you should have a spare in case of breakage or loss. A pair of regular sunglasses can serve as a spare if some sort of side shield can be rigged. The lenses should be as dark as possible. At 5000 metres, the sun is intense both visually and non-visually and ultraviolet rays can severely damage unprotected eyes. Be sure that you have a metal case to store them in because, even in your rucksack, they can be crushed.

Sun Screen for Lips

To protect your lips at high altitude you need a true sun screen, like Labiosan, which keeps out all of the sun.

Duffle Bag

If you travel with porters you should protect your gear with a duffel bag. Several companies make good duffle bags that have a zipper along the side for ease of entry. Be sure your bag is durable and has a strong zipper. Do not buy a cheap model. A bag 35 cm in diameter and about 75 cm long is large enough to carry your gear and will usually meet the weight limit – typically 15 kg. If you are trying to save money, an army surplus duffle bag will serve, but they are inconvenient because they only open from the end (but it will have no zipper to jam or break).

Most of your equipment will be carried by a porter. During the day, you will carry your camera, water bottle, extra clothing, and a small first aid kit in your rucksack. Do not overload the rucksack – especially on the first day of the trek.

It is impossible to describe how your duffle bag will look after a month on a trek. Load it with your equipment, take it to the second floor and toss it out. Pick it up and shake the contents to the far end then put it in the dirt and stomp on it a few times – get the idea?

Your duffle bag will be carried by porters, so when it is raining it will be carried in the rain. It will also be left outside tea shops in the rain while porters go inside to keep dry. Your duffle bag must be packed so that important items stay dry during rainstorms. A waterproof duffle bag and waterproof nylon or plastic bags inside your bag are both necessary.

Use a small padlock that will fit through the zipper pull and fasten to a ring sewn to the bag. The lock will protect the contents from pilferage during the flight to and from Nepal. It will also protect the contents on your trek. Porters make many stops during the day at tea houses and *chhang* shops and leave their loads outside. The lock prevents kids, curious villagers and your porter from looking inside and picking up something they think you won't miss. Duffel bags are not easily bought or rented in Kathmandu.

Extra Duffle Bag or Suitcase

When you depart on the trek, you will leave your city clothes and other items you use when travelling in the storeroom of your hotel in Kathmandu. You should bring a small suitcase or extra duffle bag with a lock to use for this purpose.

Additional Items

There is not much to be said about soap, scissors and the like, but a few ideas may help. If there are two of you travelling together, double up on a lot of this material to save weight and bulk.

– Laundry soap in bars is available in Kathmandu and along most trails. This avoids an explosion of liquid or powdered soap in your luggage.

– 'Wash-n-Dri's' are great for a last-minute hand wash before dinner. You can avoid many stomach problems by washing frequently.

– A pair of scissors on your knife is useful.

– Be sure your sewing kit has some safety pins – lots of uses.

– Be sure all your medicines and toilet articles are in plastic bottles with screw-on lids – reread the section about how duffle bags are treated.

– One of the most visible indications of western culture in Nepal is streams of toilet paper littering every campsite. Burn your toilet paper after use.

Optional Equipment

The list suggests a number of items that might be interesting to bring along on a trek. Do not bring all of them; you will be overloaded and very busy if you do so.

Cameras

People have brought cameras ranging from tiny Instamatics to heavy Hasselblads. While most do bring a camera, it is equally enjoyable to trek without one.

A trek is long and dusty; be sure you have lens caps, some sort of lens tissue and a brush to clean the camera and lens as frequently as possible. Three lenses, a wide angle (28 or 35 mm), a standard lens (50 or 55 mm) and a telephoto lens (135 or 200 mm) are useful if you wish to take advantage of all the photographic opportunities during the trek. But lenses are heavy, and you will be carrying them in your rucksack day after day. If you must make a choice, you will find a telephoto (or zoom) lens is more useful than a wide angle, because it will allow you close-up pictures of mountains and portraits of shy people. Don't overburden yourself with lots of heavy camera equipment; an ostentatious display of expensive camera equipment invites theft. Insure your camera.

Film is available, but is outrageously expensive in Kathmandu and is not always available at duty free shops on the way to Nepal. Make certain you have enough. On a two or three week trek, 20 rolls of 36-exposure film is not too much.

EQUIPMENT CHECKLIST
For Lowland Treks

Footgear
running shoes or boots
camp shoes or thongs
socks – nylon thermal

Clothing
down or fiber-filled jacket
wool shirt, sweater or acrylic pile jacket
hiking shorts (for men) or skirt (for women)
poncho or umbrella
sun hat
underwear
bathing suit (optional)
cotton or corduroy pants (optional)
T-shirts, cotton, for men; blouses, for women

Other Equipment
rucksack or pack
water bottle
flashlight, batteries & bulbs

Miscellaneous Items
toilet articles
toilet paper & matches
sun cream
towel
laundry soap

medical & first aid kit
wash 'n dris (pre-moistened towelettes)
sewing kit
small knife
bandana

Other Optional Equipment
camera & lenses
lens cleansing equipment
film – about 20 rolls

If you are going higher, add the following
items:

Footgear
Boots
socks – high for plus fours
socks – light cotton for under plus fours

Clothing
down-filled pants
nylon windbreaker
nylon wind pants or ski warm-up pants

plus fours
long underwear
wool hat (or balaclava)
gloves
down booties (optional)
gaiters

Other Equipment
sleeping bag
goggles or sunglasses
sun cream for lips

Other Optional Equipment
altimeter
thermometer
compass
binoculars

If you have a porter you will need:
large duffle bag with lock
stuff bags
small duffle bag or suitcase (for your city
clothes)

Preparing for a Trek – In Kathmandu

The following projects confront you if you are arranging your trek yourself.

INTERNATIONAL AIRLINE RESERVATIONS
Airline reservations are difficult to obtain in Asia, even more so in Nepal. They must always be reconfirmed or they will be cancelled. This is no idle threat, it often happens. Take the time before your trek to reconfirm your flight out of Nepal. A bit of advance planning can save a last-minute drama at the airport. All flights out of Kathmandu are usually fully booked from mid-October to the end of November and during the months of January and April. If you don't have a reservation, make a booking before you start your trek. By booking three to five weeks ahead, you can usually get a seat; if you wait until your trek is finished to book a seat you will certainly have to wait a week or two for a flight. Be sure to leave four or five days buffer if you are flying out of Lukla or Jomsom.

DOMESTIC FLIGHTS
All domestic flights in Nepal are operated by the national carrier, Royal Nepal Airlines Corporation (RNAC). RNAC operates a fleet of 19-passenger Twin Otter and four-passenger Pilatus Porter aircraft to some of the most remote and spectacular airstrips in the world. Both these planes are STOL (Short Take Off & Landing) aircraft in order to negotiate the short grass airstrips at Jomsom, Lukla, Shyangboche, Langtang and other places.

The approaches to these airstrips are difficult; they are all situated on mountainsides surrounded by high peaks. Therefore, if there are clouds or high winds, the pilot cannot land. The classic remark by one RNAC captain explains the picture perfectly: 'We don't fly through clouds because in Nepal the clouds have rocks in them.' Many flights to remote regions are delayed or cancelled because of bad weather.

If your trek involves a flight in or out of one of these remote airstrips, it is possible that you will experience a delay of several hours or (more often) several days. These delays are the price you pay for the time-saving and convenience of flights to remote airstrips in Nepal. It will be helpful to pack a good book into your hand luggage to make the inevitable waiting at airports in Nepal a little more tolerable.

Reservations for domestic flights are obtained from the RNAC office on New Rd. It is best to go there in person because seats are confirmed only when the ticket is issued and paid for; dealing by telephone doesn't work. If you are using a trekking company or travel agency, they can take care of the flight booking for you. There are numerous complications to booking a seat on a domestic flight, but the most common problem is 'no seats'. The seats to Lukla, Jomsom and Pokhara are booked up to two years in advance by groups, but seats can often become available at the last minute.

Once you have a ticket and a confirmed seat, the fun is just beginning. If you are lucky, your flight will exist when you get to the airport, your name will still be on the seating chart, your baggage will be accepted, the flight will depart and it will land at the destination. This sometimes happens. Other times, however, something goes wrong; flights are often cancelled because of bad weather or other complications. When this happens, you start again; your confirmed seat on a flight that did not operate gains you no priority for the next flight. In Lukla you go from having a boarding pass in hand to the bottom of the waiting list (if you are lucky, and your plane does come, you go ahead of those who are waiting). In Kathmandu there is no such system, but there is a complex programme of 'delayed schedule', 'non-schedule' and 'charter' flights that are operated, so it's worth continuing to look for a seat – though it takes time at the RNAC office to accomplish this.

Return flights to Kathmandu can be confirmed in Kathmandu until the seating charts are sent to remote airstrips – then the seats can only be confirmed in the outlying stations. The number of days before the flight that the chart is sent varies for each destination. If you are planning to fly out from Lukla, it would be prudent to confirm your flight back to Kathmandu before starting the trek. The trouble is that you must then purchase a ticket; if your flight is then cancelled and you decide to walk out, you can only refund the ticket in Kathmandu. Having a ticket can be useful; sometimes things are so crowded in Lukla that they just stop selling tickets.

On domestic flights there is a cancellation charge. If you do not fly, be sure to cancel your reservation on time and have it recorded on your ticket for proof. If a ticket is cancelled more than 24 hours before the flight a Rs 20 cancellation charge is levied; if less than 24 hours the cancellation charge is one third of the ticket cost. For 'no shows' there is no refund at all. An interesting loophole is that if a flight is delayed by more than one hour, there is no cancellation charge if you decide not to fly.

BUS TICKETS

Booking a bus ticket is, surprisingly, often easier than buying a plane ticket. Most bus routes are served by several companies, so the competition forces them into a bit of efficiency – at least in the sales department. Bus rates are fixed by the government, but vary with the class of service. Nepalese buses are built for Nepalis – who average 175 cm (5 feet 8 inches) in height and 65 kg (140 lbs) in weight. Anyone who has any experience with Asian travel will be familiar with Nepalese buses. Long distance buses depart from two places: the bus terminal behind the Electric Corporation near Bagh Bazaar (just across from Ratna Park) and from Sundhara, the area near the General Post Office. Tickets should be purchased a day ahead at either of these places – there are a large number of ticket outlets at both. Be sure to find out where the bus departs from, and when; the tickets are usually printed only in Nepalese script. Seats are assigned when you buy your ticket; if you are large, look for a seat in the front or near the door. Seating charts are rare, and there is no assurance that the bus that travels will have seats that match the chart (if it does exist). It might be worthwhile to go to the bus station a day or two ahead and see the buses that each company operates and find out which seats have a bit of room.

When you budget your expenses, remember that there are extra charges for luggage. Large pieces of luggage go on the roof, and you either drag it up the ladder on the back of the bus, or pay a rupee or two to have someone do it for you. The baggage charge is often negotiable with the conductor and is higher for the so-called express and deluxe services.

An 'express' bus is anything but express, but it certainly beats the local, which can take twice (or more) as long as the express. The express bus usually takes twice as long as a private vehicle. The Swiss Bus Service serves Pokhara; this is a holdover from the time when the company had a Swiss Post Bus, but this vanished long ago, so the service is only marginally better than the buses that cost ten rupees less.

Unlike airplanes, which depart with a minimum of ceremony, buses in Nepal make a great drama out of their departure. Honking horns, racing engines, last minute baggage loading and an attempt to cram a few extra passengers, chickens and goats on board make a huge production that can often delay departures. Bring a book to read.

Occasionally it is possible to sit on the roof of the bus after it leaves Kathmandu.

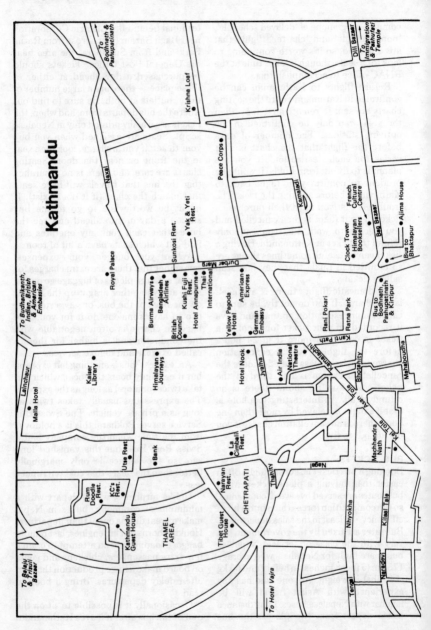

Kathmandu

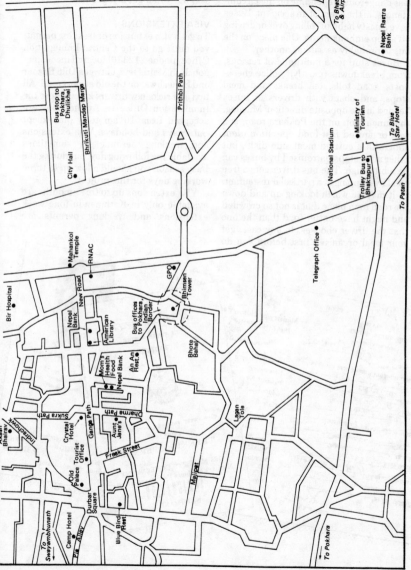

This is often an attractive spot if the weather is warm; it's also either more or less dangerous, depending on the circumstances, in the event of an accident. Buses have a nasty habit of rolling over or driving off steep embankments. One place on the bus is probably as safe as another.

Buses stop for a multitude of reasons, from breakdowns (mostly), police checkposts, road tolls, tea breaks and meal stops, and chats with drivers of buses headed in the opposite direction. Mugling, the lunch stop on the Pokhara road, is a well organised fast-food operation (*daal bhat* with a curried meat side dish), but other meal stops patronised by buses can be a bit rough. The bus driver gets a free meal by stopping at a particular restaurant, so it may be worth looking up and down the road for a place that is not so crowded and might have better food than the one that the driver chooses. In any case, get your meal organised first before you do any wandering around; it's impossible to predict how long the stop will be. You can ask, but you'll get a vague answer.

VISA EXTENSIONS

To get a visa extension or trekking permit, you must go to the Central Immigration Office (phone 212336) located inconspicuously in Maiti Devi, between Dilli Bazaar and Baneshwar on the old airport road. All taxi and rickshaw drivers know where the Immigration Office is. Applications are accepted from 10 am to 2 pm except Saturdays and holidays. Visa extensions and trekking permits are sometimes available the following day, but during the busy season you should allow up to three working days for this project.

Visa extensions up to three months are available only in Kathmandu (one week extensions and trekking permits are

available in Pokhara). Visa extension fees are high: Rs 300 (US$20) for the second month and Rs 600 (US$40) for the third month. One photograph is required and you must produce a bank certificate showing that you have officially exchanged US$5 for each day of the visa extension. The minimum visa extension period is one week. Tourist visas cannot normally be extended beyond three months, but you can leave the country and return for another three month cycle. Visa extensions are free with trekking permits, but you are supposed to get your trekking permit stamped during your trek to prove that you actually did go trekking. It would be judicious to get your trekking permit endorsed at any police checkposts that you come across if you plan to get a second trekking permit or a further visa extension. There is a fine for overstaying your visa. You cannot leave the country until the fine is paid and this can cause a fuss at the airport when you leave.

TREKKING PERMITS

A Nepal visa is only valid for the Kathmandu Valley, Pokhara and Chitwan National Park in the terai. A trekking permit issued by the Immigration Office is required for all foreigners who travel outside these regions. The permit specifies the places you may visit and the maximum duration of your trek.

A trekking permit application form, two photographs, your passport, a bank certificate or currency exchange card and a fee are all necessary to obtain a trekking permit. A trekking permit costs Rs 60 (US$4) per week for the first month of trekking and Rs 75 per week for the second and third month. Your exchange card must show that you have changed the equivalent of US$5 for each day you wish to go trekking – there is talk that this amount will be raised. Your trekking permit will be checked at several points along most trails and is sometimes checked at Kathmandu airport before you are allowed to board a flight to another

part of Nepal. There are three preprinted trekking permit forms, so it is only necessary to state 'Everest', 'Annapurna', or 'Langtang' on the application if you are headed to one of these areas. The preprinted forms allow all the possible routes in each region. For less usual destinations you should include a fairly extensive list of village or district names on the application. Be sure that the destination is shown correctly on your trekking permit; it cannot be altered except in Kathmandu or Pokhara.

It is not necessary (as it was in 1976) to have a trekking company arrange a trekking permit for you, although a trekking company can usually obtain a permit faster than you could do it yourself.

PORTER INSURANCE

Trekkers are required to insure all their sherpas and porters for Rs 25,000 (about US$1600) against accidental death although so few individual trekkers do this that the insurance companies would be surprised at the request. Trekking companies have a blanket policy that covers all their staff. Oriental Insurance Co and Rashtriya Bima Sansthan in Kathmandu can provide the required coverage for a fee of about US$8 per person. These companies can also provide (at a higher cost) insurance for sherpas if you are climbing a trekking peak.

There is no rescue insurance available in Nepal. You should organise this before you come if you want this protection for yourself.

MONEY ON THE TREK

The Nepal rupee has an official exchange rate of about US$1 = Rs 18.0. The value of the Nepal rupee is determined by the Nepal Rastra Bank (the national bank) in accordance with a 'basket of currencies' and varies day to day. The rates are announced on Radio Nepal and published in the *Rising Nepal*, the local English-language daily.

Current values are:

US$1	= Rs 18
A$1	= Rs 15
£1	= Rs 22
100 Ind. Rs	= Rs 144

Rs 10	= US$0.55
Rs 10	= A$0.67
Rs 10	= £0.45

The rupee is divided into 100 *paisaa*; in the hills the shopkeepers often do their calculations in units of 50 *paisaa*, called a *mohar*. Rs 1.50 is three *mohar*.

When you change money be sure to get a receipt or the money changer's stamp on your bank card. They don't always do this, but you will need to prove to the immigration office that you changed money officially when you apply for a trekking permit or visa extension, so you should insist on an exchange certificate.

If you will be trekking on your own, you should have enough money in rupees to cover all your expenses on the trek. It is usually not possible to change money or travellers' cheques except in Kathmandu or Pokhara. It is most important to have enough money to purchase a plane ticket (if you did not buy a ticket in advance) if you plan to fly back from Lukla, Pokhara or Jomsom. Years ago, flights to these airports operated as charters and it used to be possible to bargain the airfare or leave a passport as a deposit and 'fly now, pay later'. Now all flights are scheduled RNAC operations, so prices are fixed and tickets must be paid for in cash and in advance.

You can estimate your trekking costs in hotels at Rs 20 to 30 per day for food and Rs 5 to Rs 12 per day for lodging in the lowlands; these costs are a bit higher above about 4000 metres. You should estimate US$20 per day or more per person if you have porters, sherpas and all the trappings.

The money you take on the trek should be in notes of from one to 100 rupees.

There is a 500 and a 1000 rupee note; it is usually difficult to change these in the hills, but even these can often be changed at banks in Namche, Chame, Jomsom and Pokhara. If you are going to a particularly remote area (the Arun River or far west Nepal) you should carry stacks of 1, 5 and 10 rupee notes, but this is not necessary on the more popular routes. Consider yourself lucky that paper money is now accepted throughout Nepal. On the 1953 Everest expedition, all money had to be carried as coins – the money alone took 30 porter loads!

THE POST OFFICE

The only practical way to send letters to Nepal is airmail; surface mail (by sea via Calcutta) takes months. Mail service to and from Nepal is not totally reliable; important letters should be sent via registered mail. Cheques should never be sent through the mail – if someone is sending you money it should be done through the bank. It is almost impossible to clear a parcel through customs – do not send packages to Nepal except in an extreme emergency. Poste restante is located in the General Post Office. Your passport is required when you collect letters. If you can arrange to have your mail sent to a company that has a post office box, that is a bit more reliable. Many embassies will receive mail on your behalf and American Express has an office in Kathmandu that handles client mail. As with all mail in Asia, outgoing letters should be taken personally to the post office and you should see that the stamps are cancelled in your presence.

HIRING EQUIPMENT

It is possible to hire in Kathmandu everything that you need for a trek – from clothing to sleeping bags, tents and cooking pots. All of the equipment that is for rent or sale in Kathmandu is left-over from mountaineering expeditions or was sold by trekkers when they had finished their own treks. There is, therefore, no reliable stock of any particular item and there is not a complete range of sizes of clothing. Large size shoes are often difficult to find as are gas cartridges, freeze-dried food (sometimes) and good socks, otherwise it is almost certain that you can arrange everything you need in Kathmandu – though it will probably take a day or two of shopping. The best trekking equipment shops are in Thamel near Kathmandu Guest House and Basantapur (Freak St). A hefty deposit is required when you hire equipment, but a guide known to the shop can occasionally make a personal guarantee that the gear will be returned and save the hassle of dealing with a deposit.

Tents, sleeping bags, mattresses and cooking pots can often be hired through trekking companies. A guide hired from the same company can certainly serve as a guarantee and avoid the deposit problem. If you are hiring a cook it may be worth making a deal with a trekking company to rent kitchen equipment – new kitchen equipment can cost upwards of Rs 200 per trekker and is difficult to sell at the end of the trek. Pots and pans, plates and eating utensils are available anywhere in the Kathmandu bazaar; if you do buy this equipment, beware that your cook does not buy lots of extra items that catch his eye. A kerosene pressure lantern is a useful but troublesome addition to the kitchen gear – it does help to extend the day by allowing breakfast to be prepared early and dinner to end late. If you have a cook and are trekking in a national park you should arrange a stove; the Indian kerosene stoves are expensive and delicate – it might be worth considering taking meals in hotels if you are planning only a short stay in the Everest or Langtang parks. Theoretically the entrance station personnel will check to see that you have a stove and kerosene if you enter the park with a group.

A limited supply of equipment is available for sale and rent in Pokhara and in Namche Bazar. There is some gear available at Lukla and at other places in the Everest region; it is usually found in private homes, not in shops. There is a need for rental equipment in Manang and Muktinath so it is likely that some enterprising person will arrange to have gear available in these places before too long. Other than these places it is unlikely that you will find any gear for rent or sale except by accident (a mountaineering expedition returning home, for example).

HIRING GUIDES & PORTERS

Nepal is still a very structured society – a holdover from the old caste system. This structure leads to people having very definite ideas ingrained since birth about what jobs they will or will not do. If someone considers himself a trekking guide, he will be reluctant to carry a porter load. A porter is often reluctant to take on camp chores or other guide duties, and if he does agree to do this, guides may work to discourage – or even prevent – him from doing this. The ideal combination of a guide/porter is a rare phenomenon, though a few do exist; if you are lucky enough to find one of these people, you can probably get away with a single employee for a trek.

Hiring only a single porter, or hiring several porters without a guide, sounds like a good idea and is usually easy to arrange at the outset, but it is not always easy to administer this sort of situation on the trail. While you can sometimes find reliable porters, most are uneducated people who are subject to whims, fears, ill health and superstition. Your porter may vanish, or he may decide that he has gone far enough and wants to return home. If you have a (hopefully) reliable sherpa, and he has hired the porter, it is his responsibility to assure the porter's performance, and he will be intimidated into carrying the load himself (the only situation in which a sherpa will carry a porter load) until he can find another porter – and you can be sure that he will do so in a hurry. If you have hired the porter yourself, you sit alongside the trail until a replacement comes along, or carry your pack yourself.

There have been endless discussions about the establishment of a porter registration system and a central recruiting agency for porters, and in 1984 the Trekking Agents Association of Nepal (TAAN) received a government grant to develop such a system. It would be worthwhile to check with the TAAN office at Keshar Mahal (tel 212618), on the road between the Royal Palace and Thamel, to see what facilities they have available. Trekking with only a porter is a bit difficult because you must constantly be aware of where he is in order to protect your possessions unless you have somehow managed to secure the services of someone whose reliablity is proven. Even this isn't foolproof – I've had a porter who had been on two treks disappear on the third trek with two duffel bags of gear.

Guides may be hired through trekking companies, trekking equipment shops or referrals from other trekkers. Out-of-work sherpas may often be found outside of the Immigration Office or in Asan Tole *momo* and *rakshi* shops. Hiring a guide directly is a hit or miss situation – you might find someone brilliant or you might have endless problems. It is not likely that you would hit upon someone whose sole purpose was to steal from you, but such people do exist and are offering their services as guides. All embassies in Nepal suggest that you go through a known middle man or else check references carefully before you employ a guide.

A good trekking guide can arrange porters, and you will find that things will work much better if you give him guidelines about where you wish to trek and the salary you are prepared to pay and have him do all the negotiations on your behalf. On a long trek a good guide will lay off porters en route as loads of food are eaten or replace porters when they get too far from their homes. Wages for porters are established by the government at a minimum of Rs 21 per day below 3700

metres and Rs 30 per day in the mountain regions, but demand from other trekkers and expeditions can drive prices as high as Rs 35, even Rs 40 or 50 per day. Roadbuilding in the hills also pushes up porter wages while the construction passes through a village. Porters are expected to buy their own food out of their wages, so you do not ordinarily have to carry food for them. Unless you do provide food and shelter for the porters, however, you will have to camp near a village where they can obtain food every night.

One important facility that must be considered when you employ porters is warm clothing and equipment for cold and snow. In Khumbu this is usually not a problem because you will probably hire Sherpas or Sherpanis (women) who have their own shoes and warm clothing – though you should ask them to be sure. The place that most problems occur is with porters crossing Thorong La, the pass between Manang and Muktinath. From whatever direction the pass is approached, the route starts in low tropical country and any porters that you hire will probably be from these lowland regions. When cold and snow is encountered, the unequipped lowland porters either quit and turn back, or continue foolishly with no proper clothing or footgear, often resulting in frostbite, snowblindness, or even death. Porters are not generally available in Manang or Muktinath, so it is really worth the extra planning and expense to purchase porter clothing and sunglasses in Kathmandu (though occasionally such items are available in Manang) if you plan to use porters on this pass. You should have some sort of shelter for them for the one or two nights that shelter is scarce. If you are going into snow, you must provide goggles, shoes, shelter and clothing; porters are not expendable. You must also provide plastic sheets (available in Kathmandu) for porters to protect themselves, and your baggage, from rain.

When you do provide equipment for porters, be sure to make it clear whether it is a loan or a gift. In reality it will be very hard to get equipment back that you have loaned unless you are very determined and thick-skinned; the porters and sherpas have special techniques to make you feel guilty and petty when you ask for equipment to be returned to you.

Health & Safety

MEDICAL EXAM

The worst place on your adventure to discover that you have a medical problem is on the trek itself. The medical section below makes some suggestions about a medical exam. Most trekking agents supply an examination form that is designed to outline to your doctor some of the potential problems of a trek and to ensure that he views the examination a little more seriously than a routine life insurance exam. Be sure that any abnormalities, chronic problems, or special medicines are listed on the form. This will help you to identify the problems in case you exhibit any symptoms along the trek. If you are trekking on your own, it's a good idea to carry a brief outline of your medical history and notes on any special problems or allergies with you in case you do have an accident or illness in a remote region.

PHYSICAL CONDITIONING

Obviously, the better the shape you are in, the more you will enjoy a trek. You do not have to be an Olympic athlete, but you should be in condition for the activity you are going to do – a lot of walking.

The best way to get into shape for trekking is to walk. If you take a strenuous hiking trip every other weekend for a few months before the trek, you will be in good condition. Try to climb – and descend – as many hills as you possibly can. Walk up stairs rather than take a lift. Walk or bicycle to work. Be sure your boots fit and are well broken in; if possible, make your training jaunts in the same boots you will wear on the trek. This will also give you a chance to find out whether the nylon/wool socks are comfortable for you and whether tennis shoes or running shoes give enough support to your feet during long walks.

If you have the opportunity to climb a mountain to get used to high altitude, this conditioning will certainly help, although it does not guarantee that you will not have trouble at high elevations.

Although a trek is usually not particularly strenuous at any given time, and you are waited upon almost to the point of embarrassment, even if you stay in hotels, a trek is long; probably longer than you have ever been in the outdoors. The continual day-to-day grind up and down hills can be a relaxing experience or just a nightmare. Be sure you do enjoy walking and are willing to put up with the regimentation of walking each and every day – whether you feel like it or not, although if you trek on your own you can always spend a day resting if you arrive some place you really like.

MEDICAL CONSIDERATIONS

By David R Shlim, MD
Medical Director,
Himalayan Rescue Association

Whenever a person returns from a trip to Nepal, he or she is usually greeted by two questions: 'Did you have a good time?' and 'Did you get sick?' The answer to both questions is likely to be 'yes', but the percentage of travellers who become ill enough to seriously alter their plans is very small. I will try to outline some of the major problems that you will face in Nepal and how to approach them.

Preparation for a Trek

The routine physical examination is over-rated as a means of predicting problems that young healthy people will have while trekking. However, it is worth your while to investigate little nagging problems or any unexplained recurrent symptoms before you go, because problems have a way of escalating under the stresses of travel. Hemorrhoids can become markedly worse with diarrhoea or constipation. Most developing tooth problems can be detected by a thorough dental checkup. This is highly recommended because reliable dental care is difficult to obtain in Nepal. Repeated urinary tract infections in women, ear or eye problems, abdominal problems such as gastritis or ulcer symptoms, a chronic cough or wheezing, and particularly chronic musculoskeletal problems such as tendinitis or bursitis should be investigated or treated prior to a long trip to Asia that involves trekking in remote, difficult terrain.

People over age 40 often worry about altitude and potential heart problems. There is no clear data that altitude is likely to bring out heart disease or heart attacks that have not previously been suspected. However, having your first heart symptoms in a remote village at 4200 metres and two weeks walk from a hospital increases the anxiety and difficulty of obtaining treatment. If an older person runs or hikes regularly on difficult terrain, there is no reason at present to think that altitude will be an increased risk for that person. If you would like reassurance because you are not very active in your daily life, a stress electrocardiogram obtained near the time of your trip will bring you to your maximal heart-rate and exertion under a controlled situation and detect any heart strain. Physical training, particularly walking up and down hills, is the best method of preparing for trekking in Nepal. Jogging helps, but does not really prepare you for the hills unless you run on hills. Weight training, particularly on Nautilus equipment, can help build leg strength for the relentless 2000-metre climbs that occur on some treks. It is not just aerobic conditioning that is important, but you must try to condition your joints, particularly the knees, to continual up and down hill travel. The only way to do this is to take walks up and down hills. Cycling builds thigh strength but doesn't condition the legs to the pounding they can take.

Immunizations & Prophylaxis

Nepal currently has no official vaccination requirements for entry. However, you should make an effort to protect yourself from some of the serious infectious diseases that can be prevented by vaccine or prophylactic (preventive) measures.

It is often said that you should consult a doctor regarding immunization advice before travelling to Asia. In all fairness to your doctor, it is very difficult to have current or accurate information about travelling in Asia unless you have a special interest in that area. By not wanting to seem unhelpful or unknowledgeable, your doctor may give off-hand advice based on old data or inaccurate memory or lack of awareness of the real problems. If you consult your doctor, give that person a chance to tell you whether he or she actually knows anything about travel in Asia. If not, see if you can be referred to a doctor or clinic that has some particular interest in the problem. It will save your doctor some embarrassment at not nowing everything, and will be well worth your while in the long run. You can use this chapter as a starting point for your discussion.

Smallpox Thanks to an incredible world-wide effort at eradication, smallpox no longer exists as a disease. The vaccination is therefore neither required nor available.

Cholera Unfortunately this vaccine can still be required to enter some countries, notably India. Health cards are not routinely checked, but can be asked for at random. The vaccine is not very effective at preventing cholera infection, and it often causes a significant reaction itself. The chances of acquiring cholera under any circumstances of travel are remote: a recent study calculated the risk at less than one in ten thousand for US travellers abroad. The incidence of tourists acquiring cholera in Nepal is much less than this. The dilemma of whether to obtain the vaccine or risk being held at a border and either sent back or given a less than sterile infection will remain until this vaccine requirement is dropped. Fortunately, as I said, Nepal does not require this or any other vaccine.

Typhoid This disease is prevalent in Nepal and the vaccine probably offers significant protection. A new oral vaccine which promises to be more effective may be available soon. Either vaccine is recommended.

Tetanus & Diphtheria The vast majority of people from western countries receive these vaccines in childhood. The tetanus and diphtheria germs are world-wide, and overseas travel is a good chance to catch up on your immunity. You should take a booster if it has been longer than ten years since your last one.

Polio The current generation is no longer afraid of polio because vaccination has made it rare in the west. In fact, the disease is rising in the US because some parents are irrationally more afraid of the vaccine than the disease. However, no such eradication has taken place in Asia, and a booster for people who have been previously immunized is recommended before travelling to Nepal. If you somehow grew up without getting immunized, you should complete a series before heading out to Asia.

Immune Serum Globulin (Gamma Globulin) This is not a vaccine, but a collection of blood protein taken from other humans which is likely to contain antibodies against hepatitis A. Although there is debate about its effectiveness, particularly among doctors who see very little hepatitis, there is no debate in Kathmandu. The combined experience of all the clinics here has yet to find a case of hepatitis in a traveller who had had at least five cc's in the past four months. Not one.

Recently, because of the rise of the acquired immunodeficiency syndrome (AIDS) in the US, some travellers are electing not to use gamma globulin for fear of acquiring AIDS. The World Health Organization held a conference on this subject in 1983 and decided that gamma globulin carried no risk of transmitting AIDS. This was based on two main facts: one, that no case of hepatitis B, a blood-borne virus, was ever linked to the administration of gamma globulin (and AIDS has been proven to be caused by a virus); and two, 19.5 million doses of gamma globulin have been given since AIDS was first noted in 1980 and no cases have been linked to the injection. The risk of acquiring hepatitis A is significant while travelling in Asia, and probably increases with the length of the trip rather than decreases. Trekkers have occasionally had to be evacuated because of the disease showing up while on the trail, and one US tourist died of fulminant hepatitis which would probably have been prevented if he had taken gamma globulin.

This injection is probably the single most important of all I have listed in terms of protecting both your health and your trip.

Malaria There is currently no vaccine against malaria, although this may be available within the decade. Chloroquine phosphate is recommended in a single weekly dose (500 mg) in non-resistant malaria areas and Chloroquine *plus* Fansidar (one pill once a week) is necessary where resistance has been shown. The incidence of malaria in travellers is going up because of failure to take malaria prophylaxis. I recently treated a traveller who spent just two nights in a malaria area without prophylaxis and developed malaria two weeks later. Except for the terai, or lowland area of Nepal near the Indian border, there is no risk of malaria in the rest of the country above 1000 metres.

Rabies Vaccine In recent years a new rabies vaccine derived from human cells in the laboratory has obviated the need for repeated painful injections into abdominal muscles. The use of the Human Diploid Cell Vaccine (HDCV) differs from the use of other vaccine in significant ways. A pre-exposure series (before any suspicious animal bite) of three injections spaced over a month can produce anti-rabies antibodies. However, the level of these antibodies is inadequate to give complete protection *after* a bite. An additional two shots are mandatory after exposure to a potentially rabid animal. If the person has not taken pre-exposure shots, the post-exposure treatment follows a different regimine that can be very difficult to obtain in Nepal and is quite expensive. This post-exposure schedule involves five injections of HDCV over a period of one month *plus* a one-time injection of rabies antibodies purified from other people's blood. This injection is given in the first few days after the regimen is started and protects you during the time that it takes for your own body to start making antibodies in response to the vaccine. It is this injection, called Rabies Immune Globulin (RIG) that is so difficult to obtain and is so expensive. An average single injection in Kathmandu can cost US$400 to US$600 depending on the body weight of the patient.

As you can see, there is an advantage to having the pre-exposure series if you are going to be travelling for a long time in an endemic area. (Nepal is an endemic area.) If you are coming to Nepal for a relatively short time (less than a month) and mainly going trekking at high altitude, your risk would not warrant the pre-exposure series. If you are planning to travel for months across Asia and want to worry less about the consequences of a dog or monkey leaping out and biting you, you should consider the pre-exposure series. Just remember that a bite must still be followed by post-exposure treatment even if you take this series.

Hygiene on the Trek
As perverse as it sounds to put it this way,

the germs that cause diarrhoea are acquired mainly from eating someone else's stool. One of the major medical advances of western countries was to develop a sure way of keeping stool out of the water supply. This problem has not been solved in Nepal, and all water must be viewed as being potentially contaminated. While there is no consensus on fool-proof methods of purifying water, here are some of the considerations.

All of the stool pathogens (disease producers) can be killed if water is boiled hot enough and long enough. Hot enough would not ordinarily be a consideration, but at the impressive altitudes of up to 5500 metres that trekkers routinely travel to, the boiling temperature of water may be inadequate to kill some organisms. I am not aware of specific data on this problem. Chemicals can be added to water to kill these pathogens, and currently iodine seems to offer the best chance of killing all the major germs including the hepatitis virus.

There are four practical ways to carry iodine on a trek.

1. Tetraglycine hydroperiodide tablets
2. Logol's solution
3. Tincture of Iodine
4. Iodine crystals

Tetraglycine hydroperiodide tablets are not available in Nepal, are hard to find anywhere, although REI in the USA stock them, and can deteriorate in as little as six months in their original containers. If you can find a fresh supply of these tablets, they are the best choice; if not, you'll have to take your chances with one of the other methods.

Lugol's solution is a water-based iodine concentrate; eight drops per litre of water is sufficient to purify reasonably clean, cool water. It is available in Kathmandu at many pharmacies, especially the larger ones on New Rd. Tincture of iodine is an alcohol-based iodine solution; you must use more of this to purify a given amount of water; it tastes even worse than other sources of iodine.

To use iodine crystals, place five to seven grams of crystals in a 30 ml glass bottle with a bakelite cap (do not use a plastic bottle – the iodine eats it). The iodine is available from some pharmacies in Kathmandu and this amount will treat about 500 litres of water. Fill the bottle with water, shake it for a few minutes, then let the iodine crystals settle to the bottom. The resulting concentrated solution, *not the crystals*, may be added to your water bottle to purify the water for drinking. After using some of the solution, refill the iodine bottle with water and shake it again to make more concentrated solution.

Nothing is without its drawbacks. If you have a few grams of Iodine in a bottle, you have two to four times a lethal dose of Iodine. If you accidentally dump the whole dose into your water bottle and drink the crystals, you could die.

Recently some filtering devices designed to purify water for backpackers and trekkers have come onto the market. Filtering eliminates suspended particles that might hamper the effects of iodine, and micro-filters can actually trap bacteria and some cysts, but again, not the hepatitis virus. A combination of treatment with iodine and filtering may prove to be the most reliable, but the filters have not yet caught on widely.

Unfortunately, just treating your water carefully will not eliminate the chances of eating someone else's stool. Contamination of food from people's hands remains a major source of infection, and vegetables and fruits can also be contaminated from the soil they are grown in. The general rule is to not eat any vegetables that cannot be peeled or freshly cooked unless you are certain of the methods that have been used to soak them. Many restaurants in Kathmandu now soak their vegetables in an acceptable manner to make them safe, but if you are not sure, don't eat them. The locally brewed *chhang*, a fermented brew

made from corn, rice, or millet, is reconstituted with untreated water and is a source of infection for unwary travellers. However, since the drinking of *chhang* is so tied up in social custom, many travellers are forced to put aside their judgment so as not to offend generous hosts.

Making a point of washing your own hands frequently can also help prevent illness. I have not found a solution to the problem of dishes in tea houses being washed in untreated water, except to observe that the amount of contamination received that way is likely to be minimal. My overall feeling is that you should always do your best to avoid known sources of contamination, but don't worry excessively about those areas in which you have no control.

One area you *can* control is the disposal of toilet paper. Bury, burn (put matches or a cigarette lighter in with your toilet paper), or carry it in a plastic bag for later disposal. While not a health menace, scattered pink toilet paper along the trail and in the woods represents the worst form of visual pollution.

Diarrhoea

Diarrhoea remains the novice Asian traveller's biggest fear. Experienced travellers learn that the consistency of their stools is likely to change throughout their trip, but that they will rarely be seriously ill. Almost all diarrhoea in travellers is caused by eating or drinking something that is contaminated by someone else's stool. You must make up your mind to be conscientious about what and how you eat, and to *never* drink untreated water. New travellers tend to be overcautious – I've seen people putting iodine in their tea – but all too often experienced travellers tend to be too casual, mistakenly believing that some kind of 'resistance' has developed. These people occasionally develop serious illness as a result.

In general, most cases of diarrhoea that you would develop while travelling will go away without treatment. If they go on for several days, or you are concerned because you are leaving for a trek, a stool exam can be helpful to see if there is a treatable cause for your symptoms. If you are trekking and develop diarrhoea, the guidelines for treatment that I have given can be applied. Trekking, however popular and familiar it is becoming, still involves being many days from any form of medical help or evacuation, and therefore some idea of how to diagnose and treat someone on the trail can be of significant value.

The intestines of normal people harbour trillions of micro-organisms of many different types. These generally live in harmony with each other and their host, and the body produces a consistent amount of formed stools without abdominal discomfort. When certain other organisms are accidentally ingested they can irritate the bowels either through the production of a toxin or by directly invading the wall of the bowel. The bowel reacts by secreting extra fluid hoping to wash out the unwanted invaders. This results in loose, watery stool and often crampy abdominal pain as the intestines react to the new germs. The process of fighting off foreign germs in the intestine is remarkably successful, and almost all viral or bacterial diarrhoeas in previously healthy people are self-limiting, meaning that they will cure themselves without having to take medication. Certain other parasites, notably giardia and some species of amoeba are harder for the body to combat and medication plays an important role. In general the causes of gastro-intestinal upset while travelling in Asia are as follows:

Gastrointestinal Viruses Viruses are the smallest of all germs, and the hardest to treat with medication. They can cause diarrhoea for one to several days, but the body is universally able to fight them off. The stool exam is usually reasonably normal, without pus cells or blood, and no antibiotic treatment is necessary or even

helpful. Specialized experimental laboratories are needed to prove which viruses are involved, but this is of interest only in an epidemiological sense.

Gastrointestinal Bacteria Although the intestines are inhabited by trillions of 'normal' bacteria, certain species of germs cause significant problems when ingested. These germs have names such as shigella, salmonella, and campylobacter. The diarrhoea can occasionally be severe, and pus, muscus, and even blood can sometimes be seen in the stool. Occasionally nausea, vomiting, and fever are present. If the afflicted individual can take in enough fluids to account for all the water being lost in the stool, recovery without treatment is the general rule, with illness lasting one to seven days or so.

Recently there has been increased interest in preventing and treating these diarrhoeas with antibiotics. Although the benefits and risks have not been clearly established, some researchers found that people travelling for a short time (two or three weeks) in underdeveloped countries could prevent a certain amount of diarrhoea by taking one antibiotic pill each day. The first pill tested, doxycycline, is quite expensive, can cause nausea on an empty stomach, and can sensitize the skin to the sun producing a painful rash. However, it did offer significant protection against some kinds of *bacterial* diarrhoea. However, there are no studies published which show whether the protective effect can be continued for several months, or what the negative effects of taking full doses of antibiotics for a long time might be. Certain other antibiotics have been tested in the same way and found to be effective also.

A group of researchers who were concerned about masses of travellers taking antibiotics daily for long periods tested the effectiveness of taking an antibiotic as soon as the traveller developed symptoms, but not before. They found that this method significantly shortened the time that the person was bothered by the diarrhoea, often cutting five days of symptoms down to one or two. The antibiotic used was a combination of trimethoprim and sulfamethoxasole marketed as Bactrim DS or Septra DS. This method has obvious advantages over taking medication daily throughout a long trip.

These studies were aimed at people who had been in a new country for a short time and the diarrhoea that they developed has been termed 'traveller's diarrhoea'. When a person has been travelling for a number of weeks or months in an area of risk, the development of diarrhoea can be due to many different causes and a more rigorous view should be taken. At this point the problem can more aptly be called 'diarrhoea in travellers', rather than 'traveller's diarrhoea.' However, if you have been well and experience the sudden onset of crampy, watery diarrhoea, my approach is to wait two days and if symptoms persist, begin Bactrim DS at a dose of one every 12 hours for three to five days. This is a sulfa drug and should not be taken by someone allergic to this class of drug. An alternative is tetracycline 250 mg, four times a day for five days. This should not be given to children under nine years old. If the symptoms persist after three or four days, consideration should be given to another diagnosis.

Taking a curative pill at the first sign of diarrhoea is a nice thought, but unfortunately, there are still several more causes of diarrhoea that would not be treated by this method. These include:

Food Poisoning Some bacteria, if deposited on food that is conducive to their growth, produce a very potent poison as they grow. If you eat this portion of food, you can become violently ill within four to eight hours, with the sudden onset of nausea, vomiting, fever, and profuse watery diarrhoea. Fortunately, most of these victims are well on the way to recovery by the time they are strong

enough to leave their rooms and seek help, usually within 12 to 24 hours. In these cases the body is reacting to the poison, not the germs themselves and therefore no antibiotics are necessary. Attempting to drink as much as possible to prevent dehydration is the only therapy necessary.

Giardia This organism was once thought to be rarely associated with illness. Now we are quite clear about its role in disease, and it is becoming common in many developed countries as well. They are much larger than bacteria, and tend to live in the upper part of the intestine where few bacteria generally live. They are oval shaped and propel themselves around with a tail when they are in the host. When they decide it's time to move to another host, they secrete a sturdy shell and become a non-active cyst. These cysts are strong enough to survive in mountain streams, in dust, and to pass through the intense stomach acid of a new host. They can be killed in water by boiling or by adding iodine.

Once ingested they begin causing symptoms after one or two weeks. Upper abdominal discomfort, 'churning intestines', foul smelling burps and farts, and on and off diarrhoea are the main characteristics of giardiasis. Often people have symptoms for a week to a month or more before deciding to seek treatment because it seems like it is going away, only to recur in a few days. Sometimes the only symptoms are one to three urgent loose bowel movements in the morning followed by a symptom-free day and night, repeated day after day. Because the organisms live in the upper part of the intestine, they don't consistently show up in stool exams, although it is definitely worth looking. If a giardia infection is suspected, and a stool exam is either unavailable or negative, it is often reasonable to treat yourself anyway. If you have guessed right, the relief of symptoms is often dramatic.

In Nepal, the drug of choice is tinidazole (brand name Tiniba), readily available without prescription. The dose is two grams all at once, one time only (four 500 mg tablets). This single dose is 95 percent effective at curing a giardia infection. The medication can cause a bad taste in the mouth, headache, loss of appetite, and nausea, and must never be taken with alcohol. However, these side-effects rarely last more than a day, and can be partly ameliorated by taking your dose at night and sleeping through them.

Amoeba The term 'amoebic dysentary' still strikes fear into the heart of the Asia traveller, even though the percentage of people who get very sick from an amoebic infection is quite low. Amoebas are shapeless protozoans that live in the large intestine. There are many different species, but only a few can cause symptoms. Occasionally, amoeba can migrate through the blood stream to the liver and cause a serious abscess characterized by fever and pain in the liver. Symptoms of an amoebic infection include abdominal pain, diarrhoea (which occasionally alternates with constipation), sometimes fever, and sometimes blood in the stool. Weight loss and chronic fatigue can accompany long-standing infections. I have found it difficult to diagnose an amoebic infection on the basis of symptoms alone. Fortunately, when diarrhoea is caused by amoebas, the stool exam is almost always positive.

The treatment of amoebic infections is also tinidazole, two grams taken as a single daily dose repeated on three consecutive days. Ideally the three days of tinidazole should be followed by 21 days of diodoquin 650 mg three times a day to thoroughly rid the intestines of the organism. Diodoquin has no significant side-effects and can be taken with alcohol.

Worms These intestinal parasites are never the cause of diarrhoea and rarely the cause of any symptoms. They can occasionally be associated with vague mild abdominal discomfort. It is very easy to get infested, and a dose of worm medicine at the end of your trip is a reasonable thing to do, even without a stool test. The medicine is mebendazole (Wormin in Nepal) one pill twice a day for three days.

Other Illness
Even when things are going well, travel is stress. Stress can make your body more susceptible to illness, particularly the new strains of viruses that you will be encountering for the first time. The crossing of time zones, all night train, plane, and bus rides, tropical heat, Himalayan cold, noise, dust, and culture shock all combine to occasionally bring the most hardened traveller to his or her knees. Most illnesses acquired in this manner are short-lived and minor, and in the course of a long trip are barely remembered, although they seem devastating while they are happening. On shorter trips they can interfere with tight schedules, but other than being aware of stress and taking what steps you can to reduce it, there is little you can do to prevent occasional illness while travelling.

Mountain Sickness
The Himalayan Rescue Association has a saying that 'the Himalayas begin where other mountain ranges leave off.' This refers to the fact that even if you trek to the height of 5500 metres, you are still only at the base of most mountains. The exposure over a period of days to weeks to these altitudes requires some adjustment by your body, a process called acclimatisation. If you move up in altitude too quickly, a syndrome known as Acute Mountain Sickness (AMS) can develop.

In the early '70s, when trekking was just becoming popular in Nepal, many groups had the shock of watching someone become ill with what seemed like the flu or a chest infection and then die within a day or two. As many as five to 10 people a year died in the Everest region alone out of a total of only 500 trekkers annually. Since then, mainly through efforts of the

Himalayan Rescue Association and the cooperation of trekking agencies in Kathmandu, increased awareness has limited the deaths from AMS in Nepal to one or two per year out of more than 30,000 trekkers. The risk in the Khumbu, the highest of the routine trekking areas, is approximately one death out of 5000 tourists.

AMS occurs as the result of failure to adapt to higher altitudes. Fluid accumulates in between the cells in the body and eventually collects where, unfortunately, it can do the most harm: in the lungs and brain. As fluid collects in the lungs, you become breathless more easily while walking, and eventually more breathless at rest. A cough begins, initially dry and irritative, but progressing to the production of pink, frothy sputum in its most severe form. The person ultimately drowns in this fluid if he doesn't descend. This syndrome is referred to as High Altitude Pulmonary Edema (HAPE). When fluid collects in the brain, you develop a headache, loss of appetite, nausea, and sometimes vomiting. You become increasingly tired and want to lay down and do nothing. As you progress, you develop a problem with your balance and coordination (ataxia). Eventually you lay down and slip into coma, and death is inevitable if you don't descend. This syndrome is called High Altitude Cerebral Edema (HACE). HAPE and HACE can occur singly or in combination.

Awareness of these syndromes has caused some trekkers to be unnecessarily anxious as they trek. The progression of symptoms is usually steady, but quite slow if symptoms are ignored, taking 24 to 48 hours or more. The onset of early symptoms, particularly headache or breathlessness should be a warning that you have reached your limit of acclimitization for now and not to ascend further until the symptoms have cleared, usually in one or two days. If you continue up with symptoms, they will inevitably become worse. If symptoms don't clear within 24 to 48 hours, or you are steadily getting worse, then you should descend at least to the last altitude at which you felt well. When you feel well it is safe to continue back up. However, if you have become quite ill before you descend, requiring someone else to help you down, you should not try to re-ascend on that particular trek.

AMS has been reported at any altitude over 1800 metres, although it occurs more commonly and more severely at higher altitudes. In general you should not ascend more than 300 metres per day above 3000 to 4000 metres. Instead of walking for short distances, most people spend an extra day at say 3700 metres before moving up to 4300 metres, thus averaging 300 metres per day. But no schedule will guarantee the individual trekker that he or she will not have symptoms.

People who elect to trek with organized groups have the problem of sticking to a group schedule. If they fail to acclimitize on a given day they often have to be left behind. Trekkers arranging their own treks have the luxury of being able to take an extra day at will if they don't feel well, and you should take advantage of this when necessary. Trekkers tend to be very goal oriented, and *ambition* can lead you to want to deny your symptoms. Over the years people have come to me with AMS symptoms which they explain away as being due to the sun, dehydration, hitting their head on a low doorway, sleeping in smoky teahouses, medicine they have taken, bronchitis, the flu, in fact *anything* except mountain sickness. None of these substitute conditions can be fatal; ignored AMS can be consistently so. If you feel ill at altitude and you are not sure why, assume it is AMS and react accordingly. Guessing wrong can have serious consequences. The Himalayan Rescue Association aid posts in Pheriche and Manang can give you helpful advice, but if you are on your own, be cautious. All of the fatalities in recent years have been in people who persisted in ascending despite symptoms that should have been recognized as AMS. AMS rarely strikes suddenly to the unsuspecting trekker. Relax and enjoy your trek if you are feeling well and be prepared to rest an extra day or so if you are not.

The treatment of AMS is first to not ascend with symptoms, and if symptoms are more severe, to descend. Descent will always bring improvement and should not be delayed in order to try some other form of therapy in serious cases. The one drug that has so far proven useful in the treatment of mild AMS is called Diamox (acetazolamide). It is useful in treating the headache and nausea associated with mild AMS, and it also can improve your sleep at altitude if you are being disturbed by the irregular breathing and breathlessness that can occur normally in sleeping people at altitude. Diamox can also help prevent symptoms of AMS if taken before ascent, but the HRA does not recommend its routine use for this in the Himalaya since treks often last for a month, and the majority of people will not need any drug. It could also promote a false sense of security against developing AMS. My recommendation regarding Diamox is to carry it with you, use it to treat mild symptoms, and use it prophylactically only if you have had experience before with AMS on a certain schedule. The usual dose is 250 mg every eight to 12 hours as needed. Mild tingling of hands and feet is common after taking Diamox and is not an indication to stop its use. Some people fear that Diamox can somehow 'mask' the symptoms of AMS. There is no basis for this fear. If you take Diamox and improve, you have improved. If you don't improve, consider descent.

Dr Peter Hackett, the former Medical Director of the Himalayan Rescue Association for many years, and one of the foremost researchers in the field, has written an excellent, concise book designed to be useful to trekkers and trek doctors alike, called *Mountain Sickness: Prevention Recognition & Treatment* published by the American Alpine Club in New York. It should be read and carried by anyone trekking in the Himalaya.

Diagnosing and responding to AMS involves making a number of key decisions. To outline how this process can take place, and to give some hints about the subtlety of AMS at times, I will go step-by-step through an actual case of AMS and point out some of the decisions that could have changed the outcome.

A 41-year-old fit and experienced man set off trekking with his wife and a group of friends from Kirantichhap to Kala Pattar. He experienced some dizzy spells at lower altitudes, but this had occurred occasionally throughout his life and did not raise concern. They aproached altitude gradually, and took a rest day at Namche (3440 metres). They then ascended to Thyangboche monastery at 3870 metres. The next morning he noted a headache, but continued on to Pheriche.

Note One Any headache that develops at altitude *must* be considered an early sign of AMS and the person should not ascend. People occasionally get headaches for other reasons at altitude, but since there is no way to distinguish these from AMS headaches they should be treated the same. In my three seasons working at the HRA Aid Post in Pheriche I found that any symptom of AMS invariably became worse with ascent.

The group spent the night at Pheriche and walked up the neighbouring Imja Khola Valley the next day, returning to Pheriche to sleep. The headache persisted, but his appetite was apparently all right. He visited the HRA doctor at the Aid Post.

Note Two The persistence of the headache only helps confirm its relationship to altitude. Often early AMS is accompanied by loss of appetite, but the absence of a specific symptom does not rule out AMS. This is why I don't stress a list of symptoms, but just a general sense of not doing well. However, headache is a symptom that must never be ignored. The man did in fact visit with the HRA doctor, but spoke with him only in general terms and did not confess having a headache. If he had, he would have been told not to ascend the next day.

The man moved up to Lobuje the next morning at 4930 metres. Along the way he began to have trouble with his balance, but remained apparently in good spirits. He decided that the balance trouble was either his old dizziness returning, or a reaction to some medication he had taken for his headache. He spent the night at Lobuje.

Note Three Difficulty with balance, or ataxia in medical terms, is an ominous sign of AMS and demonstrates increasing brain swelling. Because of his previous problem with balance, and the possible obscuring effect of taking medication, he chose to believe that there was an alternative explanation for his symptoms other than AMS. However, two of the explanations are harmless if ignored, one can be fatal. Which explanation would you want to believe at this point? In addition, most people suffering from AMS begin to become irritable and anti-social after a while. The man's good spirits unfortunately helped obscure the growing seriousness of the problem.

They set out early the next morning for the planned round trip to Kala Pattar (5545 metres). He found he was too weak to make it even to the base of Kala Pattar, and eventually had to be helped back to Lobuje, arriving there at 4.30 in the afternoon. Because it was late in the day (they were trekking in December), they decided to have him rest overnight at Lobuje and descend the next day.

Note Four As we have already decided that he should not have ascended to either Pheriche or Lobuje, his decision to try to reach Kala Pattar in light of a headache, difficulty in balance, and increasing weakness can only be seen as tragic. By now the group was suspecting AMS and considered descent, but were worried about the difficulties of following the trail in the dark and the cold.

The man went straight to bed at 4.30 pm and had no interest in dinner. At 7.30 pm he was checked and found to be able to answer questions. At 1.30 am, his wife could not awaken him. He was examined and found to be deeply comatose and unresponsive to any stimulation. In the next 20 minutes, while he was still being examined, his pulse suddenly stopped, and although cardiopulmonary rescusitation was tried for two hours, the man was dead.

Note Five Once the diagnosis of AMS is considered, and a person's condition is deteriorating at altitude, it is *never* too late in the day or night to descend. Sherpas are phenomenal at carrying people on their backs, and yaks can often be found that can be ridden. It is quite likely that if the victim had begun descending at 4.30 in the afternoon and kept going until there was some sign of improvement (often just 500 metres or less), he would have lived.

This true story demonstrates the subtlety of AMS at times, and the danger of guessing that symptoms might be due to something else. Trekking at altitude should be a very safe activity. It will be if you pay attention to your body and to the behavior of your friends and allow time to adjust to the extreme altitudes that seem deceptively low because of the height of the surrounding peaks. The fact that 5000 tourists a year rather than 500 now trek to Kala Pattar has not lowered its altitude.

RESCUE

If you walk into the mountains for two weeks from Kathmandu, you are two weeks' walk from Kathmandu. This fact often does not impress itself on trekkers until they become sick or injured on the trail and the desire to return to Kathmandu arises. Radios are few and far between in Nepal, and roads are just beginning to be extended into the hills. The Himalayan Rescue Association provides medical clinics and doctors in Pheriche near Mt Everest, and in Manang, on the Annapurna circuit, and there are a few other health posts. But in general, once you head into the hills, it will be up to you to get yourself out. Here are some hints for accomplishing this.

First of all, don't panic. If someone falls, take some time to assess the situation; suspected broken bones may only be bruises, a dazed person may wake up and be quite all right in an hour or two. If the problem is severe diarrhoea, try to follow the guidelines on the Diarrhoea section. If it is severe mountain sickness, descend with the victim; do not wait for help. If the illness is severe, but not diagnosable, evaluate your options. In most areas of Nepal, some animal will be available to help transport a sick or injured trekker. In the west of Nepal, ponies are common; in the mountains, yaks are usually available. As extraordinary as it may seem, many Nepalis are both willing and capable of carrying westerners on their backs for long distances. An Australian woman who broke her leg by slipping on some ice on Poon Hill above Ghorapani was carried for three days by a series of porters and later became tearful as she recalled how kind and thoughtful they had been, demonstrating concern for *her* comfort while *they* were struggling under a 60-kg load.

Sometimes either the seriousness of the injuries or the urgency of getting care will make land evacuation impractical. The next best option is trying to get to one of the STOL air fields that have regular flights by either Twin Otter or Pilatus Porter aircraft. By negotiation, space can usually be found for a seriously injured or ill trekker, or a charter flight might be arranged, but the airport officials are quite unsympathetic to trekkers who are merely demoralized by the unexpected hardships of trail life and hope to jump the queue to get out sooner. If there is no nearby airfield, or if you know the flights are only once a week and just went yesterday, then the only alternative is to request a helicopter rescue flight. Before you use this option, you should be aware of the following facts that govern rescue flights in Nepal.

All helicopters are operated by the Royal Nepal Army. There are six small Alouette choppers and two large Pumas. The Alouettes are used for most rescues and cost the *victim* US$600 per hour of flight time. A typical rescue flight will cost between US$1500 and US$2000. Once a request is sent, and a helicopter actually leaves Kathmandu, you must pay for it, whether in fact you still need or want rescue or whether the helicopter is unable to find you. The helicopter will not leave Kathmandu until someone in Kathmandu has paid cash in advance for the flight. In practice this is usually a trekking agency, if the victim has been trekking with an agency, or the victim's embassy. Depending on the rules of the embassy, sometimes the victim's parents or family must be contacted in their home country to guarantee payment before the embassy will front the money. Registering with your embassy on arrival in Kathmandu can greatly expedite the rescue process. Arranging all of this can take a day or more. Given that it usually takes at least a day to have someone hike to a radio post or send a message out of an airstrip, it can take one or two days for a helicopter to arrive once a decision has been made that it is necessary. Rarely, a helicopter will not be available at all due to mechanical troubles or prior commitments or the message cannot be passed due to a religious festival.

Flying on rescue flights has made me familiar with some of the difficulties involved. One of the most important pitfalls is the rescue request itself. Give *details*! Try to assess the patient's condition and give the degree of urgency. If he has frostbite injuries and can't walk, but is otherwise stable, say this. If he is unconscious and has an apparent broken hip, send this in the message. On the basis of your rescue request alone, the pilots and the doctors involved will have to decide whether to take a chance and fly through bad weather, or wait for the usually better weather in the morning. The army pilots do not receive extra pay for rescue flights, and are often forced to take unusual chances while trying to perform rescues. Don't risk other lives needlessly with unnecessary flights or inadequate information. Place-names in Nepal are often confusing, and rescue requests sometimes mistakenly give the name of a district rather than a village, forcing rescuers to comb large tracts in sometimes unsuccessful efforts to find someone. Once a request is sent, stay put for at least two days, or make it clear in the message where and how you will be travelling. If you see the helicopter, make elaborate efforts to signal it. It is very difficult to pick out people on the ground from a helicopter moving ninety miles an hour and unsure where to look. Try to locate a field large enough to land a helicopter safely, but do not mark the centre of the field with cloth, as this can fly up and wreck the rotors on landing. If you are a trekker who has not sent for a helicopter, *do not wave at a low-flying helicopter*! We have made a number of unnecessary and occasionally dangerous landings only to find that the people had nothing to do with a victim and were just waving!

When I was working at the Pheriche Aid Post near Mt Everest, the sight of a rescue helicopter in a desperate situation was the sweetest thing I can ever remember seeing. If you are ever rescued in Nepal, make a point of thanking the pilots and doctors who are often risking their lives to help you out of a tight spot. If there are alternatives for getting out of that tight spot, don't ask others to risk their lives for you.

The helicopters cannot land above 5500 metres. There is currently no way to expect to be rescued from trekking or mountaineering peaks. Insurance which specifically covers rescue costs is available at low cost in your home country, but not in Nepal. It is highly recommended.

TREATING NEPALIS IN THE HILLS
Almost every trekker will encounter a situation where he or she is asked to give medical treatment to a sick Nepali. The potential patient may just have a headache, or may be covered with severe burns from which he will most likely die. The moral dilemma that the trekker is occasionally faced with can remain with the person for long after the trek. There is no simple answer, but I will offer some guidelines to help you think about the problem before you encounter it.

The Nepal government is attempting to establish and maintain health posts in remote areas. So far, this has not brought medical care to the majority of the people. The local people often have their own healers, beliefs, and practices regarding health. When these prove ineffective, or out of growing curiosity, the local people may consult passing trekkers, whether they are doctors or not. In many areas there is no understanding at all of the basis of western medical practice. Ideas that we take for granted, such as the relationship of germs to infection, have no meaning to these villagers. A pill can be seen as a form of magic, the shape, size, and colour often having more meaning than an attempted explanation that the medicine will kill the germs.

Thus, some of the medical interactions are based on villagers' desire to get closer to a form of western magic. This has created a form of medical begging, whereby it is not clear whether the person is indeed ill at the time of the encounter. It

At Thyangboche Monastery
Top: Masked dancer during *Mani Rimdu* festival (SA)
Left: Monk (*lama*) with a two-sided drum (SA)
Right: Long Tibetan horns are used in religious ceremonies (SA)

Women in the hills
Top: Chhetri women watching trekkers watch them (KS)
Left: Tamang women (KS)
Right: Sherpa girls in Solu (SA)

is fair and advisable under these circumstances to say that you have no medicine. Otherwise the pills are indiscriminately given out at later times, possibly doing someone some harm.

The Nepali who is clearly suffering from a problem presents another level of dilemma. If you can clearly recognize the problem and know that your treatment will be effective, and have a way of explaining this to the people involved, there is no reason to withhold this treatment from someone who can clearly benefit. If you do not know what is going on, or are not sure of the right treatment, you may do more harm than good, or the treatment failure may lead the villagers away from seeking appropriate western medical care at a health post in the future.

The fact that you are trekking through at that moment does not mean that you suddenly have to take on the continuing insoluble problems of remote village life. The feelings of compassion and wanting to help are natural, but if you see that you truly can't offer anything that is likely to improve the situation, don't feel obligated to 'do something'. The fact that there are large populations in the world that can't call an ambulance and be rushed to a hospital with serious illness is a reality that catches the western trekker emotionally unprepared. The discovery of these feelings and the processing of your reactions are part of the reason for trekking.

In summary, the problem remains a difficult one. Try to be aware of, and refer to, local health posts whenever possible (the Kunde Hospital in the Khumbu is a good example). If this is not possible, determine whether you can definitively help someone and then do so if your resources allow. If you are not sure what to do, you can express your concern but admit that you don't have anything to offer. The Nepalis can usually accept this gracefully.

A PROBLEM-ORIENTED FIRST-AID KIT

The question of what to bring with you as a medical kit for trekking arises so commonly that I have included a rather detailed discussion of such a kit. Because trekking in Nepal can place you one or two weeks from outside medical help, the kit contains the medication that you would ordinarily need to treat most trail problems. The kit is presented in three parts: 1) An overall list of contents to help assemble the supplies and medications; 2) A list of potential problems grouped with the medications and supplies that would be associated with that problem; and 3) A discussion of each of the medications included with details of its use, dosage, and major side-effects. In part 1 of the list the medicines are listed according to their trade name in Nepal. The proper generic name is included in the description of the drug in part 3. The kit listed is designed to treat up to four people for two weeks. You should freely adjust the amounts of medicine and supplies you take to meet specific needs.

Almost all of these medications are available from pharmacies in Kathmandu without prescription and most cost much less than they do overseas with the following exceptions: suppositories in general are not available; the quality of the supplies (tape, dressings, band-aids, etc) is poor in Nepal and these items should be imported if possible.

If a doctor is accompanying your trip, he or she may elect to bring additional, more sophisticated supplies including urinary catheters, oral airways, injectible medications and syringes, and suturing materials. These types of additions can be quite useful if someone in the group knows how to use them.

Trekking First Aid Kit (for four people)

Supplies
1	Low Reading Thermometer
1	Scissors
1	Tweezers
1	Tape – 1 inch Adhesive or Paper

1	Sewing Needle
10	4 inch x 4 inch Gauze Pads
1	Large Sterile Dressing
2	4 inch Rolled Cotton Bandages (kling)
1	3 inch Rolled Cotton Bandage (kling)
20	1 inch Band Aids
1	Muslin Triangular Bandage for Sling
1	bottle Betadine Antiseptic (Piodin)
1	4 inch Ace Bandage
2	2 packages Steri-Strips

Optional

1	4 inch x 18 inch Wire Mesh Splint
5	Safety Pins
1	Pad of Paper
1	Pencil

Medications

20	Actifed
40	Ampicillin (250 mg tablets)
10	Anusol-HC Suppositories (or tube of cream)
40	Antacid Tablets
20	Aspirin
30	Bactrim DS
10	Benadryl (50 mg)
60	Codeine (15 mg)
1	bottle Cortisporin Otic
1	tube Daktarin Cream
10	Dulcolax pills
40	Erythromycin (250 mg)
1	tube Hydrocortisone 1% Cream
6	packets Jeevan Jal
20	Lomotil
14	Mycostatin Vaginal Tablets
20	Paracetamol
6	Phenargan Suppositories
40	Sporidex (250 mg)
1	bottle Sulamyd 10% Eye Drops
12	Throat Lozenges (Strepsils)
12	Tiniba (500 mg)

Injectables (Optional)
Promethazine (Phenergan) 50 mg/1 cc
Meperidine (Demerol) 50 mg/1 cc
Adrenaline 1:1000
Syringes and Needles
Alcohol Swabs

Solving Problems with the First-Aid Kit

Diarrhoea & Vomiting
Bactrim DS
Tiniba
Jeevan jal
Lomotil
Promethazine Suppositories

Upper Respiratory Infections (colds)
Throat Lozenges
Actifed
Codeine
Ampicillin
Bactrim DS

Blisters or Skin Infection
Antiseptic (Betadine)
Tape
Moleskin
Sporidex or Erythromycin

Rash or Insect Bites
Benadryl
Daktarin Cream
Hydrocortisone Cream

Trauma (wounds)
Band Aids
Gauze Pads
Rolled Cotton Bandages
Aspirin or Paracetamol
Codeine
Splint
Steri-Strips

Hypothermia
Low Reading Thermometer

General Medical Problems

Complaint	Drug
Gastritis	Antacids
Constipation	Dulcolax Pills
Urinary Tract Infection	Bactrim or Ampicillin
Vaginitis	Mycostatin Vaginal Tablets
Hemorrhoids	Anusol-HC Cream or Suppositories
Conjunctivitis	Sulamyd Eye Drops
Internal Ear Infection	Bactrim or Ampicillin
Ear Canal Infection	Cortisporin Otic

Use of Medications

All medications are potentially harmful. Some have very rare but serious side effects (penicillin), while others have very common but not serious side effects (Tiniba). Every decision to use a medication must weigh the risk versus the benefit. The medications listed here are generally safe to use *if the patient has no history of allergies to the drug.* You must ask them several times before you use the drug.

In general, there are two reasons for using medicines: *symptomatic* – to relieve the ill effects of a disease without treating the cause (eg. Lomotil), and *therapeutic* – to treat the underlying cause and thereby relieve symptoms (eg. Ampicillin).

Symptomatic drugs can be used as needed. Therapeutic drugs should be given as a course. The list below states which kind of medicine it is, the usual doses, and potential side effects.

Drug nomenclature can be confusing: some drugs are best known by their proprietry brand name, others by their generic name (eg. Asprin). I have chosen to use the most common name (be it proprietry or generic), with the alternative name in parentheses. The brand name is given in italics while symptomatic and therapeutic are indicated as (Symp.) and (Thera.). Also, some proprietry names are specific to various countries; if those listed here are not available in your country they may still be available but under a different brand name.

Actifed (triprolidine HCL with pseudoephedrine HCL)
(Symp.) A decongestant for relief of discomfort due to colds, sinus infection, or internal ear infection.
Side Effects: Jitteriness, sedation.
Dose: One tablet every eight hours as needed.

Adrenaline
(Symp. & Thera.) Injectable (Epinephrine) – For the treatment of severe or life-threatening allergic reactions.
Side Effects: Tachycardia, nervousness.
Dose: Adults: 0.5 cc injected subcutaneously. May be repeated in one hour if needed. Children: 0.01 cc/kg of body weight; not to exceed adult dose.

Ampicillin
(Thera.) Antibiotic for treatment of suspected internal ear infections, sinusitis, bronchitis,

pneumonia, urinary tract infection. It is related to penicillin and *must not be given to people allergic to penicillin.*
Side Effects: Rash, diarrhoea.
Dose: 250 mg every six hours. For severe infection 500 mg every six hours. Usual course seven to 10 days.

Anusol-HC Suppositories
(Symp.) For relief of pain and itching due to hemorrhoids.
Side Effects: Essentially none.
Dose: One inserted rectally two or three times per day as needed.

Antacid Tablets
(Symp. & Thera.) For the treatment of burning stomach pain due to gastritis or suspected ulcer.
Side Effects: Essentially none.
Dose: two or three tablets every hour as needed.

Aspirin
(Symp.) For relief of mild pain and to help reduce a high fever.
Side Effects: Burning stomach pain.
Dose: two tablets every four hours as needed. *Do not exceed usual dose.*

Bactrim DS (trimethoprim/sulfamethoxasole double strength)
(Thera.) Antibiotic for treatment of suspected bacillary dysentary, inner ear infection, sinusitis, bronchitis, urinary tract infection. This is a *sulfa* drug and *should not be given to people allergic to sulfa drugs.*
Side Effects: Rash.
Dose: One pill every 12 hours. Usual course – five to 10 days.

Benadryl (diphenhydramine)
(Symp.) For the relief of severe itching due to allergic reactions. Can also be used as a mild sedative for sleeping.
Side Effects: Sedation.
Dose: 50 mg every six hours as needed.

Keflex or Sporidex (cephalexin)
(Thera.) An antibiotic particularly effective against staphylococcal skin infections which can be resistant to other medications. A relative of penicillin and *must not be given to people allergic to penicillin.*

Side Effects: Severe allergic reactions, rash, both rare.
Dose: 250 mg every six to seven hours for seven to 10 days.

Codeine
(Symp.) A narcotic pain reliever that can also serve as a cough suppressant. For moderate to severe pain.
Side Effects: Nausea, vomiting, stomach pain, rash, sedation, constipation.
Dose: 15-30 mg every four hours for cough suppression; 30-60 mg every four hours for pain.

Cortisporin Otic (Otisporin in Nepal)
(Symp. and Thera.) A liquid combination of antibiotics and cortisone for the treatment of external ear infections (eg. 'Swimmer's Ear').
Side Effects:: Essentially none.
Dose: five drops in affected ear four times a day.

Daktarin Cream (miconazole cream)
(miconazole) An anti-fungal skin preparation for suspected fungal infections.
Side Effects: Possible local allergic reaction.
Dose: Apply to rash three to four times per day until rash is gone.

Demerol (Meperidine)
Injectable (Symp.) A *potent* narcotic pain reliever for the relief of severe pain.
Side Effects: Respiratory depression, nausea and vomiting, rash, dizziness, sedation.
Dose: 5-75 mg intramuscularly every three to four hours as needed.

Diamox (acetazolamide)
(Thera.) A mild diuretic that also acidifies the blood. For the treatment of mild symptoms of acute mountain sickness. *Not to be taken by people allergic to sulfa drugs.*
Side Effects: Tingling of fingers and toes. This is common and does not mean you should stop taking the medicine.
Dose: 250 mg up to every eight hours.

Dulcolax (bisacodyl pills)
(Thera.) A relatively strong laxative for the relief of constipation.
Side Effects: Abdominal cramps, diarrhoea.
Dose: One or two at night and 12 hours later if no relief.

Erythromycin
(Thera.) An antibiotic for the treatment of skin infections, bronchitis, suspected strep throat. An alternative to Sporidex for persons allergic to penicillin.
Side Effects: Abdominal pain, rash.
Dose: 250 mg every six hours for seven to 10 days.

Hydrocortisone 1% Cream
(Symp.) A steroid skin cream for the relief of itching insect bites or other rashes.
Side Effects: Essentially none unless used for more than a month.
Dose: Apply to lesions as needed.

Jeevan Jal
(Symp. & Thera.) A balanced electro powder for mixing with boiled water to replace salts and fluid lost through vomiting and/or diarrhoea.
Side Effects: None.
Dose: Should be encouraged in anyone suspected of becoming dehydrated.

Lomotil (diphenoxylate HCL with atropine sulfate)
(Symp.) A medication derived from a narcotic which paralyzes the bowel for the symptomatic relief of diarrhoea. Should not be used casually.
Side Effects: Constipation
Dose: Two to start, then one after each loose stool until relief, then one every four to six hours to maintain. *Not to exceed eight in 24 hours.*
NB: Paralyzing the bowel can allow infections to get worse and prolong the illness. *Do not use if patient has a fever or a bloody stool.*

Mycostatin Vaginal Tablets
(Thera.) For the treatment of yeast vaginitis. This condition can develop relatively suddenly and is easily treated. Untreated, a woman can be quite uncomfortable.
Side Effects: Essentially none.
Dose: One in the morning and one at night for seven days.

Tylenol or Paracetamol (acetamenophen)
(Symp.) A mild pain reliever and fever reducer of similar strength to aspirin, but chemically unrelated and can be used in people allergic to aspirin.
Side Effects: Essentially none.
Dose: Two pills every four hours as needed.

Phenergan (suppositories) (promethazine suppositories 125 mg)
(Symp.) An antinausea medication for the symptomatic relief of nausea and vomiting to help prevent dehydration.
Side Effects: Sedation.
Dose: One in rectum every eight hours as needed.

Phenergan (Injectable) (promethazine)
(Symp.) Same as above.
Dose: 25-50 mg intramuscularly every six hours as needed.

Locula (Sulamyd 10% Eye Drops)
(Thera.) An antibiotic solution for the treatment of bacterial conjunctivitis (eye infections).
Side Effects: Possibly local allergy.
Dose: One to two drops every three hours for three to five days.

Strepsils (throat lozenges)
(Symp.) Candy-like dissolvable lozenges for soothing inflamed throats.
Side Effects: None.
Dose: One every half hour as needed.

Tiniba (tinidazole 500 mg)
(Thera.) An antibiotic for the treatment of the intestinal parasites, giardia and amoebas.
Side Effects: Predictable nausea, headache, metallic taste on tongue, weakness. *Cannot be taken with alcohol.*

Dose: Two gms once for treatment of giardia, two gms each day all at once for three days for treatment of amoebiasis.

IODINIZATION OF DRINKING WATER
Iodine kills all common forms of water carried diseases including amoebic cysts, salmonella and some hepatitis virus.

The inclusion of an iodinization kit in your medical supply will allow you to fill your water bottle from any stream, treat it, and 20 minutes later have safe, cold drinking water. This saves having to wait for boiled water at night and saves scarce firewood by eliminating the necessity of preparing boiling water each evening. The amount to be added depends on the temperautre and degree of pollution of the water. If the water is heavily contaminated or cold, either add more of the iodine solution or wait more than 20 minutes before drinking the water.

For more details of this method, see the *Western Journal of Medicine*, May 1975, for the article 'Water Disinfection in the Wilderness' by Frederick H Kahn, MD and Barbara R Visscher, MD and another article in the same *Western Journal of Medicine*, August 1981.

Meningitis
In March 1985 the US Centre for Disease Control issued an advisory recommending vaccination against meningococcal meningitis for all travellers to Nepal. This consists of a single dose of Meningococcal A/C vaccine, which provides five-year immunity in adults and two-year immunity in children under five.

This protection is important if you will be trekking, but is hard to obtain in many countries. The vaccine is available in Kathmandu at the International Clinic or the Infectious Disease Hospital in Teku.

The International Clinic has American doctors and caters primarily to expatriates living in Nepal, but will assist travellers as well, although it is more expensive than clinics that cater to locals. It is located in Balawatar, Kathmandu, across from the north end of the Russian Embassy, phone 410893.

The Himalayan Rescue Association has an office in the Kathmandu Guest House. Advice and information on altitude sickness and rescue is available here.

On the Trail

DEALING WITH HOTELS

When you arrive at a hotel for the night you should establish the costs for sleeping and see what facilities are provided. In many inns the sleeping charge is waived if you eat your meals there. In other inns the sleeping charge can be as little as Rs 2, though generally Rs 5, and up to Rs 10 or 20 per person for more sophisticated lodges. During times of heavy demand, such as during a flight back-up at Lukla or when snow on the pass has caused a backlog of trekkers at Manang or Muktinath, innkeepers charge what the traffic will bear and accommodation becomes expensive and difficult to find, but generally, it is safe to assume that costs will be in the Rs 2 to 10 range and that you will be able to find accommodation without too much trouble. During the busy trekking seasons in October/November and March/April it may be difficult to find bedding every night on the Jomsom trek. Mattresses, but not blankets or quilts, are available on the Everest trek. If you are going to Everest or beyond Muktinath, you should have your own sleeping bag. In April 1984 trekkers who were relying on locally supplied bedding were waiting in Chhomro for as many as five days for a sleeping bag so that they could visit Annapurna Sanctuary.

Usually the innkeeper keeps an account of all the food and drink that you consume and collects for everything in the morning. It's worth keeping track yourself because other trekkers' food often makes its way onto your account when things get busy. Meals typically take an hour or two to prepare unless there is stew or *daal bhaat* already cooked, so you should order your meal and establish a time for eating soon after you arrive. There are some pretty sophisticated short order kitchens that operate in the hills (the best being at Namche, Lukla and along the Kali Gandaki); if you patronise one of these, you can often

get a western-style meal that suits your taste, but often the choice is between *daal bhaat* with vegetables (*tarkari*) or *daal bhaat* with meat (*maasu*). Eggs (*phul* or *andaa*), when available, cost Rs 1 or 2 each.

Most Nepalis have only tea when they arise and then have a heavy brunch of rice and vegetables at about 10 am. When staying in a local inn, you will probably find it faster to operate in this manner than to get a large breakfast ordered and prepared early in the morning. The more sophisticated inns will usually be able to deal with short orders in the morning, though it is still best to organise it the evening before. A lot of time can be saved by carrying some granola or muesli (both available in Kathmandu) for breakfast, though *chiuraa* (beaten rice), available locally, makes a less tasty substitute. You should be able to move for several hours on tea and biscuits, arriving at 9 or 10 am at a place that may have *daal bhaat* already prepared.

If you want to have lunch at 12 or 1 you will almost certainly have to wait an hour or two while rice is cooked specially for you. Depending on your mood and fitness this may or may not be an attractive break in the day. If you find yourself with a long wait, it is best to accept it and use the time for a good rest rather than agitate and try to get things moving faster in the kitchen. Often a hotel can become totally chaotic with 20 people, each ordering different things. This can confuse even a western cook who uses order slips and has a complete stock of goods. In a small hotel where everything is cooked over a single wood fire with a limited supply of pots, it can get crazy. You can often save yourself a lot of time and hunger by talking to other trekkers and combining the orders into two or three dishes.

Many hotels have menus that show all

their prices, including the charges for sleeping. In most hotels there is no bargaining and the menu really does represent a fixed price. You should check the prices before you order to avoid later hassles. Strangely, the places most prone to bargaining are the fancy hotels – the US$10 a night and up variety – that have lost a lot of their business to smaller and cheaper facilities.

In inns along the main trekking routes you can generally behave just as you would in any small hotel anywhere. In remote regions where the hotels cater mainly to locals, special care should be taken to follow the customs of the people.

At high altitudes where things become more expensive (tea is 50 paisa in the lowlands, 1 rupee in places more than three or four days from the nearest road, and 2 rupees in high places such as Lobouje) it is tempting to economise and eat and drink less. It is important that you resist this temptation because a large

liquid intake is one of the primary considerations in the prevention of altitude sickness and a low food intake can leave you weak and subject to hypothermia.

Dealing with an inn when you have a guide is another matter. Theoretically a guide is more sophisticated than a porter, but this sophistication may be a mastery of ways to make money with a minimum of work, though it may also be the ability to organise an inexpensive and trouble-free trek. Tradition dictates that a guide receive transportation, food and accommodation throughout the trek. Porters receive only transportation and are responsible for arranging and paying for their own food and accommodation out of their daily wages. If you are staying in hotels, the easiest approach is to have your guide arrange everything and then pay the bill yourself in the morning, but with many guides you may find yourself paying for several glasses of *chhang*, extra food and the losses at last night's card party when you settle the bill. In such a case, often the best solution is to agree on a per diem rate for his subsistence and then pay for your own food and accommodation separately. It should cost no more than Rs 20 per day for a guide to live on a trek, and adding another Rs 5 for drinks and cigarettes makes a generous allowance.

A DAY WITH A TREKKING GROUP

A day begins about 6 am with a light breakfast of Darjeeling tea, coffee, porridge and eggs or pancakes. While the trekkers are eating, the sherpas take down the tents and pack up loads for the porters. The entire group is usually on the way by 7 am in order to take advantage of the cool morning to accomplish most of the day's hike. In spite of the size of the group, many trekkers find an opportunity to hike alone for much of the day. The porters are slower and the sherpas, especially the cook crew, race on ahead to have lunch waiting when you arrive. There are numerous diversions on the trail and it is not unusual to find sherpas and fellow trekkers in shops or *bhattis*, or for the entire group to be diverted by a festival or some other special event along the way. At a suitable spot, about 11 am, there is a stop of an hour or two for lunch: the inevitable tea, a plate of rice, potatoes or noodles, some canned or fresh meat and whatever vegetables are in season.

The afternoon is shorter, ending about 3 pm, when you round a bend to discover your tents already set up in a (hopefully) flat field near a village. Tea and coffee are again prepared soon after arrival in camp and there is an hour or two to nurse blisters, read, unpack and sort gear, wash or explore the surrounding area before dinner.

Trekking groups usually have a western diet with chicken, goat, mutton or buffalo meat frequently, but not daily, and vary the rice by substituting potatoes, noodles and other items. (The cow is sacred in regions of Hindu influence, so beef is unavailable.) The food is tasty and

plentiful, but may seem boring to a western palate after two weeks or so. Yet meals will tax the imagination of the cook as he provides a variety he has never experienced in his own meals. Most trekkers feel healthy and fit on this diet; the food is fresh and organic, with no preservatives.

After dinner the sun sets early. There is time to read by candlelight in tents or to sit around talking in the dark. Since wood is scarce there are no campfires. Occasionally, a visit to a nearby village provides an opportunity to sample *chhang* and *rakshi*, the local brews. Most trekkers are asleep by 8 or 9 pm.

DEALING WITH GUIDES & PORTERS

If you are travelling with porters, your progress will be limited by their ability to cover the required distance each day. Porters who carry 30 kg up and down hills cannot move as fast as a trekker who carries only a light rucksack. Other factors such as the weather, steepness of the trail, sickness and festivals (beware especially of the *Dasain* festival in October) can turn a schedule upside down.

You will rarely experience a strike, but you may often find that the evening discussion of the next day's destination will turn into a delicate negotiating session. On major trails there are accepted stopping places, and it is difficult to alter them. I once congratulated myself on covering three days walking by lunchtime the third day, and anticipated covering a good distance after lunch. An embarrassed sardar then informed me that our lunch spot would also be our camp for the night because by definition it took three full days to reach Ghandrung from Pokhara. Whether it had taken us that long or not was immaterial. Nothing I could say (or pay) would entice the porters to go further until the following day – when we were able to depart early in the morning, on schedule.

You may buy or bring some special food 'goodies' that you are saving for high altitudes or an important occasion. If you hand these over to a cook at the outset of the trek, you are likely to find them (despite any instructions to the contrary) cooked during the first few days of the trek or, worse yet, served to the sherpas. You should keep any special food in your luggage to prevent such mistakes.

ROUTEFINDING

It isn't easy to get totally lost in the hills, but finding the trail you want, particularly through a large village, can sometimes be a challenge. If you follow one of the major trek routes, most local people know where you are going. If you see children yelling and pointing, you probably have taken a wrong turn. Watch for the lug sole footprints of other trekkers and watch for arrows carved into the trail by guides with trekking parties. It is always worthwhile to talk to local people and ask them about the trail to your next destination and discover what facilities you can expect to find on the way.

If you are in a less frequented area, you must ask people; in such a case, be sure to phrase the question in a way that forces *them* to point the way. 'Kun baato Namche Bazaar jaanchha?' (which trail goes to Namche Bazar?) will usually do the job. If you point to a trail and ask if it goes where you want to go, most Nepalis will say yes, because they like to please you. When asking directions, ask the name of the next close village. People near Jiri probably have no idea where Namche Bazar is, but they know the trail to Shivalaya, the next village.

In particularly remote areas, be ready for confusion about destinations and times. I've seen situations where asking directions has developed into a huge argument involving 10 or more people, each one having an opinion on the best route and the time involved.

FOOD & DRINK

You may have heard a lot of talk about sickness and intestinal problems in Asia.

If you are reasonably careful, you should not have any problems – even in the more remote regions of Nepal – except perhaps a day or two of adjustment to a new environment somewhere during the trip. There is a minimal danger of problems if you stick to boiled or treated water and cooked food throughout your trek and follow a few hygiene precautions.

Getting boiled water can often be a problem. Even if you ask if the water is boiled, for example, you might be assured that it is, even if it has just been taken from the river. This illustrates several interesting facets of Nepalese culture and personality. The germ concept is not widely known or understood amongst the hill people. The desire of westerners that water be boiled is accepted good naturedly, but is not understood – they often believe that we like only hot water. Besides, the locals always drink unboiled water, why don't we? Another consideration: Nepalese like to please and dislike answering any question negatively. So, you get a 'yes' answer to almost every question, particularly 'is this water boiled?' The best solution is to drink tea. Good tea must be made from boiling water. It is an easy way out. Hotels also do not like to prepare boiled water because it uses fuel and takes up space on the stove – and they can't charge for this. Treating water with iodine solves the boiled water problem – this is discussed in the Health & Safety chapter.

Perhaps the best technique for preventing stomach and intestinal problems ('Delhi-belly' or 'Kathmandu crud') is to keep your hands clean (a supply of pre-moistened towelettes and frequent wash stops at streams helps). A lot of stomach problems come from germs transmitted by dirty hands.

ALTITUDE SICKNESS

Trekkers who have not previously experienced high altitude and who attempt to trek to places such as the Everest base camp may feel uncomfortable with headaches, nausea, and lethargy, although many make high altitude trips with few problems. Those in good physical shape who slow down their pace as they trek above 4000 metres seem to feel better. There is never any assurance, however, that anyone will be comfortable at extremely high altitudes. You should be emotionally prepared to retreat to a lower camp if your condition is such that continuing might endanger your health. You should also watch yourself and other trekkers for visible signs of deterioration. Most fatal cases of altitude sickness have resulted from people pushing themselves beyond their capabilities when they were severely affected by altitude problems. Be sure to read the section on Acute Mountain Sickness in the Health & Safety chapter.

SAFETY & THEFT

In 1974 I wrote 'there is virtually nothing to fear in Nepal from thieves, hijackings or the other horrors of our urban civilisation'. Unfortunately this has now changed, and it pays to be cautious about your companions – whether fellow trekkers or your porters – and with your belongings, especially when you camp. There are now frequent reports of items being stolen from the tents and hotel rooms of trekkers, even in the most remote villages. There have even been incidents of violent crime – something previously unheard of in Nepal. The US Embassy in Kathmandu makes the following suggestions:

While Nepalese are generally friendly and present no threat to trekkers, the number of violent incidents in recent years against trekkers has unfortunately increased. Crime, while still low by Western standards, does exist on the trails. Westerners have been the victims of murder and violent assaults. All of the victims have been travelling alone or as a couple. The general motive seems to have been robbery, even though the possessions of some of the victims were insignificant by American standards. To help you enjoy your trek and to minimize the risk of unpleasant incidents, the Embassy recommends that you take the following precautions:

a) Register with the Consular Section, giving the trek itinerary and dates of the trek.

b) Do not travel alone. Join up with other Westerners going along the same trail if you are alone in Nepal. Do take a porter or guide. Backpacking by yourself may seem the noble thing to do but it is dangerous. You will also be doing a disservice to Nepal by not contributing to the local economy.

c) Arrange for porters and guides with a reputable trekking agency, friends, or Embassy so that they can be traced if you have trouble. Do not just pick up a porter or guide off the street, no matter how friendly he may appear to be.

d) Do not make ostentatious displays of your cash or possessions. Store all valuable items in Kathmandu at your hotel or lodge. Be sure to obtain a detailed receipt of your items from the hotel or lodge.

e) Camp at night near other trekkers, if possible. Do not walk along trails after dark.

f) Don't leave your passport as collateral for renting trekking equipment. You may need it in an emergency.

g) Be sure to register at all the police and immigration checkpoints along the trail, and go only on the route prescribed in your trekking permit.

h) If you encounter problems along the trail, report them to the nearest police or immigration post. When you return to Kathmandu, report any unresolved problems to the appropriate trekking agency or hotel as well as the police and the Ministry of Tourism.

The Embassy recommends that you not take night buses in Nepal. There have been serious problems recently with bandits holding up these buses.

There were a few incidents in early 1984 of violent theft, including one trekker who was shot dead on the Manang trek. It is almost certain that there is a gang of thieves who watch trekkers and go after those who display valuable items or who have large amounts of cash. Most thefts have been from those who had things worth stealing – with the possible exception of boots; these seem to be high on the list of desirable items (along with money and cameras). Do not leave your boots near the door of your tent or outside your hotel room. The most frequent thefts occur in Naudanda, Ghandrung, Dhampus and Hyangja on the Annapurna trek and near Seopuri at the beginning of the Helambu trek, but it pays to be cautious everywhere – especially within two or three days of a road.

WEATHER

Nepal is in the northern hemisphere, so the seasons are the same as in Europe. Because it is quite far south (the same as Miami or Cairo) the weather is warmer and the winters much milder at lower elevations, including Kathmandu (elevation 1400 metres). It rarely snows below 2000 metres.

The seasonal weather pattern is governed by the monsoon in the Bay of Bengal. The monsoon creates a rainy season from about the middle of June through the middle of September. It is hot during the monsoon and it rains almost every day, though not continuously. During this season, trekking is difficult and uncomfortable. The mountains are usually hidden by clouds and the trails are muddy and infested with leeches.

To avoid the monsoon, most trekkers travel during the winter season from October through May. Temperatures are generally comfortable during this period: in the high 20°C during the daytime and falling to 5°C at night while trekking between 1000 metres and 3500 metres, and from about 20°C down to –10°C at higher altitudes. Mornings are usually clear with clouds building up during the afternoon, disappearing at night to reveal spectacular starry skies. It is about 10 degrees colder than this from December to February.

It usually does not rain for more than one or two days during the entire fall season. During spring treks, there may be a week or so of rainy evenings. The Himalaya makes its own localised weather. Despite the assurances of Radio Nepal and the *Rising Nepal*, the local English language newspaper, that the weather will be ' . . . mainly fair throughout the Kingdom,' you should always expect clouds in the afternoons and be prepared for occasional rain (thunderstorms in the spring), though there is much less likelihood of rain from mid-October to mid-December.

Most of the precipitation occurs during the summer, so there is less snow on the mountains during the winter. Everest itself is black rock during the trekking season, becoming snow-covered only during the summer. Of course, there are exceptions to this weather pattern – you should be prepared for extremes. During December and January, occasional winter storms blanket the mountains with snow and produce rain in the lowlands. This snow may make an early spring pass-crossing difficult and can present an avalanche danger, especially on the approach to the Annapurna Sanctuary.

In the winter the days are short; first light is about 6 am and it is daylight up to about 6 pm. By March you can gain an hour on each end and could walk from 5 am to 7 pm if you wished.

CULTURAL CONSIDERATIONS

No matter what style of trekking you choose, you will have a chance to meet and become acquainted with Sherpas and members of other Nepalese ethnic groups – people whose background is completely different from what you are used to in the west. Treks are a fascinating cultural experience, but are most rewarding when you make some concessions to the customs and habits of Nepal.

Nepal is officially a Hindu country, although the Sherpas and most other high mountain people are Buddhists. In Kathmandu, you will be refused entry into a

Hindu temple if you are wearing leather shoes or a leather belt; there are other temples that you will not be allowed to visit at all. Generally, Buddhist temples, or *gompas*, are less restrictive, but you should still ask permission to enter and remove your shoes when you do – and definitely ask permission before taking photographs in any temple.

During the trek you will have many opportunities to photograph picturesque local people. Some people, however, will not want to be photographed. There are always cases of shyness which can be overcome by a smile, a joke or using a telephoto lens – but don't pay people for taking their picture. They are not afraid that a camera might 'steal their soul', as some African people are; instead, it is too much contact with photographers and cameras that causes the problem. Many photographs of hill people in Nepal, especially Sherpas, have been printed in books, magazines and brochures. The Sherpas, in particular the women, are afraid that a photo of them will be reproduced in quantity and eventually be burned, thrown away, or even used as toilet paper. This is a major reason for local people to refuse photographs and it is probably legitimate.

Nepal represents a culture far older and in many ways more sophisticated than our own. The more you listen and observe the more you will learn and the more you will be accepted. If you must try to teach Nepalese hill people something, try teaching them English. This is one element of our culture that is universally desired. Spending your time conversing with a sherpa or porter in English as you stroll the trail together will be a good start towards a lasting friendship. You are not visiting a museum – you are visiting a country that is vibrantly alive, where the people live more comfortably and, in most cases, more happily than we do.

A few other suggestions and considerations that will make your trek more enriching:

– Don't pollute. Pick up papers, film wrappers and other junk.
– Burn all your toilet paper and bury your faeces.
– Don't pass out balloons, candy and money to village children. It encourages them to beg. Trekkers are responsible for the continual cries of children for *mithai* (candy), *paisaa* (money), and 'boom boom' (balloon). Well-intentioned trekkers have thought they were doing a service by passing out pens for use in school, so clever kids now ask for pens.
– Don't tempt people into thievery by leaving cameras, watches and other valuable items around camp. Keep all your personal belongings in your tent. This also means that you should not leave laundry hanging outside at night.
– Don't make campfires; wood is scarce in Nepal.
– Don't touch food or eating utensils that will be used by local people. Most Hindus cannot eat food that has been touched by a non-Hindu foreigner; this problem does not apply to Sherpas, however.
– Do not throw things into the fire in any house – Buddhist or Hindu.
– Nudity is unacceptable and brief shorts are not appreciated.
– Public displays of affection are frowned upon.
– Most Nepalis eat with their hands. In many places you will not be offered a spoon, but they are often available if you ask. Only the right hand is used for eating. If you eat with your hand, you are expected to wash it before and after eating; a jug of water is always available in *bhattis* for this purpose.
– Nepalis will not step over your feet or legs. If your outstretched legs are across a doorway or path, pull them in when someone wants to pass. Similarly, do not step over the legs of a Nepali.

ENVIRONMENTAL STRESS

The population of Nepal is growing at a furious rate. In the 10 years from 1974 to 1984 the population has increased from

12 to more than 16 million. Development is moving ahead at an even faster pace. During the five years from 1978 to 1983 the number of vehicles in the country increased from less than 7500 to more than 53,000; half of these are in the Kathmandu Valley. There are now true traffic jams in Kathmandu and the unnecessary noise and pollution caused by these vehicles is immediately noticeable. There are few days with clear mountain views; 10 years ago the Kathmandu Valley was usually framed by towering white mountains and clear blue skies. You can see the smog from your plane as it approaches Kathmandu.

In the hills, this growth is manifesting itself in many ways. There was a furore 10 years ago about garbage left by trekkers and expeditions along the Everest route; this was never really an important issue compared to the current problems of sanitation, overgrazing, deforestation, landslides and uncontrolled development – mostly of hotels for trekkers. There is no systematic waste disposal system in the hills, and many hill people are importing more and more manufactured items from Kathmandu; a look at the stream of worn-out shoes and broken toys in the streets of Namche will show that litter is not only a trekking problem. The piles of garbage and human waste at Ghorapani and on the route to Annapurna Sanctuary and the relentless clearing of rhododendron forests between Ghorapani and Ghandrung to allow even more hotel construction are, however, caused by trekkers. Yet the proposed solution, a protected area or even a national park, can lead to greater pressures (it takes a staff of more than 100 army personnel to manage and enforce the regulations of Sagarmatha National Park – which has a local population of less than 2500 people).

It is naive to think of maintaining the ecological balance of the Himalaya in a pristine state. There are simply too many people living in the hills; it would be necessary to relocate entire villages (this

was done in both Lake Rara and Royal Chitwan national parks) in order to accomplish this.

The primary reason for the destruction of forests throughout the Himalayan hill region is the pressure of a population that requires natural vegetation for food, fodder, fuel and even shelter. The lack of roads and other development, combined with the lack of any local deposits of fossil fuels, allows no easy alternative. The inevitable result of the destruction of forests is increased erosion and loss of topsoil, causing huge landslides that carry away fields, houses and occasionally entire villages. As you fly or trek in Nepal you can easily spot many examples of these landslides. One solution would be a massive tree-planting campaign, but to hill people this is expensive and unrewarding because the plantations must be fenced off to cattle and goats for several years. Fencing is expensive and the financial returns are a long way off.

Tourists, particularly trekkers, contribute to the mess. A typical hotel burns from three to eight loads (of about 25 kg each) of firewood per day and a large trekking party can consume three to five loads a day. National park regulations that ban the use of firewood do not apply to those who use hotels. This exempts individual trekkers and the porters of trekking parties from any limit on fuel consumption. The influence of trekkers is small in the Everest region (6752 trekkers in 1983) compared to the Jomsom and Annapurna Sanctuary areas which attracted more than 20,000 trekkers during the same year.

Everyone should agree that the hill people have a right not only to live in their traditional homesites but also to try to improve their standard of living. Their lifestyle may be picturesque, but it is a meagre subsistence-level lifestyle that could be improved in numerous ways by many aspects of development. Trekkers can contribute to this development, not only through their cash but through their example. Solutions to the energy problem such as hydroelectric plants, biogas generators, solar energy units and wholesale import of fossil fuels all take time and cost money. As solutions are developed and implemented they will cause change in the trekking experience and will certainly increase costs. When attempts are made in this direction, it would seem reasonable to support them, even when the result is a more expensive trek. It will cost more to eat at a hotel that has a new energy-efficient wood stove (or even a kerosene stove) and a proper latrine, or to trek with a group that uses no firewood. It is through this kind of direct economic encouragement that hill people can be assisted and taught.

In 1984 there were only the faintest stirrings in this direction amongst hoteliers; hopefully they will find the means to continue the attempts and, with the encouragement of trekkers, revamp the entire hotel system in the hills into something that not only turns firewood into cash, but also serves as a demonstration for all villagers of the need and advantages of limiting their dependence on the forests. One good start would be to spurn the offers of hot showers. You can talk to other trekkers and try to order the same food at the same time so that a hotel can do all the cooking at once instead of keeping a fire roaring throughout the day. You can purify your water with iodine instead of ordering boiled water. The process will take time and effort; old habits and traditions are hard to change.

Even in Kathmandu and Pokhara where alternatives are readily available many homes, hotels, and restaurants rely on firewood for cooking. Hundreds, perhaps thousands, of loads of wood are carried into the cities, not only by porters, but also by the truckload.

Route Descriptions

The teacher can but point the Way,
The means to reach the Goal
Must vary with each Pilgrim

This quotation is one of the Tibetan 'elegant
sayings' attributed either to Nagarjuna, the
Indian mystic who lived in the second century
AD, or to the Head Lama of the Sakya
monastery in Tibet, 1270 AD.

SCOPE & PURPOSE

This section provides descriptions of the
best-known trekking routes in Nepal. The
purpose of these descriptions is to provide
some insight into the type of country and
culture to be encountered on specific
treks. They may help you to choose the
area you wish to visit because they provide
some indication of the difficulty of each
trek, and the number of days required to
follow a particular route.

As you trek these routes, you can refer
to the route descriptions for cultural
background notes, but they are *not* self-
guiding trail descriptions. If you are not
travelling with a Nepalese companion, you
must always ask questions on the spot of
hotelkeepers or other trekkers in order to
find the correct path; if you are with a
guide, he or she will be asking questions as
you travel. What to us may be a major
trekking route may be, for the people of a
village, only a path from Ram's house to
Bir Bahadur's house to Dawa's house. In
our minds we string all these sections of
trail together to form a major route to
some place that the village people may
never go. Since most trekking routes are in
the east-west direction or in the high
mountain regions, they are not generally
followed by locals since most trade routes
are south to north and avoid the higher
elevations. There is nothing more frustrating
than wandering around the hills of Nepal
looking for the correct trail; and it is
impossible, no matter how detailed the

route description, to document every
important trail junction and *trails do
change* for a multitude of reasons. The
descriptions that follow portray what you
may expect if you follow the shortest
available routes, but it will be all too easy
to get lost if you try to walk through Nepal
using only this (or any other book) as a
guide. Develop the habit of talking to
people and asking questions.

Just as it is impossible to document
every trail junction, it is also impossible to
describe every possible trek. What follows
is a description of the major routes, a few
optional side trips, and some alternative
routes that avoid backtracking. You
should seriously consider backtracking,
however. Often the second time over a
particular trail provides insights and
views not seen or appreciated the first
time through.

If you are making your first trek in
Nepal, it is likely that you will choose one
of these. Not only are they the best known,
but they are generally the most interesting
places to go. There is good reason for the
fame of the Everest trek, the Jomsom trek
and other well-known routes. Most of the
routes described (with the exception of
the Khumbu-Dhankuta route, the Lamidanda trek and the Barahbise-Mali option)
have hotels of some sort available every
night and the trails are reasonably well
defined. You may at first be tempted to go
to some other region where there won't be
so many tourists because of stories and
articles you may have read about the
'freeway' to Everest. When you listen to
these discussions it is important to place
them in their proper perspective. In 1983
the so-called overcrowded conditions in
the Everest region consisted of 6000
trekkers over a period of eight months –
this is fewer people than occupy a typical
United States national park campground
on a single weekend night. Getting to

remote and unexplored areas has little meaning in Nepal.

The following routes are described here:

The Mount Everest Region
Jiri to Everest Base Camp
Gokyo
Thami
The Lamidanda Escape Route
A Way to Avoid the Jiri Road

Eastern Nepal
Solu Khumbu to Dhankuta

North of Kathmandu
Langtang
Across Ganja La
Helambu Circuit
Gosainkund

Central Nepal
Pokhara to Jomsom
Annapurna Sanctuary
Ghorapani to Ghandrung
Around Annapurna

Western Nepal
Jumla to Rara Lake

Other Destinations
In each of the sections there is a brief introduction outlining some of the many options possible in that region. There are many parts of Nepal that are closed to foreigners. Many trips that a map may suggest are in restricted areas; you cannot obtain a trekking permit for those regions. Some areas specifically closed to foreigners are: Mustang (north of Kagbeni), Larkya La (a circuit of Manaslu is not allowed), Dolpo (a circuit of Dhaulagiri is not allowed), Humla, Kanchenjunga Base Camp, Rolwaling and the route to Nangpa La in Khumbu. When you plan your trek, assume that these areas will remain closed; do not count on a last-minute change in the rules. Police checkposts are frequent in the hills and you will get turned back if you try to proceed where

foreigners are not allowed. There are numerous reasons why the restricted areas exist. In some cases it is a holdover to a time when the border with China was more sensitive than it is now, but environmental groups, particularly the Nepal Nature Conservation Society, are pressuring the government to keep some places closed for ecological reasons to avoid both cultural and environmental degradation. Trekkers require assistance when something goes wrong (accident, illness or theft); the government restricts some areas because they are doubtful that they could provide the security (to trekkers) that they would require. There are also political reasons for some restrictions; you do not want to be the centre of an international incident.

There are many routes that proceed over high passes. Two of these – Ganja La and Thorung La – are described here. These treks have the dangers of rockfall, avalanches and high altitude. It is important for all members of the party – including the sherpas and porters – to be well equipped before attempting these routes. The possibility of snow increases from December through April and you may be forced to turn back if the pass is snowbound.

Day by Day
The route descriptions here have been separated into daily stages, a device useful to make them readable and to estimate the time required for a particular trek. The suggested night stops are the ones most trekkers use; in all cases wood, water, food for porters (and usually *chhang* for sherpas) and a place large enough to pitch four or five tents is available at each place mentioned. Food and accommodation is available for those relying on local inns.

You will find when you trek these routes yourself, either with an organised group or alone, that you may not be able to spend the night at the places suggested. Your actual stopping places will depend on your

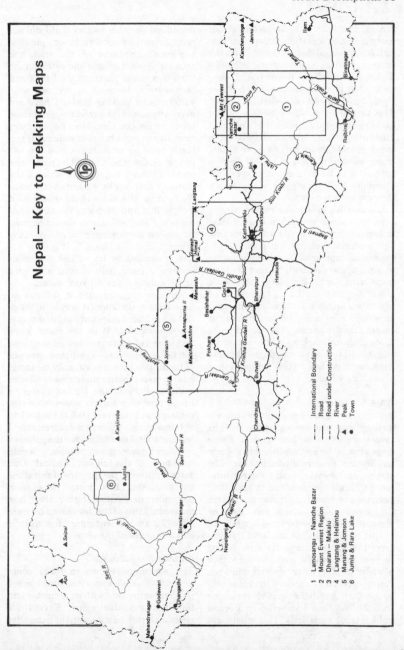

Nepal – Key to Trekking Maps

1 Lamosangu – Namche Bazar
2 Mount Everest Region
3 Dharan – Makalu
4 Langtang & Helambu
5 Manang & Jomson
6 Jumla & Rara Lake

International Boundary
Road
Road under Construction
River
Peak
Town

fitness, whether you or someone in your party is sick on a particular day, weather, trail conditions and arrangments with the porters. Porters can severely influence the speed with which you can travel, since their 30-kg loads make them much slower than a trekker with only a light rucksack. This variance from the schedule should cause no concern; you are not on a planned itinerary and your trek should allow the freedom and opportunity to move as fast or as slowly as you wish. A trek is supposed to be a vacation; don't carry schedules and timetables along where they are not necessary.

It is possible to alter the number of days suggested here. Perhaps you can cut a day or two off the time if you walk from first light to sunset each day, but since a trek is a continual experience, not simply progress to a particular destination, there is little point in rushing the trip just to get to some place that may not be as interesting as where you are now. At high altitudes it is important to proceed no faster than the ascent times recommended here in order to avoid altitude sickness. The trek can be lengthened to almost any degree by side trips, rest days and further exploration of interesting villages.

TIME & DISTANCE

In the following route descriptions there is no list of approximate walking times. The routes are listed in daily stages. These stages can all be accomplished in a single day by any moderately-fit trekker. The stages do, however, tend to get a little more difficult farther along in each trek, because you (and I) get fitter as the trek progresses. Each stage can also be accomplished by porters in a single day.

I did go through the exercise of trying to record walking times. It is a boring project, incidentally, trying to keep track of when you stop, when you walk and when you rest. When I compared the times on a particular trip with the times for that same trek the last time I travelled it, I found unbelievable variations. This must have

depended on other factors that I did not record, such as my own mood, physical condition, condition of the trail, the number of other people and cattle on the trail, how many photographs I took and the weather. Because of my own wide variations in walking times, I have not even attempted to project approximate times for anyone else. Most days require from five to eight hours of walking. If you really need to know times, you can ask people on the trail. The hill Nepalis use a unit of distance called a *kos*, which is the distance that can be walked in one hour. *Namche Bazar kati kos chha?* should elicit a reply that approximates the number of hours to Namche Bazar (as should *Namche Bazar kati gantaa laagchha* – 'how many hours to Namche Bazar?'). It is more fun and rewarding to try to talk to people instead of continually looking at a book and checking it against your watch.

Another statistic that is difficult to determine is distance. It is easy to judge distances from a map, but a printed map is two-dimensional. With the many gains and losses of altitude – and all the turns and twists of the trail – a map measurement of the routes becomes virtually meaningless. In researching a guidebook to Glacier National Park in the United States, a friend pushed a bicycle wheel-odometer contraption over every trail in the park to obtain accurate mileage measurements. I have neither the ambition nor the patience for such a project, and besides, it would take most of the fun out of a trek. One gains a different perspective of travelling by discussing how many days to a particular destination rather than how many km. Most of the days listed here are 10 to 20 km, depending on the altitude and steepness of the terrain.

On Measuring Altitude

The elevations shown in these route descriptions are composites, based on my own measurements with an altimeter and the best available maps. Except for specific elevations shown on the Schneider map series, all elevations have been rounded to the nearest 10 metres. The elevations of peaks are those shown on the official mountaineering regulations of Nepal.

This uncertainty over precise elevations will cause no problems during a trek. The primary reason that a trekker needs to know the elevation is to learn whether the trail ahead goes uphill or downhill and whether it is a long ascent (or descent) or a short one. The elevations shown here fulfill that purpose. The idea of precise elevations becomes even more complicated because villages are spread out over such large areas. What is the 'correct' elevation of a village like Bung, which extends almost 500 vertical metres up a hillside?

Changes

Between 1980 and 1984 there were major new roads opened to Jiri, Gorkha, Dhankuta, and along the Narayani River from Mugling to Narayanghat. The Dumre – Besi Sahar road (at the start of the trek around Annapurna) is being worked on – slowly – and the Trisuli Bazaar – Dhunche road takes several days off the Langtang trek. If the Hyangja – Suikhet road is ever improved, the service here will become more viable and change the route to Jomsom. It is interesting to note that every major trek in this book is two to four days *shorter* than it was four years ago. There is a road planned from Pokhara to Mustang via Jomsom and even talk of a road up the Dudh Kosi to Namche Bazar, but this one hasn't even reached the drawing board stage yet. The roads also change the relative importance of villages. Lamosangu, for example, was a major roadhead from 1970 to 1981; it lost its importance, and many of its facilities vanished when Kirantichhap became the roadhead. The same will probably happen to Dumre when bus service begins up the Marsyandi. Roads also bring about an increase in theft. Before a road is built, travel must always be on foot. After a road reaches an area, no self-respecting Nepali

will walk when a bus is available, but the bus fares on the new roads are expensive – making a new demand for cash. For many, the only source of easy cash is theft, and the road offers a quick getaway. Be especially watchful of your posessions within a few days walk of any road.

Trail and bridge construction is also proceeding at a furious pace in the hills. Many trails have been reconstructed or widened with local government money or foreign aid assistance. In the case of the Everest trek, the new trail has changed the route significantly, bypassing some places and visiting villages that the old expedition route did not reach before. The Swiss are planning an extensive new series of bridges in the hills. Landslides and flood damage is becoming more frequent as the forest cover is removed and topsoil washes away. These phenomena can alter trek routes drastically; whole villages can disappear and trails can require extensive detours to cross slide areas.

Many hotels are being constructed in the hills. There seems to be an impression that 'moderate' inns, charging US$3 to US$10 per person per night, can be successful. This may be true, but most hotels charge much less, or even allow you to sleep for free if you buy a meal from them. Trekkers who have a completely arranged trek generally prefer their tents to even a reasonably priced hotel room. The fancy hotels at Poon Hill, Jomsom, Phakding, Lukla and Phaphlu are slowly going to seed and won't offer much of an option until there is enough of a chain to allow sleeping in high standard hotels every night. But these establishments are exerting their own influence on the trekking routes and the trekking experience, so this will bring changes in the future.

The construction of small trekkers' hotels, and the conversion of private homes into hotel facilities, is proceeding at an even more frantic pace. New hotels spring up every week on the major trek routes; they also vanish when the inn-keeper or his wife gets bored or discovers that the costs are higher than the potential returns. The competition for trekkers' rupees is intense, so prices are driven down in order to attract customers, and it becomes hard to make a hotel pay its way. There are pressures for hotels to improve the way they deal with fuel usage and sanitation, particularly toilet facilities, so this may change the number and location of hotels before long.

In many cases specific hotels are mentioned by name; when you get to these places, you may find a hotel with a different name. This confusion is caused by a funny system in Nepal that allows a hotelier to avoid tax by changing the name of his company. Often the *Namaste Hotel* becomes the *New Namaste Hotel*, but sometimes the new name is much less similar.

There are many influences on the decision to open or close certain parts of Nepal to foreigners. Recent changes have liberalised both trekking and climbing, and there is considerable pressure to open more areas to trekkers. Rumours that the Kanchenjunga area and the Larkya La will open are frequently heard; there are continual (and still seemingly unfounded) rumours that Mustang and Dolpo will be opened soon – but this rumour has been continuing for more than 10 years. You should check with a trekking agent or the Central Immigration Office before planning any unusual trek, but you can assume that the treks listed here will not be affected.

A trek route changes because of the season. The routes described here work in the trekking season from October through May, though some high passes may be open only in October-November and again in May. If you trek during the monsoon, the trails may not bear any resemblance to what is described here. Bridges can get washed away and trails can get flooded during this season. In early October, and again in April and May, rice is growing in many of the terraces along the trek route. Many campsites that are excellent in November and December are under water in the rice growing season. Hotels in high places, particularly Gorak Shep, Annapurna Sanctuary, and along the Ghorapani – Ghandrung route often close in the coldest winter season (December to March) and monsoon.

TREKKING NOMENCLATURE

These route descriptions list many places that do not correlate with names in other descriptions of the same route or with names on maps. The diversity occurs because there is no universally accepted form of transliterating Nepali and Tibetan names into English, so the same place name may be spelled in many different ways. To make matters more complicated, a place may have several different names. Mount Everest, for example, is also known as *Sagarmatha* (Nepali) and *Chomolungma* (Sherpa). The same situation obtains for many village names.

His Majesty's Government has assigned new Nepalese names to 31 peaks and three tourist places that had been known before only by English names. The new names are mentioned in the text, but the old English names are used to avoid confusion.

Many maps made before 1960 had very little ground control and village names had little resemblance to reality. This is particularly true of the maps prepared by the US Army Map Service that have been subsequently copied and distributed as trekking maps in Kathmandu.

In the route reports that follow, names and descriptions have been translated in most cases, but to avoid a lot of repetition, several Nepalese and Tibetan words have been used throughout the text. These include:

Tamang, Chhetri, Brahmin, Rai, Sherpa, Gurung, Limbu, Newar and *Magar* – names of some of the many ethnic groups that populate Nepal's hills *khola* – a river

Kosi – one of the seven major rivers flowing into the Arun River

yak – the wonderful domestic beast that provides wool, milk, fuel and transportation in Solu Khumbu

nak – a female yak

gompa – a Tibetan Buddhist temple

mani wall – a stone wall, or even a large rock, carved with prayers. The correct phonetic spelling is *maani*.

chorten – a Tibetan Buddhist monument

kani – an arch-shaped chorten that is built over a trail

la – pass (Tibetan)

bhanjyang – pass (Nepali)

terai – the flat plains area along the southern border of Nepal

kharka – an alpine pasture

goth – an animal shed or small hut near an alpine pasture, usually inhabited only during the summer months. Pronounced like 'goat'.

bhatti – a local inn that caters primarily to Nepalis

chautaara – a stone wall that serves as a resting place built around a large piple or banyan tree

MAPS

The maps included in this book are based on the best available maps of each region. As with everything else here, they are reasonably accurate, but not perfect by any means. In order to make them legible, most villages and landmarks not included in the route descriptions have been eliminated. In some cases, even major villages and mountains have vanished from the maps. No elevations are shown; these may be obtained from the route descriptions. Instead of contour lines, only ridge lines have been depicted. This is the line of the highest point on a ridge; if the trail crosses one of these heavy black lines, you have to walk uphill; if the trail leads from a ridge line to a river, you must walk downhill. Peaks are shown in their true position, but villages may not always be located accurately – the problem

occurs because of the size of villages. Where does the dot go for a village that is three km from end to end and that has no real centre or town square? The trails and roads follow the general direction indicated on the maps, but small switchbacks and twists obviously cannot be shown in anything of this size.

For more detailed maps, there are several sources. The best series is the 1:50,000 series produced by Erwin Schneider for Research Scheme Nepal Himalaya and printed in Vienna. They are available from many map shops overseas and at most bookshops in Kathmandu. The fantastically coloured maps are also fantastically expensive – about US$8 a sheet, but if you are doing any serious trekking they are worth it; if you are planning a climb, they are absolutely necessary. The available maps include: Khumbu Himal, Shorong/Hinku (Solu/Hongu), Dudh Kosi, Tamba Kosi/Likhu Khola, Rolwaling Himal, Lepchi Kang and Kathmandu Valley. There is a Langtang/Jugal Himal map in the works.

Other maps are available as blueprints of traced maps in Kathmandu. They aren't really very accurate, but they will give you some idea of where you are going. The Police Adventure Foundation has also produced a series of blueprinted maps. A few other printed maps, including an excellent series by Dr Harka Bahadur Gurung, formerly Nepal's Minister of Tourism, are available in Kathmandu. There is a US Army Map Service series (Series U502 at 1:250,000) and an excellent Survey of India series at one inch to a mile, both prepared between 1950 and 1965, but these are restricted and hard to obtain.

A map titled *The Mount Everest Region* is published in England and covers about the same region as the map of the same name in this book in the section on the Everest trek. This map is available by mail from the Royal Geographical Society, 1 Kensington Gore, London SW7 at a cost of £5 per copy.

The Mount Everest Region

Interesting and justifiably famous, not only for its proximity to the world's highest mountain, but also for its Sherpa villages and monasteries, the Everest, or Solu Khumbu area is the second most popular trekking destination in Nepal. The primary objective of Everest treks is either the Everest base camp, about 5340 metres, or Kala Pattar, an unassuming 5545 metre bump on the southern flank of Pumori (7161 metres), which provides a fine view of Everest (8848 metres).

One of the biggest problems with the Everest trek is the high liklihood of Acute Mountain Sickness (AMS), commonly known as altitude sickness, a potentially deadly illness caused by too rapid an ascent to high elevation. Be sure to read the section on Mountain Sickness if you are planning an Everest trek. If you suffer any symptoms of altitude sickness it is still possible to make a fascinating trek to less ambitious destinations including Namche Bazar, the administrative headquarters of the Khumbu region; Khumjung or Thami, more typical Sherpa villages; or Thyangboche monastery, from which an excellent view may be had of Everest and its more spectacular neighbour Ama Dablam (6856 metres).

The Everest region may be reached by STOL (short take-off and landing) airstrips at Lukla (2800 metres), Shyangboche (3700 metres), or Phaphlu (2364 metres) or by an eight-day trek from the roadhead at Jiri, 188 km from Kathmandu. Those who fly to Lukla miss the historic and culturally fascinating route followed by the Everest expeditions of the '50s and '60s although the trek has changed substantially in the past 30 years. It is best to take the time to walk from Jiri, then after acclimatisation and conditioning afforded by the trek, visit base camp or climb Kala Pattar and either fly out from Lukla or walk back by an alternative route

to Kathmandu. Those who insist their time is limited can fly to Lukla and spend as little as six days to visit Namche Bazar and Thyangboche. It is ill advised to attempt a quick visit to base camp, because of the lack of time for acclimatisation, if you fly in to one of these airstrips. You should allow at least eight or nine days to reach the base camp region if you fly to Lukla; the return from base camp to Lukla can be made in as few as four or five days, so an absolute minimum of two weeks is required for a safe trek to base camp. The timing is further complicated because flights to Lukla often do not work as planned, so those with a tight schedule would do well to allow a few spare days for both the flight in and the flight out. Shyangboche has been virtually closed since 1982 and is used only for the occasional charter flight and Phaphlu has only two flights weekly with six-passenger aircraft, so the best chances of flying to the Everest region are to and from Lukla. Phaphlu airport is being extended (in 1985) to accommodate Twin Otter (19-passenger) aircraft, so by 1986 or '87 Phaphlu may become a viable alternative.

JIRI TO EVEREST BASE CAMP

This section details the route and suggested camping spots on a 21-day trek from Kathmandu to Everest base camp and a flight back to Kathmandu from Lukla. If you are flying to Lukla, begin reading on Day 8 and spend your first night at Phakding, but be sure to take a day at Namche Bazar or Thyangboche for acclimatisation. An excellent 32-day trek may be made by walking on to Dhankuta instead of flying out from Lukla. This route is described in another section.

The Everest trek involves a tremendous amount of up and down walking. A glance at the map will show the reason why. All the rivers in this part of Nepal flow south and the trek route proceeds east. Therefore the trail must climb to the ridge separating two rivers, descend to the river itself and ascend the next ridge. Even though the trek begins at an elevation of 1860 metres, on the sixth day it crosses the Dudh Kosi at an elevation of only 1500 metres – after considerable uphill walking. If you total all the uphill climbing, it will come to almost 9000 metres (29,000 feet) of elevation gain from Jiri to Everest base camp. The Jiri road saves almost 4000 metres of uphill walking over the old Lamosangu route and the new trail up the Dudh Kosi Valley has saved another 500 metres of climbing.

The first part of the trip is by road along the new 110 km long road from Lamosangu to Jiri. The development of roads has been a characteristic of this trek since the first Everest expedition in Nepal. In 1953 the British Everest Expedition started from Bhadgaon. By 1963 the American Expedition could begin from Banepa, saving a day of walking over the British. The Chinese road to Kodari allowed the trek to begin from Dolalghat in 1967 and from Lamosangu in 1970. The road reached Kirantichhap in 1980 and by 1984 it was finally possible to drive all the way to Jiri. There is talk of continuing the road further, perhaps to Phaphlu or even to Namche Bazar, but this is still only a dream and no firm plans exist. The Jiri road was built by the Swiss Association for Technical Assistance (SATA) as part of the Integrated Hill Development Project, a large program of agricultural development in this region. The road was built by hand instead of machine in order to have a beneficial economic impact by employing hundreds of workers. A direct effect of this approach to road building is that it has raised porter wages and created a porter shortage in the region.

Maps and route descriptions for the Everest trek become confusing because of conflicting names for the same place. Many of the villages along this route have both Sherpa names and Nepali names. This applies to both Sherpa and non-Sherpa villages. The Nepali names are used here because these are the ones shown on all official maps and records. The Sherpa names for the villages along the route are given in parenthesised italics after the more common Nepali name.

Day 1: Kathmandu-Lamosangu-Jiri

Buses leave Kathmandu throughout the day for Lamosangu; the first one is at 5.30 am. It requires 2½ hours by private vehicle to cover the 78 km from Kathmandu to Lamosangu on the Arniko Rajmarg, the Chinese constructed Kodari highway, which links Nepal's capital with Tibet. If you are travelling by public bus, allow up to five hours for the trip. There are direct buses to Jiri from Kathmandu; in 1984 there were two buses daily at 6 am, but this schedule will change as the road is completed and demand increases. The road follows the Chinese trolley bus route to Bhaktapur, then passes extensive brick-making factories, finally leaving the Kathmandu Valley and passing by the old Newar towns of Banepa and Dhulikhel – which offers an excellent panoramic view of the eastern Himalaya (including Langtang Lirung, Dorje Lakpa and Manaslu) on a clear day. The road descends to Panchkal, the starting point for Helambu treks and then follows the Indrawati River to its confluence with the Sun Kosi at Dolalghat, crossing the river on a large bridge 57 km from Kathmandu. It then follows the Sun Kosi north to Lamosangu, a bustling bazaar about 50 km south of the Tibetan border. Close to Lamosangu is a hydro-electric power plant built with Chinese aid.

Buses stop at the silver-painted bridge that spans the Sun Kosi. Here, about two km short of the main bazaar and the 'long bridge' that gave the town its name, the new Jiri road begins. If you did not take one of the direct buses from Kathmandu to Jiri you will have to change here to one of the Indian short wheelbase buses that ply the narrow and circuitious route to

Jiri. The 1984 schedule had two buses daily from Lamosangu at 8 and 10 am, reaching Jiri in the early evening. The cost is a hefty Rs 65 from Lamosangu to Jiri with extra charges for baggage. By some bizarre calculation method the fare from Kathmandu direct to Jiri is Rs 61.50. The bus fare from Kathmandu to Lamosangu is Rs 13.

From Lamosangu the road begins to climb towards the top of the 2500-metre ridge that forms the watershed between the Sun Kosi drainage to the west and the Tamba Kosi drainage to the east. The trip from Lamosangu to the eastern Himalaya, proceeding as it does from west to east, cuts across the grain of the country, crossing six major ridges en route to Namche Bazar. The villages in this area are of mixed ethnic and caste composition. Most of the population is either Chhetri or Brahmin, who speak Nepali as their mother tongue, or Tamangs, who speak a Tibeto-Burman language among themselves, but speak Nepali – the *lingua franca*, or trade language of the country – as a second language. Chhetris and Brahmins are Hindus, while the Tamangs practise a form of Tibetan Buddhism. Generally, Tamangs live at slightly higher elevations than their Hindu neighbours, but there is a great deal of overlap.

After some initial switchbacks that take the road out of the Sun Kosi Valley, the road turns east and heads up a canyon towards the top of the first ridge. The first large settlement that is reached is Pakhar at 1980 metres elevation. This is a predominantly Tamang village, and is the site of a Swiss vehicle and road maintenance centre. There is little mineral wealth in Nepal, but near Pakhar there is an economically viable source of magnesite, a mineral that is used in refractories. Ore is mined here, and there are plans to export it to India and other countries with the aid of a ropeway that is under construction from here to Lamosangu. From Pakhar the road climbs along the top of a ridge towards the pass. Buses

often stop at Muldi, 3540 metres, for tea or lunch; there are several bhattis here. The road continues to climb, more gently now, past a stone quarry that produced much of the stone for construction of the road and the wire mesh-enclosed embankments that keep it from sliding back down the hill.

After crossing the pass at 2440 metres the road makes a long sweep around the head of the valley, finally reaching Charikot at the road junction for Dolkha at km 53. Dolkha is a large and interesting bazaar that is situated a few km to the north. This is the jumping-off place for treks to Rolwaling. There are several hotels here and it might be prudent to grab a snack if the wait is particularly long. Trekking permits are checked here by the police. Though buses are often late because of breakdowns, road problems or an excess of bureaucratic formalities, it is usually not necessary to spend a night in a hotel along the road because the buses continue their trip at night, no matter how late. The Swiss project has published a pamphlet entitled *Dolkha* that describes several short treks and excursions in the region near Charikot.

The road descends from Charikot through a region of heavy settlement to Kirantichhap at 1300 metres elevation, 64 km from Lamosangu. Kirantichhap used to be a pleasant little market with a few shops built in a semicircle around a pipal tree, but the road now cuts the village in half and has turned this delightful hill bazaar into a nondescript roadside village. Just east of the village there is a reasonably good camping spot in the shade of another huge pipal tree. The road makes a circuitous descent from Kirantichhap into the Tamba Kosi Valley; this is a fertile area, containing a good deal of terraced land for irrigated paddy cultivation. The population is mainly Brahmins and Chhetris, but there are also Tamangs and a few Newars. Crossing the river on a large steel bridge at 800 metres, the road makes a steep ascent to Namdu; the only part of

Namdu that is seen from the road is the large school. Namdu and its neighbouring village, Kabre, are large and spread out; there are some reforestation and agricultural projects that are part of the Swiss development scheme in both villages.

Sometimes private vehicles are stopped at Kirantichhap or Mina Pokhari. If so, you can either wait for the bus (which has a special permit) or you can walk. From Kirantichhap the trail descends from the bazaar, crosses the river on a suspension bridge at Busti, a bit upstream from the road bridge, then climbs to Namdu. From Namdu the trail stays lower than the road, climbing to Kabre, Yarsa and Chisopani before crossing the ridge at 2510 metres, then descends to the Sikri Khola. From the Sikri Khola you can either go to Jiri or follow the trail downstream, cross a ridge and reach Shivalaya via Those. If you are stopped at Mina Pokhari you can descend to the trail and avoid the longer route that the road follows.

The road climbs above Namdu through scrub forests, switchbacking as it climbs higher and higher, past Mina Pokhari, one of the road project stations. This settlement is a good example of a phenomenon that takes place as roads are constructed. Mina Pokhari hardly existed before the road was conceived. For several years the road ended here, and Mina Pokhari became a boom town; when the road finally reached Jiri, Mina Pokhari again lost its importance. Many villages have suffered such rise and fall – Dumre on the Pokhara road, Betrawati on the Langtang road and Pakhar and Kirantichhap on the Jiri road.

The road finally reaches the top of the forested ridge at 2500 metres. It remains high and contours around the head of the valley in forests above the village of Thulo Chaur, then descends along the top of a ridge above Jiri. This is the Jiri bazaar, elevation 2100 metres, where a weekly market is held on Saturdays; there are a few hotels here. It is a short descent to the main village of Jiri, 1860 metres, where

the road ends at the Swiss dairy and agricultural project. The people of Jiri and the surrounding area are Jirels, a group whose language is related to that of the Sherpas. Although their culture and religion have been influenced by the Sherpas, in many ways they conform to regional practices in this part of the hills.

Bus service to Jiri began in 1984 and many new hotels have been constructed to accommodate trekkers and locals. There are a few cheaper hotels in the bazaar area on the ridge, but the larger and better facilities are in the village at the end of the road. Buses stop at the bazaar at the top of the hill, then descend to the town itself. The trek route has not had time to evolve with its new starting point at Jiri. If you are on your own, you can reach Thodung or Bhandar on the first day (though it is a long hard day) and Sete on the second day according to the schedule that is suggested here. If you have porters or are not in good shape, you may have trouble reaching Bhandar the first day and might settle for Shivalaya the first day and Bhandar on the second day. You should plan on spending a night at either Sete or Sagar to break the long climb to Lamjura Pass into two stages because the total elevation gain from the river to the pass is almost 2000 metres – a pretty difficult climb to make in a single day unless you are in outstanding condition.

Day 2: Jiri-Bhandar

The route to Solu Khumbu starts at the end of the road and heads down the valley towards the hospital, above the Jiri airstrip. The trail starts behind the hospital with a climb in forest, ascending the side of the valley past the few houses of Bharkur and Ratmati, and finally emerging into pastureland as the trail nears the top of the ridge. There is a bhatti at Chitre, only just below the pass. Crossing the ridge at 2400 metres, the trail begins to descend into the Khimti Khola Valley. From Mali, a small Sherpa

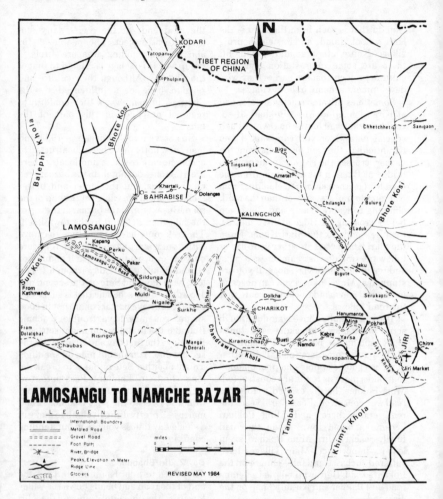

LAMOSANGU TO NAMCHE BAZAR

LEGEND

- International Boundary
- Metalled Road
- Gravel Road
- Foot Path
- River, Bridge
- Peaks, Elevation in Meter
- Ridge Line
- Glaciers

miles
0 1 2 3 4 5 6

REVISED MAY 1984

settlement at 2200 metres, the trail descends alongside a stream, crossing it on a small wooden bridge, then emerges into the main valley where a suspension bridge leads to Shivalaya, a small bazaar at 1800 metres elevation. Food and accommodation here is mediocre – it is close enough to Jiri and Those that few people stay here.

The old trail went via Those and provides an alternative to the newer direct route. To reach Those from Jiri, follow a trail downstream along the east side of the Jiri Khola. The trail climbs a bit in forests, then drops to join the old route from Lamosangu. The trail descends past Kattike to the Khimti Khola then follows the river upstream to Those at 1750 metres. There is a good camp just beyond the iron suspension bridge that crosses

the Khimti Khola, and there are several hotels in the village itself. Beware of second floor rooms above smoky kitchens here. Those (pronounced 'toe-say') (*Maksin*) is a large pleasant bazaar with a cobblestone street and whitewashed houses. It was once the largest market on the trail between Lamosangu and Namche Bazaar, but its importance has greatly diminished now that the Jiri road has been completed,

so many of the shops and hotels here are closed or abandoned. Most of the shops are owned by Newar merchants. It is possible to buy items manufactured locally from the nearby sources of low-grade iron ore. Rooster lamps are a speciality. From Those the trail leads upstream to Shivalaya where it joins the route from Jiri.

From Shivalaya the route ascends

steeply towards the next pass. It is a climb of 350 metres to a school house at Sangbadanda, elevation 2150 metres. There is a small bhatti here; there are three others between here and the pass, and several more on the pass itself. On this trail the first mani walls are encountered. These are stones covered with the Tibetan Buddhist inscription 'Om Mani Padme Hum', which is most easily translated as 'hail to the jewel in the lotus', though its true translation is much more complex and mysterious. You should walk to the left side of these walls as the Buddhists do. Leaving Sangbadanda, the trail climbs less steeply past several isolated – but large and prosperous – houses. Just above a large house with blue windows is a mani wall that has some unique and well-preserved stones on its south side (peek around the wall after passing it on the left). One of these stones was pictured in the book *Everest, the West Ridge*. There is a small tea shop at Kosaribas, 2500 metres, then the trail becomes reasonably level, and even descends a bit, as it goes towards the head of the canyon. Crossing a stream on a wooden bridge, the trail ascends steeply in forests to another tea shop, crosses another stream, this time on two logs, then makes a final climb through forests to the pass. On the top of the pass at 2705 metres there is an impressive array of long mani walls, indicative that the trek is now entering an area dominated by Tibetan culture, and there is an excellent view of the Likhu Khola Valley and the village of Bhandar (*Chyangma*), a large Sherpa settlement, far below in a hanging valley.

An interesting side trip may be made to Thodung either by climbing north for about 1¼ hours from the pass or by detouring from the main trail just beyond Sangbadanda. Thodung, at 3090 metres, is the site of the first cheese factory built by the Swiss in the 1950s. It is now operated by the Nepal Dairy Development Corporation. The long hard climb to the factory is rewarded by cheese, yoghurt and yak (specifically nak) milk for sale, although fresh dairy products are usually available only in the autumn season. The return route from Thodung rejoins the main trail at the top of the pass, then descends to Bhandar. Good food and accommodation is available in Thodung if you have the courage to seek out the manager and his huge mastifs.

Just below the pass there is an important trail junction. One or two minutes' walk below the pass, take the left-hand trail to reach Bhandar. If you continue straight you will stay high on the ridge and reach the village of Roshi; this is the route to the Solu region and crosses a pass to the south of Lamjura. It is a route that is almost never used by foreigners.

After an initially steep descent, the trail to Bhandar reaches the outskirts of the large village and descends gradually through fields and pastures to the village gompa, surrounded by two imposing chortens, at 2200 metres elevation. A chorten is literally a receptacle for offerings, and often holds religious relics. Each of its elements has a symbolic meaning. The square or rectangular base symbolizes the solid earth. On the base is a half-spherical dome, symbolizing water. On top of the dome is a rectangular tower, the four sides of which are painted with a pair of eyes, the all-seeing eyes of Buddha, and what appears to be a nose, but is actually the Sanskrit sign for the number one, symbolizing the absoluteness of Buddha. Above the rectangular tower there is a conical or pyramidal spire (symbolizing fire) with 13 step-like segments, symbolizing the 13 steps leading to Buddhahood. On top of the 13 steps is an ornament shaped like a crescent moon symbolizing air, and a vertical spike symbolizing ether or the sacred light of Buddha. The two chortens at Bhandar are usually freshly painted and are well preserved; one has a pyramidal spire and one has a circular conical one. A large chorten is called a *stupa* and may be seen at Bodhanath or at Swayambunath in Kathmandu.

There are some hotels just below the gompa, and there is an excellent camping spot in a large meadow about 15 minutes walk beyond the village. The three hotels that surround the village square in Bhandar are really the first true hotels since Jiri; there is also a large new hotel under construction just below these, and – imagine this – the *Shobha Hotel* has a radio repair shop on the premises.

Day 3: Bhandar-Sagar
From the hotels at Bhandar the trail descends through the lower fields of the village, then follows a small stream, crossing it on a covered wooden bridge, and descends through deep forests for a while. Leaving the forests, the trail drops into a steep canyon, passing the settlement of Baranda, then finally meets the same stream, crossing it on another covered bridge at Tharo Khola. There is a chance of getting food here, but better food is available in Kenja, about 1½ hours away. The trail turns north, following the Likhu Khola, crossing the river on a suspension bridge at 1580 metres. This bridge replaces an ancient chain link bridge that collapsed under a load of 12 porters during the approach march for the American Mount Everest Expedition in 1963; the remains of the abutments for this bridge may be seen just downstream of the high suspension bridge. As you follow the trail up the east bank of the river to Kenja it is possible to see grey Langur monkeys in the forests. The trail continues along the east bank of the river, climbing over a spur, through the settlement of Namang Gaon, before crossing a small suspension bridge at Kenja, 1630 metres, a small village inhabited by Newars and Magars. Several shops and hotels have been constructed here to cater to both trekkers and local people. In 1969 there were no shops here; now there are more than 15 shops, restaurants and hotels operated by Sherpas who have migrated from the village of Kyama, several miles to the north. There is a weekly market on Sundays; one speciality of Kenja's market is instant tailoring performed on hand-operated sewing machines.

Leaving Kenja, the ascent towards the high Lamjura ridge begins. The first part of the ascent is very steep, then it becomes less severe as elevation is gained. After about two hours of climbing there is a large house. This is not a hotel, but food and accommodation is sometimes available. There is also a welcome supply of water. This is a trail junction; the left fork leads to the north and climbs around the hillside to the Sherpa settlement of Sagar (*Chandra*), 2440 metres, a large village with two-story stone houses and an ancient village gompa. It is possible to camp in the yard of the school, one of the projects of the Himalayan Trust, headed by Sir Edmund Hillary of New Zealand. In 1984 there were no true hotels in Sagar, but this is a Sherpa village, so many people are willing to take guests into their homes. The trek is now completely in Sherpa country. With only one exception, all the remaining villages up to Namche Bazar are inhabited by Sherpas.

If you are trekking on your own, you should take the right fork, which is the trail to Sete, elevation 2575 metres, a small defunct monastery where there are three small hotels. Camping is difficult in Sete; the campsite can accommodate only four or five tents and there is a water shortage, especially in the spring.

Day 4: Sagar-Junbesi
From Sagar or Sete it is a long, but fairly gradual, climb – although in spots it gets steep – to the top of the 3530-metre Lamjura Pass. The way is scenic and interesting; it is one of the few parts of the trek that has no villages. The trek gets into really fine, moist mountain forest, with huge, gnarled, moss-covered rhododendrons, magnolia, maple and birch trees. There is often snow on the trail and the mornings are usually frosty throughout the trekking season. It is said that snow occasionally blocks the pass for a few days

at a time, but I have not heard of this in the last 15 years. In the spring the ridge is alive with blooming rhododendrons; the white, pink, and red blossoms cover the entire hillside. The flowering is limited to a band of a few hundred metres of elevation that moves up the hillside, starting in mid-February and finally reaching the highest elevations in mid to late April. This day is also a delight for the bird lover – Nepal has more than 800 species of birds, and many of the most colourful are found in this zone – sunbirds, minavets, flycatchers, thrushes etc.

The trail from Sagar joins the Sete trail at a small settlement of three houses near two small ponds. The forest changes from pines to rhododendrons here and the trail continues to climb to Goyem, two smoky, but clean and well-maintained hotels, at 3300 metres elevation. Although Goyem is only about two hours from either Sagar or Sete, it is best to have lunch here because the next hotel of any consequence is at Tragdobuk, at least three hours away, although there is a small bhatti about a half-hour below the pass on the other side. The trail climbs steeply up the ridge, finally reaching a mani wall where the trail leaves the ridge and begins to contour towards the pass on a trail that is always muddy and often covered with snow or ice. Passing through a forest of large trees with silver bark, the trail passes three *kharkas*, each consisting of a *goth* or two and a mani wall; these are used by herders in the summer season and are uninhabited from October to June. The houses have no roofs, so they cannot be used as shelter. Since you will probably be crossing the pass about noon or early afternoon, it will be cloudy, cold and windy; there is no view of Himalayan peaks from the pass, although there are glimpses of the top of some snow peaks on the way up. If you are here in the early morning, you will undoubtedly see planes crossing the pass en route to Lukla – so close to the ridge that you can almost reach out and touch their wheels.

The pass is the highest point reached during the trek between Jiri and Namche Bazar and is marked by a tangle of stones, twigs and prayer flags erected by devout travellers. On the east side of the pass the route descends steeply for about 400 metres through fragrant fir and hemlock forests to a stream and a small hotel. The trail then enters open grassy country and descends gently through fields and pastures where horses graze to the small settlement of Tragdobuk, 2860 metres. There are two hotels here, but they are likely to be closed on Saturdays when the owners go to the market in Salleri, about three hours walk to the south. The trail climbs up from Tragdobuk to a huge rock at the head of the valley, then climbs over the ridge to a vantage point overlooking Junbesi (*Jun*), a splendid Sherpa village located amidst beautiful surroundings at 2675 metres. Numbur (6959 metres), known in Sherpa as *Shorong Yul Lha*, God of the Solu, towers over the large green valley above Junbesi. This village is at the north end of the Sherpa region known as Solu (*Shorong* in Sherpa). On the whole, the Sherpas of Solu are economically better off than their cousins in Khumbu, because the fertile valley here is at a lower elevation so a wide variety of crops can be grown. In recent years, however, employment with expeditions and trekking parties has done much to improve the lot of the Khumbu Sherpas.

A short distance below the ridge there is a trail junction marked by a sign:

> The big building in front of you is a monastery called Serlo. All are welcome to drop in. We speak some English and (real!) fruit juice are available. You might enjoy seeing the statues, taking some pictures, or asking some questions about the things we do here.
>
> We can offer food and lodging also.

If you do not visit the monastery, stay on the main trail and descend gently to Junbesi, keeping to the left of a huge mani stone, and enter the village near a small hotel. There is an abundance of hotels in

Junbesi so it is worth a bit of exploration before settling in. Several hotels offer hot showers and other enticements; there is a large new hotel under construction. Trekking groups usually camp below the village on the banks of the river; camping is not allowed in the school yard. The school here is one of the largest and most active of the Hillary schools.

The region near Junbesi is well worth exploring, and a day spent here can offer a variety of alternatives. To the north of Junbesi, about two hours away, is the village of Phugmochhe, elevation 3100 metres, where there is a 'Traditional Sherpa Art Center'. En route to Phug-mochhe, a short diversion will allow a visit to Thubten Chhuling, a huge Tibetan Buddhist monastery about 1¼ hours' walk from Junbesi. The trail to Thubten Chhuling starts in Junbesi village in front of the gompa and follows the Junbesi Khola upstream, crossing it on a bridge, then makes the final climb to the monastery at 3000 metres. The central gompa here is large and impressive and often has more than 200 monks chanting both inside and outside. An offering is expected and no accommodation or food is available. There are small cells all over the hillside that are the residences of monks and nuns; you probably won't be welcomed at these because many of the inhabitants are on extended meditation programmes. The monastery was founded in the late 1960s by Tushi Rimpoche, who travelled to Nepal with many monks from Rongbuk monastery in Tibet. It is a large, active and impressive religious community.

To rejoin the main trail without returning to Junbesi you can follow a yak trail that climbs from Thubten Chhuling to the Lapcha La, a pass marked by a large chorten and many prayer flags at 3475 metres. The Schneider map does not show this trail and Thubten Chhuling is shown as Mopung. A guide is helpful here, but you can probably find the way yourself if you proceed generally south-east and always go up. The trail from the Lapcha La is another herders' trail that drops steeply to the Ringmo Khola, passing through the yards and fields of several houses. It requires about three hours of tough walking to reach Ringmo from Thubten Chhuling.

Day 5: Junbesi-Nuntala

Below Junbesi the trail crosses the Junbesi Khola on a wooden bridge at 2640 metres. Just beyond the bridge there is a trail junction; the right-hand or downhill trail leads to Phaphlu, the site of a hospital (operated by the Himalayan Trust) and an airstrip. South of Phaphlu is Salleri, the administrative centre for the Solu Khumbu district. The route to Khumbu takes the left-hand trail leading uphill. After it has climbed high on the ridge, at about 3080 metres, there is an excellent view of Everest (this is the first point on the trek where Everest may be seen), Chamlang (7317 metres) and Makalu (8463 metres). The trail turns north, descending through Salung, 2980 metres, (a small hotel here) to the Ringmo Khola at 2650 metres. This river provides one of the last opportunities to wash clothes and bathe in a large river; the next river, the Dudh Kosi, is too cold for all but the most determined.

From the river the trail ascends to Ringmo where Dorje Passang, an enter-prising (and very patient) Sherpa has succeeded in raising a large orchard of apples, peaches and apricots. The fruit has become so abundant that many fruit products – including delicious apple *rakshi*, apple cider, dried apples and even apple pickles – are available at reasonable prices from the 'Apple House'. At Ringmo the trail joins the 'road' from Okhaldunga to Namche Bazar that was built with the assistance of several aid programmes. From here to Namche the trail was widened and levelled between 1980 and 1984 by local labourers who were paid with food instead of cash. The result will probably never be a motorable road, but you can now walk side by side with your friends on the wide trail and the route avoids many steep ascents and descents that had characterised the old expedition route.

Just beyond Ringmo the trail passes two mani walls. The second wall hides another unexpected opportunity to get lost. Go to the left of the mani wall, make a U-turn and head uphill; the straight trail heads north through unpopulated country (not even a single house), eventually reaching Ghat in the Khumbu Valley after five days – it is not a practical trekking route (several porters perished on this trail during the approach march for the 1952 Swiss Everest Expedition). It is a short ascent from Ringmo to Trakshindo Pass, 3071 metres, marked by a large white chorten. A bit above Ringmo is a sign advertising a 15-minute walk to Trakshindo cheese factory. It is worth a visit, if only to experience the hospitality of the vivacious Ang Phorba Sherpani, the wife of the cheese-maker. Cheese is available year round (the 1984 price was Rs 54 per kg), but fresh dairy products like yoghurt (*dahi*) and milk (*dudh*) are available only in the summer and fall. There is food and accommodation available at the cheese factory and also at the pass itself in three tiny hotels.

A few minutes below the pass, on the east side, the trail passes the isolated monastery of Trakshindo, a superb example of Sherpa monastic architecture – certainly the most imposing building so far encountered on the trek. There are two hotels here, outside of the monastery grounds. The trail then descends through a conifer and rhododendron forest alive with birds. There are a few herders' huts alongside the trail, but the route is mostly in dense forest. Several picturesque streams are crossed on wooden bridges just before the trail reaches Nuntala (*Manidingma*) at 2320 metres. Here there are stone-walled compounds enclosing numerous hotels that range from mediocre to crummy. There is also one small shop. As you enter the village there is a large new hotel that was under construction in 1984.

Bhakta Bahadur Srestha, the school-teacher, is also the region's impresario. He often stages evening cultural shows performed by the school children. He expects a hefty donation to the school, but perhaps this is a better system that the Junbesi school approach of opening a donation book in your lap as you drink tea.

Day 6: Nuntala-Khari Khola

From Nuntala the descent continues to the Dudh Kosi ('milk river') – the largest river met since the Sun Kosi. The trail is generally well graded, though it sometimes passes through terraced fields and the yards of houses, then it descends steeply through forests to a chautaara overlooking the river. From here it drops on a rough and rocky trail for about 100 metres to the suspension bridge, built by the Swiss, that crosses the Dudh Kosi at 1500 metres. The trail now concludes its trip eastward and turns north up the Dudh Kosi Valley. Beware of stinging nettles (*sisnu*) from here to Chaunrikarka. These are used as cattle fodder, as a vegetable (they are picked using bamboo tongs) and to make rough cloth. They inflict a painful rash the instant you touch them. At the end of the bridge, turn left and climb through fields of barley, wheat and corn to the large spread-out village of Jubing (*Dorakbuk*) at 1680 metres. This village is inhabited by an ethnic group known as Rais. Like the Tamangs and Sherpas, the Rais speak a Tibeto-Burman language of their own and are basically of Mongoloid stock, but they have a very different culture and practice an indigenous religion of their own that is neither Buddhist nor Hindu, although it has been influenced by Hinduism in certain aspects. Rais have very characteristic facial features which make them easy to recognize. Other signs of Rai influence in this area are the garlands of marigolds that decorate the Dudh Kosi bridge and the use of traditional bamboo pipes instead of plastic hose for the village water supply. The Rais (along with Limbus,

Top: Chhetri homes near Pokhara (KS)
Bottom: Gokyo Lake and Cho Oyu (elevation 8201 metres) (SA)

In Sherpa country
Top: Spinning a prayer wheel (SA)
Left: Carved *mani* stone (SA)
Right: Closely spaced houses in Junbesi (SA)

Magars and Gurungs) are one of the ethnic groups that supply a large proportion of the recruits for the well-known Gurkha regiments of the British and Indian armies.

The trail stays below the village; the Amar Hotel (and the post office) is at the north edge of the village at 1800 metres. Beyond Jubing there is a short climb across a side valley, then a steep climb over a spur. From this ridge you can see Khari Khola (*Khati Thenga*) at about 2070 metres elevation. This is a predominantly Sherpa village, though it also has a small Magar community. Descend a bit on a sandy trail; it is then a pleasant walk into the main Khari Khola bazaar. There are several hotels here; the *Quiet View Lodge* and the *River View Lodge* are the upmarket hotels; the *Milan, Annapurna, Sagarmatha* and *Mayalu* hotels are pretty much shared accommodation with the proprieors. There is a campsite beyond the village just across the bridge (there is no camping allowed in the schoolyard).

You can save a day on the trek in by continuing on to Bupsa today, then Ghat the following day and Namche the day after that. This is made possible by the new trail that has eliminated several steep climbs. If you have porters, however, you may have trouble convincing them to change the schedule because tradition dictates that the camping places should be the ones described here.

Day 7: Khari Khola-Puiyan

From Khari Khola you can see the white chorten on the ridge in Bupsa. The trail descends from Khari Khola village and crosses a stream with the same name on a suspension bridge near some water-driven mills at 2010 metres, then makes a steep climb up to Bupsa (*Bumshing*), at 2300 metres. There is a hotel on the ridge and two others about 10-15 minutes up the trail.

The trail then climbs steadily, but gently, through forests to a ridge. The Dudh Kosi canyon is extremely steep here

and in many places you can see all the way to the river, a thousand metres below. The trail climbs to a cleft in the rock, then into another canyon before reaching a ridge at about 2900 metres overlooking Puiyan (*Chitok*), a Sherpa settlement of about 10 houses completely surrounded by forests at 2730 metres. Much of the forest near this village was cut down in the '70s to make charcoal which was burned for fuel in the Khumbu region before kerosene became easily available.

From the ridge, the trail turns almost due east as it descends into the deep canyon of the Puiyan Khola. This portion of the trail is totally new and in many places it is narrow and exposed, especially where it was blasted out of a vertical rock wall. At one point a collection of logs and shrubbery provides a false sense of security as the trail crosses a rock face above a precipice. After crossing a large slide area, the trail climbs on a stone staircase, then crosses two streams on wooden bridges (all the bridges built under the trail renovation programme are identical in design). There is a shelter under a rock that is used by porters, and a few minutes beyond is a small stone hotel and a camping place. The owner of this hotel, Passang Phuttar, is likely to be away or drunk, so it might be wise to continue on to the *Holiday Inn*, the last house in the village, about 15 minutes up the trail.

A trail was once constructed that goes directly from Khari Khola to Surkhe and avoids the long climb through Puiyan, but it is in disrepair and subject to rockfall. There is no food or accommodation on this route and even the local people don't use it. There are conflicting reports about the future of this trail; some people say it is cancelled and others say that it will be improved.

Day 8: Puiyan-Phakding

The trail climbs for about an hour after Puiyan to a ridge at 2800 metres then up to another ridge. Lukla airstrip can easily be recognised from here by the large metal roof of the Sherpa Co-operative Hotel and by the remains of one of the two planes that crashed there. The trail descends to Surkhe (*Buwa*), 2293 metres, located on a small tributary stream of the Dudh Kosi. The trail stays above the village, circling it like an expressway. There are a few tea shops near the bridge, but these cater mostly to the local porters that serve the Namche market. There is a trekkers' hotel off the trail as you first enter the village. Beware of Friday and Saturday nights in Surkhe and the nearby villages. The porters to and from the Namche market start to travel at first light, and if there is a full moon, this can be at 2 am, causing a total uproar in every hotel.

From Surkhe the trail climbs for about 15 minutes to a junction where a stone staircase leads off to the right. This is the trail to Lukla; it requires about an hour of steep climbing to reach the airstrip. It is not necessary to go to Lukla at this point unless you want to make a reservation for a return flight, although they can only waitlist you at this end. The Khumbu trail goes north up the steep canyon on a route that was blasted out of the rock, crossing the large stream that comes from Lukla, then climbs steeply up some wobbly stone steps past several caves to another stream where there is a small bhatti. It is a short walk uphill through a jumble of boulders to a series of mani walls, finally emerging at two brightly painted houses, the beginning of Mushe (*Nangbug*). There are numerous mani stones and walls along the trail and Mushe blends almost imperceptibly into Chaunrikarka (*Dungde*), a large village at 2680 metres. The region from Khari Khola to Jorsale is called Pharak. The Sherpas in this area have slightly different traditions from their neighbours in Solu and Khumbu and have better agricultural opportunities due to the gentler climate in the Dudh Kosi Valley. Pharak villagers raise large crops of corn (maize) and potatoes in the summer; they grow wheat, turnips, cauliflower and cabbage in the winter season;

and they raise herds of cows and yak cross-breeds, as well as sheep and goats.

The major hotel in Chaunrikarka is the wooden building on the right of the trail just after the short steep climb from Mushe. The house just before the stone kani over the trail to the north of the hotel (which isn't much of a hotel) also offers food and accommodation. There is a shop of sorts further on, around the corner near the first large chorten. There are three more chortens and some wonderful mani walls, then the trail passes through fields to Chablung (*Lomdza*), where the trail from Lukla joins the route, then continues north to Ghat (*Lhawa*), at 2550 metres, on the banks of the Dudh Kosi, then climbs a bit above the river, passing several scattered houses, descends a steep stone staircase and climbs again to reach Phakding, which is situated on both sides of the river at 2800 metres elevation.

In September 1977, an avalanche from Ama Dablam fell into a lake near the base of the peak. This created a wave of water 10 metres high that raced down the Dudh Kosi and washed away large parts of the trail, seven bridges, and part of the village of Jorsale, killing three villagers. At Phakding the first signs of this devastation become apparent; the river is crossed on a long wobbly wooden cantilever bridge just beyond the village at 2650 metres. There is a fancy new suspension bridge south of Phakding, but nobody uses it because the trail from this bridge climbs steeply over a ridge; there is no climbing necessary if you use the old bridge. From Phakding to Jorsale the trail is continually undergoing repair and improvement, so portions of the trail between here and Jorsale may be different from what is described because of recent modifications to the trail. At Phakding the *Khumbu Alpine Camp* has been under construction for more than eight years. You can stay here in a reasonably comfortable hotel room for about US$10 a night.

Day 9: Phakding-Namche Bazar

There is another part of Phakding just above the Khumbu Alpine Camp; there are two or three smaller hotel/tea shops and a campsite there. From Phakding the trail continues north up the Dudh Kosi Valley, staying a hundred metres or so above the river on its west bank, crossing a small stream where a tiny hotel sits on the opposite side of the wooden bridge, then up the river to the village of Benkar at 2700 metres. There is a bhatti here just behind the huge mani stone in the centre of the trail. Past Benkar the trail crosses the river on another wooden bridge. There is a spectacular and intricately carved mani stone just on the other side of the bridge, but to walk to the left of this one would require swimming the Dudh Kosi. The trail follows a pleasant route alongside the river then climbs to the village of Chomoa, the site of an agricultural project that was set up to serve the Hotel Everest View, and the *Hatago Lodge* run by funny old Mr Hagayuki who makes peach wine, bean salad and other unique concoctions. It's a bit more expensive than some of the other hotels along the way, but the Hatago Lodge (Hatago means Inn in Japanese) has good food and one of the most colourful of Nepal's many strange characters in residence.

From the lodge at Chomoa, the trail climbs a bit to another hotel (there are more than 100 inns and hotels in Khumbu) and a campsite, descends to cross a stream and climbs up to Monjo. The *Monjo Hotel* (which once had a sign proclaiming itself to be the Monjo Sheraton) is up a little rise at the north end of the settlement of only three or four houses. Beyond the hotel, the trail makes a steep rocky descent to a large farm, then turns left in front of two houses and drops to a suspension bridge that the US Peace Corps built to span the Dudh Kosi. A short distance up the west bank of the river is Jorsale *(Thumbug)*, 2850 metres. All along this part of the trail, villages are interspersed with magnificent forests –

rhododendron and magnolia trees and giant firs. In both the early fall and late spring seasons, the flowers on this portion of the trek make it a beautiful walk. On the cliffs above the river it is possible to see musk deer and Himalayan tahr.

There are numerous hotels packed together along the main street of Jorsale, and you usually have to detour around cows and crowds of porters hanging around the village. It is a good spot for lunch because there is no reliable food available between here and Namche – a good steep two or three-hour climb away. At Jorsale the trail enters the Sagarmatha (Everest) National Park. There is an entrance station just beyond the village where a fee of Rs 60 (about US$4) is collected from each trekker. The rules printed on the back of the entrance ticket are as follows:

Children below 12 years of age shall pay half the entry fee. This permit is non-transferable and good for one entry only. You enter the park on your own risk. His Majesty's Government shall bear no liability for damage, loss, injury or death. Trekking is an acceptable challenge, but please do not:
- litter, dispose it properly.
- remove anything from the park.
- disturb wildlife.
- carry arms and explosives.
- scale any mountain without proper permission.
- scale any sacred peaks of any elevation.

Please keep all the time to the main trek routes. Please be self sufficient in your fuel supply before entering the park. Buying fuel wood from local people or removing any wood materials from the forest is illegal. This will apply to your guides, cooks and porters also.

Park personnel are entitled to arrest any person in charge of having violated park regulations or search his belongings.

For further information visit Park headquarter or ask any park personnel.

National Parks Family Wishes Your Trip Pleasant.

The degree of enforcement of these regulations varies, especially with respect to the use of firewood. It is sometimes difficult to obtain kerosene to use as a fuel, and almost impossible to obtain petrol or cooking gas. There is a kerosene depot at Jorsale that also rents plastic jerrycans, but not stoves. Kerosene is also available in Namche at the Saturday market; the price varies from Rs 275 to Rs 350 (US$22) per 16-litre tin. Lesser quantities are available from shopkeepers in Namche throughout the week. If you do plan to use kerosene, bring along a filter – both dirt and water can mess up stoves, and both are present in most of the locally available kerosene. Trekkers on their own may eat in houses and hotels that cook over wood fires – but theoretically this will also be prohibited eventually.

From Jorsale the trail climbs over a spur up a soggy trail under a weeping, moss-covered wall, crosses the Bhote Kosi on the only bridge remaining out of the six 'Hillary Bridges' in the valley, and begins the steep climb to Namche Bazar. From two places along the trail to Namche there is a view of Mount Everest, Nuptse and Lhotse, but because clouds usually obscure the peaks in the afternoon, Everest will probably not be visible. The first viewpoint is almost on the trail itself, but the second one, half an hour higher, is about 10 metres out onto the ridge at a place where the trail switchbacks. After this viewpoint the trail climbs less steeply, but still steadily, through forests to a small tea shop and a defunct National Park forest nursery. Just beyond the nursery is a small spring and a hydraulic ram system that pumps water to the National Park offices on the hill. Take the right, upper, trail to reach the main street of Namche; the left-hand trail leads to the lower pastures of the village. Namche Bazaar (Nauche), 3440 metres, is the administrative centre for the Khumbu region and has a police checkpost, headquarters for Sagarmatha National Park, a bank (you can sometimes change money here), several shops selling items of every description, and a few hotels and rest-aurants. Even a small bakery and several hotels with hot showers are situated among the hundred-odd houses of this prosperous village.

It is probably futile trying to keep up-to-date on the latest hotel developments in Namche, but not counting the small bhattis catering to locals and the homes that offer food and accommodation but do not have hotel signs, there are at least 11 major hotels here. The most popular is *Lakpa Dorje's Trekkers Inn*, which churns out yak steaks by the hundreds. The largest is *Passang Kami's Khumbu Lodge*, which offers private rooms for Rs 60. Private rooms are also available in *Karma Lama's Namche Hotel* (also called the *Cooperative Hotel* which is the large low building in the centre of town. The other popular hotels are the *Thamserku*, *Tawa*, *Kala Pattar* and the *Sherpa Hotel*. The owners of the *Khumbila Hotel*, which is near the entrance to the village, have a sister who is married to a Japanese man, so this hotel is a bit upmarket with private rooms and other amenities.

Electricity was introduced to Namche in October, 1983, when a UNESCO-sponsored hydroelectric plant located below the village began operating. Each house has two 40 watt lights; some hotels have electric stoves that they can use during the day; and all the wiring is underground. Despite technical problems caused by overloading the system, the electricity is working surprisingly well (only three or four blackouts each night) and Namche exudes a certain amount of charm in the evening. There are a total of 125 houses with electricity, including the National Park and government offices on the hill and the houses of Chhorkung, above Namche. The electricity project is part of an effort to conserve energy and reduce environmental degradation in Khumbu. The large area fenced in by stones above Namche is a forest plantation that is part of the same effort.

There is equipment available for rent in Namche, so if you discover that your jacket or sleeping bag is not warm enough, you can rent one here.

Each Saturday there is an important weekly *hat*, or market, in which corn, rice, eggs, vegetables and other items not grown in Khumbu are sold. Two or more buffalos are usually slaughtered each week, so meat is available on Saturdays and Sundays. The food is carried to Namche Bazar from villages six to ten days away by lowland porters (the buffalos walk themselves). It is an important social event, as well as the focus for the region's trade, as Sherpas from all the neighbouring villages come to purchase food and socialise and the bazaar becomes a crowded rumpus of Sherpas, local government officials, porters and sightseers. For the most part it is a cash market, in which Sherpas exchange money they have received from trekking or mountaineering parties for the goods they require. The Rais and other people carrying goods to the market are often told by fun-loving Sherpas that the money comes from Mount Everest, and it is not uncommon to find an unsuspecting lowland porter shivering with cold as he accompanies a trekking party to Everest Base Camp in search of the free money that tumbles from the highest peak on earth.

Day 10: Namche Bazar

Acclimatisation is important before proceeding higher. This is the first of two specific 'acclimatisation days' that should be built into everyone's trek schedule. The day may be spent by taking a day hike to Thami, by visiting Khunde or Khumjung, or by relaxing and exploring Namche Bazar. There is a police checkpost in Namche where trekking permits must be presented and endorsed and the details entered into a register. Usually trekkers are required to sign the register; if so, you will have to go personally to the police checkpost, but sometimes a trekking guide can take your permit and undertake the formalities on your behalf. Be sure to bring both your trekking permit and

National Park entrance ticket for the police to examine.

Above the police checkpost, at the top of the hill, is the Sagarmatha National Park headquarters which has a visitor centre that is worth a visit. There are displays about the people, forests, wildlife, mountaineering and the impact of tourism. The current park warden, Passang, was trained in New Zealand; you should try to meet him and his New Zealand wife if you want to learn more about the area.

The region above Namche, but below the National Park headquarters, is called Chhorkung. This non-village has grown a lot recently and boasts several hotels and large group campsites.

Day 11: Namche Bazar-Thyangboche

There is a direct route from Namche Bazar to Thyangboche that starts from Chhorkung, but it is more interesting to take a slightly longer route and visit Khumjung, the largest village in Khumbu, and Khunde, its smaller neighbour. From Namche Bazar it is a steep climb of one hour to the airstrip at Shyangboche, 3720 metres, which was built to serve the Hotel Everest View. The hotel has been pretty much closed since 1982, and planes rarely land at Shyangboche now. There are a few tea shops near the airstrip, but there is a water problem here, so it isn't a good choice for a place to stay for the night. From the airstrip it is a 20-minute walk to the hotel, which provides excellent views of Everest and Ama Dablam. If the hotel is operating, you can get a cup of coffee or tea or a meal here. A trail descends from the hotel to Khumjung village, 3790 metres, or you can walk from the airstrip directly to Khumjung – head for the chorten at the top of the hill and then follow the trail down through the forest. In the morning, just follow the schoolchildren from Namche to Khumjung, situated at the foot of the sacred peak Khumbila (5861 metres). The Khumjung gompa posesses what is said to be the skull of a yeti or abominable snowman. It was this

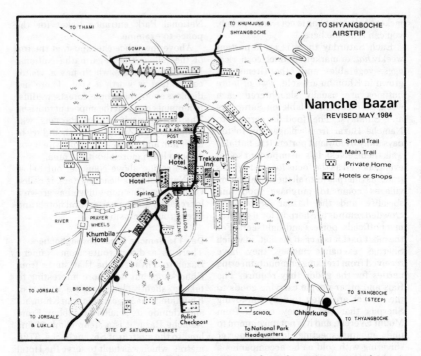

Namche Bazar
REVISED MAY 1984

Small Trail
Main Trail
Private Home
Hotels or Shops

TO THAMI
GOMPA
TO KHUMJUNG & SHYANGBOCHE
TO SHYANGBOCHE AIRSTRIP
POST OFFICE
PK Hotel
Trekkers Inn
Cooperative Hotel
Spring
PRAYER WHEELS
RIVER
Khumbila Hotel
INTERNATIONAL FOOTPATH
TO JORSALE
BIG ROCK
TO JORSALE & LUKLA
SITE OF SATURDAY MARKET
Police Checkpost
SCHOOL
To National Park Headquarters
Chharkung
TO SYANGBOCHE (STEEP)
TO THYANGBOCHE

relic that was taken by Sir Edmund Hillary, the village headman, Khunjo Chumbi, Desmond Doig and Marlin Perkins to the United States in 1960 to be examined by scientists. The scalp turned out to be made from the skin of a serow – a member of the antelope family – but the yeti legend still goes on.

Also in Khumjung is a school, built by the Himalayan Trust, that has succeeded in providing an excellent primary education for many of the children of Khumbu and was expanded in 1983 to include a high school so that Sherpa children no longer have to go to boarding school at Salleri, a week away, to complete their education. It is only a short detour from Khumjung to Khunde, the site of the Khunde Hospital, also built and maintained by the Himalayan Trust. From Khumjung the trail goes down the valley, continuously passing picturesque mani walls and chortens;

after a short descent it meets the main Namche Bazar-Thyangboche trail. Beyond a few mani stones is another group of hotels; this settlement, called Kenjoma, is inhabited primarily by Tibetans and there is always an extensive display of Tibetan (and made-in-Kathmandu) souvenirs to tempt you. Bargaining is very much in order. The trail descends gradually to Teshinga, then steeply to Phunki Thanghka, a small settlement with several water-driven prayer wheels on the banks of the Dudh Kosi, at 3250 metres. There is only one hotel in Khumjung, no hotel in Khunde, food (and lots of booze), but no accommodation, in Kenjoma, a small hotel in Teshinga and three hotels in Phunki Thanghka.

From Phunki Thanghka the trail climbs steeply at first, then becomes a gradual ascent through forests and around mani stones as it follows the side of a hill up to the saddle on which Thyangboche monastery is located, at 3870 metres, in a clearing surrounded by dwarf firs and rhododendrons. The view from this spot, seen to best advantage in the morning, is rightly deemed to be one of the most magnificent in the world. Kwangde (6187 metres), Tawachee (6542 metres), Everest (8848 metres), Nuptse (7855 metres), Lhotse (8616 metres), Ama Dablam (6856 metres), Kantega (6779 metres)and Thamserku (6608 metres) provide an inspiring panorama of Himalayan giants.

The gompa and its surroundings provide interesting insights into the way of life in this remote and peaceful monastery. The following sign used to appear near the monastery guest house:

I am happy to welcome you to Thyangboche.

This is the religious centre of the whole 'Sherpa-land', in fact the entire Solu-Khumbu area.

A very modest rest house has been built on the far end of the meadow facing Chomolungma (Mt. Everest).

It has been erected with the funds collected from friends and visitors who have come to this sacred and beautiful place. If you wish, you may contribute to our meagre funds to enable us to make it more comfortable when you come again, for we hope you will. Anything you wish to give will be gratefully accepted.

While you are a guest at Thyangboche, whether you stay in the rest house or in your own tents, I wish to request you to observe the few rules in observance of the Divine Dharma. Please do not kill or cause to kill any living creature in the area of this holy place. This includes domestic fowls and animals, as also wild game.

Please remember that this holy place is devoted to the worship of the Perfect One, and that nothing should be done within these sacred precincts which will offend or cause to hurt those who live here in humility and serenity. May you journey in peace and walk in delight, and may the blessings of the Perfect One be always with you.

Nawang Tenzing Zang-Po, The Reincarnate of Thyangboche

The sign has long since disappeared and has been replaced by a fancy carved sign directing visitors to the New Zealand-built *Thyangboche Trekkers Lodge*, a part of the Sagarmatha National Park development. No longer is it necessary to endure the simple lodging offered by the lamas – now you can sit around a stove burning charcoal (from Puiyan, outside the National Park) and write comments in the guest book either praising or damning the lodge concept.

In addition to the National Park lodge, there is a choice of other facilities at Thyangboche. The gompa-owned hotel is the most popular and has two rooms of dormitory accommodation and a huge kitchen-cum-dining room that is often the centre of social life for both foreigners and locals. It has a cozy ski lodge atmosphere and is worth visiting at least for a cup of tea or rakshi. The *Namaste Lodge* across the field is cheaper and a bit rougher, but Passang Thongdup is a personable and helpful hotelier. There is another unnamed hotel near the Namaste, but it caters primarily for locals. The gompa charges Rs 5 for each tent at Thyangboche and a lama comes around with a receipt book to be sure that you pay this fee. It is one of the few sources of revenue for the monastery— which now supports about 50 or 60 monks – so it really isn't reasonable to argue about this charge. Several trekking companies donate money to the monastery each year and in return receive the use of certain camping sites. The lamas won't let you camp in these places. There is also a camping place and a hotel at Devuche, about a 20-minute walk from Thyangboche.

Thyangboche (the correct phonetic spelling is Tengpoche, but most maps use Thyangboche) was founded about 60 years ago by Lama Gulu. The main temple was destroyed by an earthquake in 1933 and has since been rebuilt. The founding lama was killed in this earthquake and his remains are still buried inside the gompa. Thyangboche is the largest and most active monastery in Khumbu, but it is not the oldest. Buddhism is believed to have been introduced into Khumbu towards the end of the 17th century by Lama Sange Dorje, the fifth of the reincarnate lamas of the Rong-phu (or Rongbuk) monastery in Tibet, just to the north of Mt Everest. According to legend, Lama Sange Dorje flew over the Himalaya and landed on rocks at Pangboche and Thyangboche, leaving his footprints. He is thought to have been responsible for the founding of the first gompas in Khumbu, at Pangboche and Thami. The gompas of Khumjung and Namche Bazar are of a later date. None of these were monasteries; their priests were married lamas and there was no monastic community with formal organisation and discipline. The first monasteries, at Thyangboche and, at about the same time, Thami, were established as offshoots of the Nyingmapa (Red Hat) sect monastery of Rong-phu in Tibet, and young monks were sent there to study. Thyangboche's charter bears the seal of the abbot of Rong-phu. A nunnery was later founded at Devuche, just north of Thyangboche. Trakshindo was established in 1946 by a lama from Thyangboche.

There is a new library and cultural centre behind the gompa that is designed to cater to both Tibetan scholars and trekkers. The plan is to develop an extensive library of books on religion, culture and history in several languages.

Each year, usually at the November-December full moon, the Mani Rimdu festival is celebrated at Thyangboche. On this occasion the lamas wear elaborate masks and costumes and through a series of ritualistic dances, dramatize the triumph of Buddhism over Bon, the ancient anamistic religion of Tibet. There are usually large crowds of westerners at this ceremony, and hotel accommodation is at a premium. Even tent space is hard to come by. Prices creep up in accordance with the capitalist tradition of charging what the traffic will bear. The monastery charges for entrance tickets, usually Rs 10 per person, with a surcharge for movie cameras.

Day 12: Thyangboche-Pheriche

From Thyangboche there is a short, steep and muddy descent to Devuche through a forest of birches, conifers and rhododendrons. Because of the ban on hunting at Thyangboche, almost-tame blood pheasants are to be seen here and Nepal's national bird, the Danfay or Impeyan pheasant, may be encountered. This colourful bird is only found at high altitudes. The tail is reddish, it has a shiny blue back, and has a metallic green tinge and pure white under its wings. It appears almost iridescent when seen in sunlight. Another common bird in this region is the snow pigeon, which swoops in great flocks above the villages of Khumjung, Namche and Pangboche. The crow-like birds that scavenge any food that you might drop (I have even seen them fly away with a full packet of biscuits that they have stolen) are red billed choughs and occasionally ravens; both are called *goraks* by the Sherpas. Near Gorak Shep you are likely to encounter Tibetan snow cocks racing happily down the hillside. High above you may see goshawks, Himalayan griffons, golden eagles and lammergeiers circling on the updrafts from the mountains. Musk deer may sometimes be seen here, especially in the forests below Thyangboche, leaping like kangaroos.

There is a lodge near the stream at Devuche. The few houses of Devuche and the village gompa are off in the trees to the west and the nunnery (which isn't too enthusiastic about visitors) is up the hill to the east. From Devuche the level trail passes many mani walls in a deep rhododendron forest. Watch the leaves curl up in the cold and open in the morning when the sun strikes them. After crossing the Imja Khola on a steel bridge swaying a terrifying distance above the river at a spot where the river rushes through a narrow cleft, the route climbs up past some magnificently carved mani stones to Pangboche at 3860 metres. Just before the village are two chortens, a kani and a resting place. Just east of here is a monument where the footprint of the patron saint Lama Sange Dorje may be seen preserved in stone. Pangboche is the highest year-round settlement in the valley. The gompa, which is the oldest in Khumbu, has relics said to be the skull and hand of a yeti, which may be seen by visitors for a slight fee. Pangboche is actually two villages, an upper and a lower village; on the way to the Everest base camp the lower route is best; on the return trip the upper trail may be used, allowing a visit to the gompa, 120 metres above the lower village. There are three hotels in lower Pangboche, one at each end of the village and one in the centre – good choices for lunch.

From Pangboche the route enters alpine meadows above the tree line. Most of the vegetation is scrub juniper, tundra and wildflowers, including edelweiss. At Showma there is a tea shop, then the trail passes several yak herders' goths as it ascends on a shelf above the river to Orsho where there is a small hotel. Beyond Orsho the trail divides; the lower more important looking trail leads to Dingboche; the trail to Pheriche goes up to the left, through the front yards of a few herders' huts, over a stone wall, and climbs a small ridge before descending to the Khumbu Khola, crossing it on a wooden bridge. From the bridge it is a ten-minute walk, usually in the wind, to Pheriche at 4240 metres. Pheriche is windier, so it seems colder, than most places in Khumbu; be sure that you carry your warmest clothing on this day. There is a trekkers' aid post at Pheriche supported by the Himalayan Rescue Association and Tokyo Medical College. A western physician is usually in attendance during the trekking season. This establishment and the doctors who operate it specialise in the study and treatment of altitude sickness and strive to educate trekkers in the dangers of too fast an ascent to high altitudes. You should visit the clinic if you have even the slightest problem with altitude.

Pheriche is a labyrinth of walls and pastures. There are five hotels here, including the *National Park Lodge* that is an on/off operation depending on who has the contract to operate it. The biggest hotel is *Nima Tsering's Himalayan Hotel*, a two story affair with a tin roof. Other hotels are semi-permanent buildings which have evolved from sod huts with a tarp on the roof into more substantial structures that are ever expanding. Be careful when you sit down in these crowded places – that comfortable-looking cushion in the corner is likely to be a baby wrapped up in blankets. The *Snow View Hotel* has a mountaineering equipment shop. There is the usual jumble of new and used climbing equipment for sale, and there is often an unlikely collection of expedition food available, such as Bulgarian stews, Russian borscht, Yugoslavian halibut, French snails or American granola bars – it all depends on which country recently had an Everest expedition.

Day 13: Pheriche

One of the most important aspects of acclimatisation to high altitudes is a slow ascent. Therefore, it is imperative that an additional night be spent at Pheriche to aid the acclimatisation process. This is the second of the mandatory acclimatisation days on this trek.

The day may be spent in many ways. You may wish to declare a rest day and relax in camp. Or you may wish to do some strenuous exploring. A short trip may be made to the small Nangkartshang Gompa, a climb of about 400 metres above the village. From this vantage point there is a good view of Makalu, fifth highest mountain in the world, to the east.

A more strenuous trip may be made by climbing the hill to Dingboche, then up the Imja Khola Valley past Bibre to Chhukung, a small summer settlement at 4700 metres. The views from Chhukung and further up the valley on the moraines towards Island Peak, 6189 metres, are tremendous. The great south face of Lhotse towers above to the north; Amphu

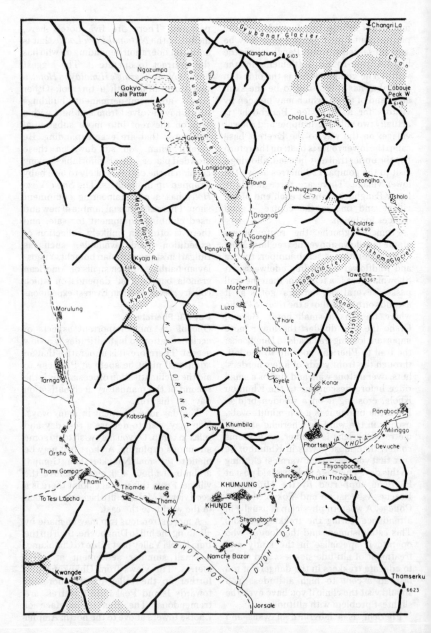

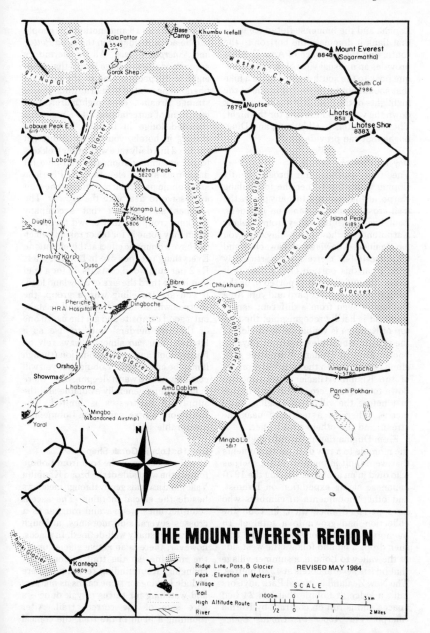

THE MOUNT EVEREST REGION

REVISED MAY 1984

Ridge Line, Pass, & Glacier
Peak Elevation in Meters
Village
Trail
High Altitude Route
River

SCALE

Lapcha and the immense fluted ice walls that flank it dominate the horizon to the south; and the east face of Ama Dablam provides an unusual view of this picturesque peak to the south-west. This is a hike that should not be missed; it is one of the highlights of the trek. It is a fast trip back down the valley to Pheriche for the night. There are hotels in Chhukung and Dingboche that can provide lunch.

Day 14: Pheriche-Lobuje

The trail ascends the broad, gently sloping valley from Pheriche to Phalang Karpo, at 4340 metres. In many places the trail crosses small streams on boulders. Look back down the valley from Phalang Karpo and see how much elevation you have gained. The views of Tawachee and Cholatse (6440 metres) are particularly good from this portion of the trail as it passes through country reported to be the habitat of the snow leopard and yeti. Ama Dablam is seen from a different aspect here and is hardly recognisable; the true top of Kantega is visible far to the left of the prominent saddle seen from Thyangboche. Beyond Phalang Karpo the trail climbs steeply onto the terminal moraine of the Khumbu Glacier then contours down to a stream, crossing it on a bridge just before the village of Duglha, 4620 metres. There is a tea shop near the stream and two others a bit higher.

From Duglha the trail climbs higher on the moraine to a row of stone monuments that were built in memory of six sherpas who died in an avalanche during the 1970 Japanese skiing expedition on Everest, and other monuments to climbers who have perished since then; in 1983 the collection had grown to a total of 18 memorials, mostly for sherpas. The trail then drops a bit and follows the west side of the valley to Lobuje, a summer village that boasts several hotels at 4930 metres. The New Zealand National Park advisors built a lodge at Lobuje that has 24 bed spaces and is run on contract by Karma Sherpa. The *Above the Clouds Lodge*

accommodates 18 and another few people can be accommodated in the *Kala Pattar* and *Sherpa* hotels. All is dormitory accommodation on huge bunks that sleep eight to 10 people. One of the common phenomena related to high altitude is very strange dreams, even nightmares, that lend a bit of entertainment to a night in a crowded lodge in Lobuje. If you are staying in hotels, you will probably get involved in a daily race with other trekkers to get accommodation; this can be a bit dangerous at this elevation. At Pheriche and Lobuje particularly, you must be a bit aggressive to deal with the crowds. The sherpas and porters that accompany trekking groups further crowd the hotels when they come in for tea or rakshi (which can have a dramatic effect at this elevation). Everything is expensive in Lobuje; tea is Rs 2 per cup; wood costs Rs 60 for a load that is one third the size of a lowland load. If you are travelling with a group, the sherpas will do the racing ahead to stake out a good campsite and get the use of one of the two herders' huts to use as a kitchen. You can almost always rely on finding food and accommodation (though it may be crowded) at Lobuje, but you will certainly need a warm sleeping bag – there is no bedding generally available and the supply of mattresses is limited. The sunset on Nuptse, seen from Lobuje, is a memorable sight.

Day 15: Lobuje-Gorak Shep

The first section of the trail from Lobuje follows the west side of the broad Khumbu Valley and ascends gently through meadows beside the glacial moraine. The ascent soon becomes steeper and rougher as it crosses several side moraines, although the trail is usually well-defined. In places, however, there is an active glacier under the moraine, so the trail is constantly changing. Routefinding techniques here include looking for stone cairns as markers and watching for traces of yak dung – a sure sign of the correct trail. After rounding a bend in the trail, the conical peak Pumori (7161 metres) comes into view; on the lower slopes of this mountain there is a ridge extending to the south, terminating in a small peak. This peak, called Kala Pattar, is 5545 metres high and provides the best vantage point for viewing Mt Everest. The ascent of Kala Pattar may be made easily from Gorak Shep in the afternoon or following morning.

The trail makes a short descent onto the sandy flat expanse of Gorak Shep, 5160 metres elevation. This was the base camp for the 1952 Swiss Everest Expedition and was called 'lake camp' by the British in 1953. At Gorak Shep there is a small lake that is usually frozen, and several monuments to climbers who have died during various Everest expeditions. The carved stone in memory of Jake Breitenbach of the 1963 American expedition and the monument for Indian Ambassador H Dayal who died during a visit to base camp after the 1965 Indian expedition are to the north-east of the lake.

Usually Gorak Shep is reached by lunch time; most people spend the rest of the day resting, but those who are not tired by the altitude can climb Kala Pattar or go to Base Camp in the afternoon. There are two herders' huts at Gorak Shep near the lake, but they are small and dirty and should only be considered emergency shelter. The *Yeti Tea Shop*, run by Ang Lamu Sherpani has a few bunks in the one room building. She often closes during the coldest months from December to February and goes back to Khumjung, so it is best to inquire at Lobuje before you count on this facility during these months. It should be possible to find food and shelter here at most other times during the trekking season. The best plan of all is to start early in the morning and go from Lobuje to Kala Pattar via Gorak Shep and return to Lobuje for the night, avoiding the necessity of staying at Gorak Shep.

Day 16: Gorak Shep-Lobuje

It is impossible to explain the discomfort of high altitude to someone who has not experienced it. Most people have an uncomfortable, often sleepless, night at both Gorak Shep and Lobuje despite the extra time taken for acclimatisation. By descending 300 metres to Lobuje, or better yet, to Pheriche, most people experience an immediate and noticeable improvement, so it is really not worth spending an additional night at 5160 metres.

Mornings are usually sparkling clear and the climb of Kala Pattar is one of the most rewarding parts of the trip. It is a steep ascent up the grassy slopes west of Gorak Shep to a shelf at the foot of Pumori. Even from this low vantage point the entire Everest South Face is visible as well as the Lho La (the pass between Nepal and Tibet, from which George Leigh Mallory looked into Nepal in 1921 and named the Western Cwm), Changtse (the north peak of Everest) and most of the west ridge route climbed by Unsoeld and Hornbein in 1963. Those familiar with the accounts of expeditions on the Tibetan side of Everest will be able to spot the north ridge and the first and second steps, prominent obstacles during the attempts on the mountain in the 1920s and '30s. Continuing on to the top of Kala Pattar, more of the peak of Everest itself comes into view, and a short walk north from the summit of Kala Pattar on the ridge towards Pumori will allow an unobstructed view all the way to the South Col.

The walk to base camp requires about six hours round trip, possibly more unless an expedition in progress has kept the ever-changing trail in good condition. The route follows the Khumbu glacier, sometimes on the moraine and sometimes on the glacier itself. The walk is especially interesting for the views of the 15-metre-high seracs of ice, a feature peculiar to Himalayan glaciers. Everest base camp is not actually a specific site; various expeditions have selected different locations for a semi-permanent camp during their assault on the mountain. Some of the base camp sites may be identified by debris on the glacier at 5360 metres or more. The trip to base camp, while interesting, is not as spectacular as the ascent of Kala Pattar because there is no view of Everest itself from base camp.

It is difficult to go to both base camp and Kala Pattar in a single day; if you wish to do both, you should use the afternoon of the day at Gorak Shep for one trip and the next morning for the other. But the exhaustion and lethargy caused by the altitude limits many people to only one of the possible options. The descent to Lobuje is easy, but seems endless because of the many uphill climbs from Gorak Shep. The night, however, will be much more comfortable than the previous one.

Day 17: Lobuje-Dingboche

To go to Dingboche, follow the uphill route back to Duglha, but then go straight up the hill from the bridge to reach an upper trail, staying high above the valley floor, past the yak pastures at Dusa to a chorten at the head of the Imja Valley. From here the views are great – you can easily recognise Island Peak because its name is an apt description. Makalu is the greenish-grey peak visible in the distance over the pass to the right of Island Peak. From the chorten descend to Dingboche, at 4360 metres, following the trail as it traverses east into the valley. The high pastures in this region are sometimes referred to as 'summer villages'. Sherpas with homes lower in the valley own small stone huts in the higher regions and occupy them in the summer months while they graze their herds of yaks in the surrounding pastures. A few crops, especially barley, are also grown in these high fields. While Dingboche does not have all the hotels and tourist facilities of Pheriche, it is a more typical summer village and the mountain scenery is outstanding. There is one real hotel in Dingboche and two houses that have hotel signboards. There are also two hotels in Chhukung, several hours up the valley.

Day 18: Dingboche-Thyangboche

The route from Dingboche descends the Imja Khola Valley, then crosses the Khumbu Khola on a wooden bridge and climbs up to rejoin the upward trail. Following the trail downhill, it is easy to make a detour and visit the upper part of Pangboche and the village gompa, then continue to Thyangboche for the night. While ascents at high altitudes must be made slowly, descents can be made safely as fast as you wish.

Day 19: Thyangboche-Namche Bazar

The trail returns to Phunki Thanghka, then ascends the ridge towards Namche Bazaar. The direct route to Namche follows the side of the ridge and avoids a lot of climbing, but it's a long walk in and out of side valleys; an alternative route through Khumjung allows a visit to either Hotel Everest View or Sherpa villages before the steep descent to Namche, but involves climbing an extra 200 metres. In Namche Bazar you will have a last opportunity to buy (mostly) phoney Tibetan jewellery from a dozen Tibetan merchants who sell their wares at campsites and along the trail.

Day 20: Namche Bazar-Lukla

From Namche, the steep descent back to the Dudh Kosi at Jorsale is a bit rough on the knees, but the warmer climate offers a good opportunity to finally shed down jackets and woollen sweaters. You must be at the airport at Lukla the night before your flight in order to reconfirm reservations if you have them – your seats may vanish if they are not reconfirmed. The trail from Jorsale to Lukla follows the upward route as far as Chablung, then turns off above the village of Chaunrikarka towards Lukla, situated high above the river on a shelf at 2800 metres elevation. Lukla is another classic paradox in determining altitudes because the runway is on a slope and there is a difference of almost 60 metres between the lower and upper ends of the runway.

Camp at Thyangboche

There is a good choice of hotels in Lukla. The upmarket *Sherpa Cooperative Hotel* halfway down the airstrip offers rooms for about US$10 a night; its dining room is decorated in Tibetan style and is the centre of Lukla's social life (and also the source of all the rumours about flight operations). *Buddha Lodge*, near the airport, also has private rooms, hot showers, and a reasonably efficient short order kitchen. Most other hotels offer dormitories and less extensive (but cheaper) menus. The RNAC office is open for one hour in the evening – usually from 5 pm to 6 pm, but sometimes 6 pm to 7 pm. They post a sign. You can reconfirm flights only at this time; if you are not present the night before the flight you probably will lose your seat. The radio message that tells the RNAC staff how many flights are scheduled for the following day usually doesn't come until after the office closes. This tends to add an atmosphere of mystery and intrigue to the proceedings, but in fact the actual flight schedule for each day is not prepared in Kathmandu until about 7 pm when they know where each plane ended up for the night. Check-in begins early and can be chaotic; if your hotelkeeper or trekking agent offers to check you in for the flight, take advantage of it. There isn't much to do at Lukla other than wait for planes or talk about when the plane will come.

Day 21: Lukla-Kathmandu
RNAC schedules three flights a day to Lukla in 19-seat Twin Otter aircraft that

can carry only 14 or 15 passengers from Lukla because of the high elevation, but there are usually either more or less than these three flights because of extra flights, charters or delayed schedule flights. The airstrip was built by a Hillary team as part of the Khunde Hospital project in 1965 and was expanded by RNAC in 1977; the control tower was added in 1983. The landing is a visual one; there are no instruments or sophisticated navigational aids. If there are clouds, no plane will come – occasionally for days at a time during periods of extended bad weather. It is interesting to note that only 60 percent of the trekkers who go to the Everest region fly in to Lukla, but 96 percent of them fly out of Lukla.

When many flights have been cancelled, those who have planned to fly to Kathmandu must wait and a backlog of people builds up, each person convinced that he or she must fly on the next available aircraft. The situation often becomes ludicrous, but provides a great opportunity to develop patience and to become acquainted with trekkers from all over the world as you wait together. The stories of overcrowding in the Everest area now become real. In the past, 350 or more people have waited here – especially in late October and early November each year. The problem usually solves itself in a few days, but it's important to be prepared for a long delay for any flight to or from Lukla. It's even possible to depart from Lukla exactly on schedule. The trek to Dhankuta becomes attractive because it avoids the pile-up at Lukla and explores some interesting country unlike any that has been seen on the first portion of the trek.

The flight from Lukla to Kathmandu takes 35 minutes and is a jarring return to the noise, confusion and rush of a large city.

TO GOKYO
The trek to Gokyo offers an alternative to the traditional trek to Everest Base Camp.

From Gokyo more of Everest itself is visible, though from a slightly greater distance, than from Kala Pattar above Gorak Shep. The mountains are generally more spectacular, the Ngozumpa Glacier is the largest in the Nepal Himalaya and from a ridge above Gokyo, four 8000-metre peaks (Cho Oyu, Everest, Lhotse and Makalu) are visible at once. The view of the tremendous ice ridge between Cho Oyu (8201 metres) and Gyachung Kang (7952 metres) is one of the more spectacular panoramas in Khumbu. There are numerous options for additional exploration and high altitude walking, including a 5400-metre-high pass into the Khumbu region.

Day 1: Namche Bazar-Phortse Bridge
Acclimatisation is essential for this trek, because it is easy to get too high too fast and run a danger of altitude sickness. Only after a *minimum of two days* in the Namche-Khumjung region is it safe to begin this trek. From Khumjung, the trek begins by descending to the west of the village down the broad valley leading to the Dudh Kosi, but soon turns north, climbing above the more frequented route to Thyangboche and Everest base camp.

There is a choice of routes in the beginning: the yak trail which climbs gently, but traverses a long distance around the ridge, or the steep staircase-like trail that is built of rocks embedded in a narrow cleft in a large boulder. The Sherpas claim that the steeper trail is better – for exercise. The two trails soon join and continue towards a large chorten on the top of a ridge at 3973 metres. This ridge descends from Khumbila, 5761 metres, the abode of the patron god of the Khumbu region. Khumbila (or more correctly *Khumbu Yul Lha*, translated as 'Khumbu area god') is often pictured on thankas and other monastery paintings as a white-faced figure riding on a white horse. Numbur, the mountain that towers over Junbesi and the Solu region, is the protector god of that area and has the

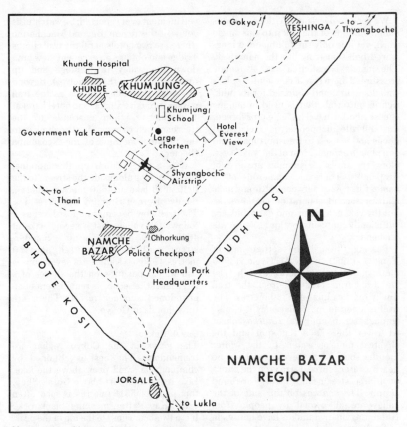

NAMCHE BAZAR REGION

Sherpa name *Shorong Yul Lha*, 'Solu Area God'.

From the ridge the trail descends in a series of steep switchbacks down a sandy slope to the Dudh Kosi. There is an excellent camping spot near the river at 3500 metres, just before the bridge that provides access to Phortse, an isolated village of about 60 houses. It is possible to go much further in a single day from Khumjung – as far as Tongba or Gyele – but it doesn't serve much purpose and it can be dangerous because of the fast increase in elevation.

Day 2: Phortse Bridge-Luza

You should make this an easy day in order to aid acclimatisation. The trail climbs steeply out of the valley through rhododendron forests which give way to fragrant stands of juniper and large conifers as the elevation increases. This portion of the trek is especially beautiful in the spring when the rhododendrons are blooming – late April and early May at this elevation. The trail passes through many summer settlements or *kharkas*, used when herds of yaks are brought to graze in these high pastures. Some of the villages in this valley are occupied as late as December by people grazing their herds.

We tend to oversimplify the numerous manifestations of the yak into this single word, yet it is only the full blooded long-haired bull that truly has the name yak. The female is called a nak. A female crossbreed between a cow and a yak is called a dzum, and is prized for its milk, rich in butterfat, that is used in making cheese and butter. The male crossbreed, the infertile dzopchuk, is (relatively) docile and is used to transport loads and as a plough animal. Most of the 'yaks' seen along the trails of Khumbu are in fact dzopchuks. There are numerous other names for crosses between cattle and naks and for second generation crossbreeds, but the yak, nak, dzum and dzopchuk are sufficiently confusing for this lesson in yak husbandry.

Passing through the settlements of Tongba (3950 metres), Gyele (3960 metres), Dole (where there are two hotels) and Lhabarma (4220 metres), the trail finally reaches Luza at 4360 metres. The trail is steep in most places as it climbs through scrub junipers. *Kharkas* occur wherever there is a flat spot and the slightest hint of water. In the winter months some of these villages have no nearby water source; Luza is on the banks of a large stream and has a year-round supply. The *kharkas* on this side of the valley are all owned by people from Khumjung; many families have houses in several settlements and move their herds from place to place as the grass becomes overgrazed and the snows melt.

The views of Khumbila and Tawachee (6542 metres) are tremendous throughout the day, and it is possible to climb a ridge behind Luza for an even broader view up and down the valley.

Day 3: Luza-Gokyo

The trail continues to climb along the side of the valley, high above the river, crossing sandy spurs to Machhermo at 4410 metres. It was in Machhermo, in 1974, that a yeti killed three yaks and attacked a Sherpa woman. This is the most credible yeti incident ever reported; be watchful as you visit this region. Beyond Machhermo (there are two hotels here) the trail climbs a ridge and obtains an excellent view both down the valley to Kantega and up towards Cho Oyu (8153 metres). Beyond the ridge the valley widens as the trail passes through Pangka (one hotel here) at 4390 metres, then descends to the riverbank before beginning the climb onto the terminal moraine of the Ngozumpa Glacier.

It is a steep climb up the moraine, switchbacking alongside the stream to the first small lake at 4650 metres, where a family of green Braminy ducks resides. The trail now becomes almost level as it follows the valley past a second lake at 4690 metres and finally up a boulder-strewn path to Gokyo itself at 4750 metres. Gokyo is a kharka of seven houses and walled pastures on the shores of a large lake; the setting is reminiscent of an abandoned summer resort. There are three hotels at Gokyo.

Day 4: Gokyo

The views in the Gokyo region are tremendous. The best is obtained by climbing the small peak above the lake. Like its counterpart above Gorak Shep, this peak of 5318 metres is also often called Kala Pattar, meaning 'black rock'. It is a two-hour climb to the top of the peak, providing a panoramic view of Cho Oyu, Gyachung Kang, Everest, Lhotse, Makalu, Cholatse and Tawachee.

For those with more time and energy, a trip may be made up the valley to another lake, marked with the name Ngozumpa on the maps, or even beyond to a fifth lake. There are several small peaks in this region that offer vantage points for the surrounding peaks and even of the Nangpa La, the old trade route into Tibet.

Day 5: Gokyo-Phortse

The descent to Phortse may be made in a single long day, or you can spend the night at Thare or Konar on the way in order to make the day less strenuous. Rather than retrace the upward route, follow the east side of the valley on the downward route to gain different views of Khumbila and generally somewhat warmer weather because the sun stays on these slopes longer in the late afternoon.

Descending from Gokyo, the route passes the second lake. About half way between the first and second lakes a trail leads off across the moraine to the east. This is the route to the 5420 metre Chola La (or Chhugyuma) Pass into the Everest region. The pass is not difficult, but it is steep and involves a glacier crossing on the east side. Allow three days from Gokyo to Pheriche on this high altitude route. An ice axe, crampons and a rope are often necessary for negotiating the small icefall at the foot of the glacier on the other side of the pass, although in ideal conditions there are no technical problems and there is a trail of sorts in the rocks beside the icefall. The western approach to the pass varies in difficulty depending on the amount of snow. It can vary from a rough scramble up a scree (gravel) slope to an impossible technical ice climb. The best conditions are when there is snow soft enough for kicking steps up the slope. The pass is not possible for yaks and usually not suitable for heavily laden porters, but you can send the porters and yaks around the mountain via Phortse and they can meet you in Lobouje or Pheriche three days later.

The main trail follows its upward route through Pangka, then climbs to Na, 4400 metres, the only year-round settlement in the valley. The descent from Na along the east side of the Dudh Kosi Valley is straightforward, with a few ups and downs where landslides and streams have carved side valleys. The trail enters Phortse at its upper part and a camp may be made in the potato fields of this large village. In 1983 there was no hotel in Na or Phortse, but there was a small hotel in Thare, about

halfway between them. With the proliferation of hotels this gap may have been filled by now. Ask locally.

Day 6: Phortse-Namche Bazar The trail descends from Phortse to the bridge and rejoins the original route from Khumjung. It is easy to reach Namche Bazar, or even beyond to Jorsale, for the night.

An alternative route may be taken from Phortse up a steep, narrow and exposed trail that leads to upper Pangboche, where it joins the trail to the Everest Region. There is also a trail that descends steeply from Phortse and climbs through forests to Thyangboche.

TO THAMI

Thami lies at an elevation of 3800 metres near the foot of a large valley to the west of Namche Bazar. The village is the jumping-off place for crossing Tesi Lapcha, the 5755-metre-high pass into the Rolwaling Valley. Tesi Lapcha should only be attempted by experienced, well-equipped and well-informed parties, because frequent rockfalls near the pass present a very dangerous complication.

From Namche Bazar the trail to Thami starts above the village, leading west past a large array of prayer flags and mani stones. The carved mani stones all the way to Thami are some of the most complex and picturesque in Nepal. Contouring around the hill on a wide and almost level trail, the route passes through Gonglha and Drama before reaching the large village of Thomde. Just before Thomde there is a trail leading uphill to the monastery at Mende. A few westerners are studying here under the tutelage of the English-speaking head lama. At Thomde there is an office building for the hydro-electric project and the beginnings of the dam that will someday generate electricity from the Bhote Kosi to provide lights for all the homes of Khumbu.

After a short climb followed by a descent to the river, which is crossed on a sturdy wooden bridge, the trail makes a steep ascent beside a stream to Thami, about three hours from Namche Bazar. Thami is situated in a large valley with good views of the snow peaks of Teng Kangpoche (6500 metres) and Kwangde (6187 metres) to the south. Just to the north of the village is a police checkpost. Trekkers are not permitted to travel further north than here. This is a trade route between Nepal and Tibet; it is a two-day trip to the Nangpa La, the 5741-metre pass that was once crossed frequently by trains of yaks carrying goods between the two countries. It is now used infrequently for the trade of yaks and wool.

About 150 metres above Thami is the Thami monastery, a picturesque gompa situated amongst many homes occupied by both lamas and lay people, perched on the side of a hill overlooking the valley. This is the site for the spring celebration of the Mani Rimdu festival, held about the middle of May each year. Mani Rimdu at Thami tends to be a little more spirited (literally) than the festival in the fall at Thyangboche, because the weather is warmer in the spring and the *Rimpoche*, or reincarnate lama, at Thami is a bit more liberal than the Thyangboche lama. The first day of Mani Rimdu involves prayers by the lamas in the monastery courtyard. The second day is the colourful lama dancing with elaborate gowns and wonderfully painted paper mache masks. Hundreds of local people attend the performance; it is an important social occasion as well as an entertaining spectacle. Along with the serious and intricate dances the lamas also stage two absurd comic sequences that make the entire performance a grand and amusing event. On the final evening of Mani Rimdu all the local people join in an all-night Sherpa dance.

It is possible to make the trip to Thami and back to Namche Bazar in a single day, but more worthwhile to spend a night in Thami in order to see the peaks in the clear morning. This side trip provides a good acclimatisation day before proceeding to higher elevations. In 1983

there was not a true hotel in Thami, but there was a hotel in Thammu. During Mani Rimdu, several temporary hotels are established near the gompa and offer *momos* (meat-filled dumplings), *thukpa* (noodles) and endless quantities of tea, chhang, and rakshi.

THE LAMIDANDA ESCAPE ROUTE

Occasionally the pile up of people at Lukla becomes unmanageable. Imagine 350 people vying for seats on planes that carry 15 passengers. Many people, having completed a great trek, make themselves miserable by fighting for seats out of Lukla. It's a helpless feeling to be in a place where no amount of influence or money can make the planes come, but you did come to an undeveloped country. If you expect things to operate on time (or sometimes to operate at all), you should head for the mountains of Switzerland.

Unbelievable things happen when people flip out at Lukla. I've seen the station manager chased around the airport by a tourist brandishing an ice axe; I've seen chanting mobs outside the airline office; I've seen rock fights on the airstrip; twice I've seen planeloads of police arrive in Lukla to get things under control; and I've heard endless tales of woe from people who *had* to be at work the following day (they weren't). If it gets like this – usually in late October and early November, and occasionally at other unpredictable times – the only way to preserve your own composure is to be sure your name is somewhere on the reservation list. Assign one of your sherpas (or better yet, your hotelkeeper or the Lukla representative of your trekking company) to assure that other names are not slipped in ahead of yours, and retire to a kettle or two of chhang to consider your alternatives.

You can wait. It might be a day (I've seen a dramatic airlift of 14 flights to Lukla in a single day), or as long as two weeks. You can walk to Jiri. If you go at a normal pace, it's six days to Jiri where you can get a bus back to Kathmandu. If you walk 10 to 12 hours a day (you save days in Nepal by walking a longer time each day, not by walking faster) you could reach Jiri in four days – perhaps even three. Some people suggest trying the airstrip at Phaphlu, two long days (or three comfortable days) from Lukla. It is an interesting walk, but it's unlikely that it will hasten your return to Kathmandu because Phaphlu is served only by six-passenger Pilatus Porter aircraft and seats are in heavy demand for government officials stationed in nearby Salleri. When the expansion of the Phaphlu airstrip is finished and it can accommodate Twin Otter aircraft, this will become a good alternative that is worth investigating. You can walk from Phaphlu south to Janakpur in six days. The 10-day trek to Dhankuta described in this book is also a way to escape from Lukla. Another alternative is described here. You can walk to Lamidanda, an airstrip five days to the south. The important thing is to not make yourself, and everyone else, miserable by fighting and bemoaning your fate. Instead, do something positive. You can always go back to Namche Bazar for a few days and wait for things to clear up, or you can climb the ridge behind Lukla, where there are some wonderful high meadows and a good view of Kariolung.

The Lamidanda escape route works in either direction; you can walk to Khumbu after a flight to Lamidanda. Although it is shown as a five-day trek, it can be done (if the porters agree) in four days. The opposite direction, however, will certainly require five days because of the long initial climb up to Aiselukharka.

Day 1: Lukla-Bupsa
A trail leads off the end of the Lukla airstrip and descends to join the main trail to Kathmandu. The descent continues on the main trail to Surkhe, then the trail climbs to Puiyan, crosses the pass and descends again to Bupsa. See Day 7 and 8 of the Everest trek description.

Day 2: Bupsa-Wobsa Khani
The trail descends steeply to Khari Khola (2070 metres). If you did not walk from Kathmandu, this will be your first view of extensive terracing and of the middle hills region of Nepal. There is a bazaar in Khari Khola on Wednesday if you need to stock up on provisions. There is only rice and daal available between here and the next bazaar at Aiselukharka. The trail climbs out of Khari Khola on a trail higher than the main route to Kathmandu, then turns south about 20 minutes beyond the village. The path climbs over a ridge, then contours south, high above the village of Jubing. The route passes through scrub forests and a few cultivated fields to Jube (2100 metres), then through forests of rhododendron and oak. The trail descends, crosses the Thana Khola, then climbs steeply out of a side valley. There are a few houses and herders' huts, but for the most part the trail is through forests and is reasonably level (for Nepal). The Rai village of Wobsa Khani (1800 metres) is reached about two hours after the Thana Khola. Below Wobsa is Tamba Khani ('copper mine') where you can see the smelter and buildings for the mine that gave the town its name.

Day 3: Wobsa Khani-Lokhim
Some oranges and rice from here are carried by porters to the market at Namche Bazar. Except for those porters, this trail is not often used by either locals or trekkers, so there are no hotels and few bhattis along the route. From Wobsa Khani the trail continues fairly level as the valley becomes wider, then it descends a bit to Waku, a Chhetri village at 1500 metres elevation. The trail descends further through forests to Suntale at 1100 metres and drops steeply to the Hinku Khola, crossing it on an old suspension bridge at 980 metres. This is the same river (also called the Inukhu) that is crossed on Day 3 of the trek to Dhankuta. After a steep climb up a series of steps cut in the rock, the trail reaches a ridge at

1290 metres and descends a bit to the Rai and Chhetri village of Khorde. The trail descends further through trees to the Hongu Khola, crossing it on a temporary log bridge at 900 metres elevation. There are the remains of an impressive cantilever bridge here, but it looks as if this bridge collapsed years ago. There is some trade up the Hongu from here, and people who live in villages as far away as Bung travel down the valley to Aiselukharka on bazaar days. Climbing steeply past the herders' huts of Utha, the trail reaches a ridge at 1590 metres. It may be necessary to camp in Utha, because it's another 1½ hours to Lokhim from here. Lokhim is a huge Rai village with beautiful stands of bamboo situated in a large side valley at about 1800 metres elevation. This being Rai country, it is usual to encounter *dhamis* (shamans) walking the remote trails, or at least to hear the echoes of their drums in the distance.

Day 4: Lokhim-Ilim

Lokhim is a large village, almost 45 minutes' walk from beginning to end. From the east end of the village the trail climbs through Chuwa towards the pass at Deorali (2400 metres). The Schneider *Dudh Kosi* map covers this part of the trek, but this section of trail is not shown on the map; the trail contours around the Dudu Khola Valley before it ascends steeply towards Deorali. There is a tea shop, the first since Khari Khola, at the pass. Descending from the pass, the route travels through Harise, a Sherpa village at 2300 metres, then descends a steep stone staircase to Aiselukharka, a large town strung out along a ridge at 2100 metres elevation. There are shops and government offices here and a very large bazaar on Saturdays. The trail descends the ridge to the south on a wide trail to Ilim at 1450 metres.

Day 5: Ilim-Lamidanda

It is a steep descent through tropical country to the Ra Khola. There is a bridge upstream at 800 metres elevation or you can wade the river. This is a rice-growing region, and the trail follows a complex and intricate route amongst a network of dykes and irrigation canals. The trail makes a steep ascent up the Pipal Danda, then contours around the valley between 1200 and 1400 metres. The route is through terraced fields and there is little shade – it will probably be hot. Finally the trail (this trail also is not shown on the Schneider map, nor is Lamidanda) passes a school and follows a ridge out towards the airport. There is a hotel near the terminal building at 1200 metres elevation. From Lamidanda there are flights three times a week to Kathmandu and three days a a week to Biratnagar. From Biratnagar you can take a bus or plane to Kathmandu. The fare from Lamidanda to Kathmandu is less than from Lukla – only US$40 each way. If you travel to Biratnagar from Lamidanda it will cost only Rs 170 (US$11) to Biratnagar and then US$65 by air from Biratnagar to Kathmandu or about US$5 by bus.

Local people say that it is a two-day walk to Bhojpur and a one-day walk to Okhaldunga from here. Those timings are probably accurate. Once, however, the Lamidanda people terrified a trekking group that had landed there by all agreeing that it required at least 12 days to walk to Lukla (where none of them had ever been). There is nothing to see or do in the Brahmin village of Lamidanda, except wait for an airplane. There is a Buddhist shrine about a day's walk away that might provide some diversion if you get stuck here for a long time. Lamidanda is the air traffic control point for this part of Nepal, so the radio is in constant use here (unlike Lukla) and it is easy to find out about flight movements.

A WAY TO AVOID THE JIRI ROAD

It takes a bit of the continuity out of the Everest trek when you drive all the way to Jiri. The following route from Barahbise to Shivalaya avoids the Jiri road entirely and visits some new country that trekkers rarely visit. This trek is seldom followed by anyone (even locals) as it is described here, so villagers will not usually be able to point you in the right direction. A local guide (or a basic knowledge of Nepali) is almost essential for this trek. There are so many trails leading in every direction that it is impossible to document all the junctions and alternatives. This description is only a suggestion; it can be modified in many ways once you are on the trail. There are some bhattis on this route, but none from Biguti to Mali, so you will be more comfortable if you carry your own food on this trek.

Day 1: Kathmandu-Khartali

Barabise is 10 minutes drive beyond Lamosangu on the east bank of the Bhote Kosi. Just south of Barahbise the Sun Kosi joins the Bhote Kosi ('river from Tibet') to form a much larger river, called the Sun Kosi, that flows south and then east across Nepal to join the Arun River near Biratnagar. Barahbise is a crowded bazaar at 820 metres inhabited mostly by Newars and Chhetris. The route begins on an unpretentious set of stone steps between two shops and begins a climb that will eventually be more than 2400 metres of uphill walking. Passing through a few scattered Gurung villages, the route soon enters country inhabited mostly by Tamangs. Most of the route is in open cultivated country with a few piple trees surrounded by stone chautaaras providing welcome shade on hot days as it climbs to Parati, a small village at about 1300 metres. Beyond Parati the trail becomes less steep – and even has a few level stretches – as it continues through heavily cultivated country to the large Tamang village of Khartali at 1680 metres.

Day 2: Khartali-Thulo Tingsang

Beyond Khartali the trail continues to traverse eastward along the ridge, high above the Sun Kosi. Few villagers use this trail except for porters carrying rice, wood

and slate for roofing down to Barahbise. The trail climbs to a ridge where the climb is rewarded by a small bhatti and a rushing stream at 2290 metres. After the ridge, the trail enters deep rhododendron forests and makes some short climbs and descents as it traverses in and out of wooded side valleys. Below the trail and across the valley houses are splashed across the hillside, but above the trail there is mostly forest. Rounding a ridge, the trail offers a view of the large-spread out village of Dolangsa, a Sherpa village with clean whitewashed houses, each surrounded by fields of corn, potatoes, wheat, and barley. From the ridge, the trail enters another side canyon (watch the stinging nettles) and crosses a stream on a bridge hewn from a huge tree – a reminder of what the forests of this region must have been before rising population forced the cutting of large amounts of firewood. A short distance beyond the bridge take the left trail which makes a steep uphill climb to the Sherpa village of Dolangsa, at an elevation of about 2380 metres. There is no hotel here, but you could probably find accommodation in a house. High above the village is a gompa.

Beyond Dolangsa the trail climbs through rhododenron forests past a few kharkas used during the summer months as pastures for herds of cattle; they are uninhabited during the trekking season but are good campsites if you have a tent. The trail then begins a steep climb to the pass, crossing the Tingsang La at 3320 metres elevation. At the pass there are good views in every direction; on a clear day Gauri Shankar (7145 metres) dominates the horizon and peaks are visible from Chhoba-Bhamare, a rock spire (6108 metres) in the west all the way to Pigpherago (6730 metres) and Numbur (6959 metres) in the east. A short distance below the pass is Thulo Tingsang, a large kharka at 3260 metres. The views from this camp are equally as good as from the pass. During the summer months this high pasture is inhabited by many people and even boasts a small shop and hotel. In the winter months it is uninhabited; the roofs are removed from the stone huts and the people remove their household effects to lower permanent settlements. There is no food or accommodation here.

Day 3: Thulo Tingsang-Amatal

From Thulo Tingsang (big Tingsang) the trail descends through conifer and rhododendron forests to Sano Tingsang (small Tingsang), another kharka at 3000 metres. The trail continues a gradual descent (a very pleasant walk – most descents in Nepal are steep and rough) through forests and past small kharkas to a stream at 2230 metres. Here is a small paper factory; frames with Nepalese paper may be seen here drying in the sun. A few minutes below is another stream crossed by a covered bridge at about 2100 metres. From this point a rough steep trail climbs 400 metres to Bigu at 2500 metres. Bigu is a Sherpa village with a large gompa and a nunnery. It is a strenuous side trip that involves a steep descent to rejoin the main trail. The direct route continues down the river valley through Tamang, Chhetri and Kami (the blacksmith caste) villages with courtyards paved with slate, to Amatal at 1680 metres.

Day 4: Amatal-Saunepani

It is a long but pleasant walk along the Sangawa Khola to its confluence with the Tamba Kosi. Stay on the south bank of the river, passing through Kopai and a few other small villages. Much of the route is in forests; here are many pines whose lower branches have been cut off for firewood – a traditional method of avoiding total deforestation. The trail ascends and descends over ridges and spurs and finally makes a steep descent to the Sangawa Khola, crossing it at an elevation of 1220 metres. The trail continues along the north bank of the river, making a few ups and downs, but generally staying level and passing a few side streams, two of which flow from beautiful tropical waterfalls.

Not only is the trail level, but the route is almost totally uninhabited during the afternoon's walk – two very unusual things in Nepal. Finally the route reaches the Tamba Kosi (here called the Bhote Kosi) at the village of Sigaati at an elevation of 1000 metres. There are a few houses and a small shop here.

Day 5: Saunepani-Serukapti

Walk south for about an hour along the west bank of the Tamba Kosi. This trail, if followed in the opposite direction, would lead to the Rolwaling Valley after a week of walking. The trail is level as it follows the river south to Bigute, situated across the Tamba Kosi on the east bank at 950 metres. There is a small shop on the west bank; across the river there is a wonderful old chain link suspension bridge. These bridges are becoming rare in Nepal, being replaced by new cement and steel cable bridges, so the swinging bridge high above the river offers an exhilirating and unusual river crossing. About five minutes south of the bridge on the west bank is a new trading centre, Gumbu Khola; the ground floor of every house here is used as a shop or hotel. If you are looking for an excuse to delay crossing the chain bridge, you can reinforce your courage with a glass of rakshi from this village.

From Biguti turn north and cross a small stream, then climb the ridge to the north-east. The trail climbs a bit and turns east as it passes through the Tamang villages of Jaku, elevation 1460 metres, and Yarsa. Unlike the brief walk along the Tamba Kosi, which is a main trade route, the trail is now on a rarely used route that climbs through forests and small villages towards the head of the valley. Because this is an out-of-the-way trail, there are places where it is steep and narrow; routefinding is a problem – ask for the trail to Serukapti when you reach a dead-end in someone's front yard. The trail becomes better and more defined as it passes through Sarsepti, a large Tamang village at 1760 metres and then continues to climb through forests of oak and rhododendron that are transformed into a place of beauty by an abundance of ferns and orchids. After more climbing, the Sherpa village of Serukapti is reached at 2300 metres.

Day 6: Serukapti-Mali

From Serukapti the trail continues up in forests. There is a trail junction about 15 minutes beyond the village; the lower (right-hand) trail goes to Jiri and the upper (left-hand) trail crosses Hanumante Danda and bypasses Jiri. Since one of the purposes of all this uphill climbing was to avoid the motor road, there is no good reason at this point to go to Jiri, so continue up the valley to a large kharka, a

beautiful high-altitude meadow surrounded by big trees, at 2300 metres. Climbing through a forest of large moss-covered pines, the trail finally emerges at the top of the ridge at 2900 metres, high above Jiri. There are many trails here. One trail descends to a cheese factory and then climbs back to the ridge above Mali. The most direct trail runs along the ridge to the east for a while, then drops slowly as it traverses below the ridgetop, making another easy descent past a few slate mines before reaching the Patashe danda (ridge) and descending on a broad trail (stay on the ridge) to Mali, a Sherpa village at 2200 metres elevation. Here the route joins the trail from Jiri and continues to Shivalaya and Bhandar.

In August 1985 another tremendous flood, this time from near Tesi Lapcha raged down the Dudh Kosi and destroyed most of the bridges and large parts of the trail. The bridge below Namche, the large suspension bridge at Jorsale, the bridges at Phakding and Benkar, and even the

bridge near Jubing that has survived since the 1950s were washed away. The trail to Everest will, therefore, be temporary in many places and may have been rerouted here and there by the time you read this.

Eastern Nepal

Treks in eastern Nepal generally begin from the village of Dharan, where the flat terai terminates at the foot of the Siwalik Hills. Destinations include Makalu base camp, an eastern approach to Everest and, if it is opened to foreigners, the area near Kanchenjunga – at 8598 metres it is the third highest mountain on earth. There is endless variety in this part of Nepal. Most ethnic groups are represented and many villages, such as Dhankuta, are large, prosperous and clean. The land includes hot, rice-growing country, the cooler tea-growing region of Ilam, the heavily populated middle-hills (gouged by the mighty Arun River at an elevation of less than 400 metres) and the major mountain massifs of Kanchenjunga and Makalu.

Treks here tend to be more expensive since the party and its gear must be transported to the east of Nepal (two days by bus) and the treks are generally longer because two weeks are required to reach the high mountains. STOL airstrips at Tumlingtar and Taplejung can shorten the time but greatly increase the expense. Inhabitants of this part of Nepal are not used to westerners and great care should be taken to avoid the mistakes trekkers have made in the more popular regions, mistakes that have contributed to theft, over-reliance on the whims of tourists to support the economy, and problems of garbage, pollution, begging and unnecessary hotel construction.

SOLU KHUMBU TO DHANKUTA

This section describes an interesting alternative to the Jiri to Everest Base Camp trek. Though shown here as a route from Khumbu to Hile, it can equally well be used as an approach route to the Everest region – in fact, the first foreign visitor to Everest Base Camp, Tilman in 1950, used this route.

By walking from Jiri to Everest Base Camp and then walking via the route described here to Hile, a rewarding 32-day trek may be made. Walking to Hile avoids the flight complications at Lukla and lends a sense of continuity to the trek that is not felt when you fly back from Lukla.

Though some trekkers have made this walk as a village inn trek, it is not easy. The first six days, from Lukla to Phedi, are through country that sees few tourists and not a lot of local travellers so there are almost no hotels and local people are not used to cooking meals for trekkers in their homes. It is most important to carry food for the nights at Gaikharka, Bung and Sanam, because facilities in these villages are poor.

Day 1: Lukla-Puiyan

Instead of flying from Lukla, take a leisurely stroll down the 550-metre long runway and drop to Surkhe, then climb back up to Puiyan at 2730 metres. If you are travelling from Namche Bazar, it is not necessary to go to Lukla; you can walk from Jorsale to Chaunrikarka, then from Chaunrikarka to Puiyan.

Day 2: Puiyan-Pangum

The trail follows the same route as the Lamosangu to Namche Bazar trail as far as Bupsa, then heads into new country. From Bupsa, climb on the old trail to the large white house at the top of Kharte, then climb over a fence and turn south-east up the broad Khari Khola Valley. There are some ups and downs as the trail gradually gains elevation through forested slopes, passing isolated Sherpa houses and small streams, to the village of Pangum (also pronounced 'Pankoma' locally), at about 2850 metres. Here is yet another Hillary school (there are 12 such schools in the region), a gompa and a paper factory that produces rice paper (actually made from the inner bark of the daphne bush), which is carried to Kathmandu in huge loads by porters.

Day 3: Pangum-Gaikharka

From Pangum it is a short climb to the 3173 metre Pangum La (also called the Satu La), the pass between the watersheds of the Dudh Kosi and the Inukhu Khola. From the pass there is a great view, not only of the Khumbu Himalaya, but also of the peaks at the head of the Inukhu (also called Hinku) Valley. The trail descends gradually to Chatuk, a small Sherpa settlement, then drops almost vertically in a series of short switchbacks to the river at 1855 metres, which it crosses on an exciting bridge suspended high above the river on two steel cables. The bridge was built by a Himalayan Trust team in 1971. One of the volunteers, when questioned about the fantastic engineering that must be required for the construction of a bridge in such a remote location commented, 'We don't engineer them, we just build them.'

The trail climbs a short distance alongside a picturesque waterfall that widens into a pool just above the river, a good place to take a bath after the cold of Khumbu. The trail then climbs up the side of the wild, sparsely-inhabited Inukhu Valley to the Sherpa hamlet of Gaikharka ('cow pasture'), at about 2300 metres. Although the only permanent settlements in this valley are those of Sherpas, the valley is also used by the neighbouring Rais for grazing their cattle and by the Gurungs to graze large herds of sheep which they bring up from the south during the summer.

Day 4: Gaikharka-Bung

The route continues to climb past the roofless goths of Najidingma, situated in a large meadow at 2650 metres, then makes a steep ascent in forests towards Sipki (or Surkie) Pass at 3085 metres. Beyond the pass the trail descends a short distance

through forests, then the valley suddenly opens up above the village of Khiraule, at about 2400 metres. There are many criss-crossing trails here used by the people of Bung when they collect wood, so it is easy to get lost; aim south and a bit east to the ridge above the gompa. Boksom gompa is surrounded by a large circle of trees and may be identified a long distance away. It is particularly sacred, but has fallen into disuse and disrepair.

The trek is now in the great Hongu Valley, one of the most fertile regions of Nepal. Much of the rice for the Namche Bazar market comes from this area and is carried back across three ridges to Khumbu. Except for some Sherpas living at higher elevations and some Chhetris and Brahmins downstream near Sotang, the Hongu Valley population is exclusively Rai. Some Rai villages are extremely large and boast 200 or 300 households; typically the villages are spread out over the hillside with trails leading in every direction. Route finding in a Rai village is always an interesting challenge. Rai people are very independent and individualistic. The two hundred thousand or so Rais in the eastern hills speak at least 15 different languages which, although closely related, are mutually unintelligible. When Rais of different areas meet it is necessary for them to converse in Nepali.

The trail descends down a ridge crest to the large village of Bung, spread out over the hillside from about 1900 down to 1400 metres elevation. The most direct route through the village follows a ravine downhill, but soon gets lost wandering among the houses and fields in the lower part of this typical Rai village. There are no hotels here and the people of Bung are a bit unhappy about trekking groups camping in the village.

A particularly interesting sight in regions of Rai influence is the *dhami* shamans who are diviners, spirit mediums and medicine men. Occasionally they may be seen in villages, but more often they are encountered on remote trails dressed in elegant regalia and headdresses of pheasant feathers. The rhythmic sound of the drums that a *dhami* continually beats while walking echoes throughout the hills; you are almost certain to hear the drum of a *dhami* in the Hongu Valley.

Day 5: Bung-Sanam

From Bung there is a steep descent through bamboo forests to the Hongu Khola, crossed by a rickety wooden bridge at 1316 metres, followed by an equally steep climb up to Gudel, another large Rai village, at about 2000 metres. It was this long useless descent and ascent that H W Tilman, travelling in the opposite direction, described poetically in his book *Nepal Himalaya*:

For dreadfullness, naught can excell
The prospect of Bung from Gudel;
And words die away on the tongue
When we look back on Gudel from Bung.

Beyond Gudel the ascent, up the side of the Lidung Khola, a tributary valley of the Hongu, continues more gradually. But it is a long and tiring climb through forests and the small Sherpa settlements of Sorung (2470 metres) and Tigare to Sanam at 2850 metres. Rai villages in the valley have a maximum elevation of about 2400 metres; Sherpa villages exploit different resources, so there is little economic competition between the two groups. Sanam is primarily dependent on herds of cattle and there is often milk, yoghurt and excellent cottage cheese available in the village, a compact settlement of houses arranged in a single row.

Day 6: Sanam-Phedi

The route continues to climb through a totally uninhabited area. The trail drops slightly to the floor of the canyon that it has been ascending, crosses the Lidung Khola, which here is only a stream, and makes a final steep climb to the Salpa Bhanjyang, the 3349-metre pass between the Hongu and Arun watersheds. This area is deep hemlock and fir forest abounding in bird and animal life, including Himalayan bear, barking deer and the Lesser Panda, a smaller, red-coloured relative of its more famous namesake. The pass is marked by a large chorten, the final influence of Sherpa culture on the route. The total climb up from the Hongu Khola is 2033 metres. The first available water is about an hour beyond the pass, making the lunch stop on this day quite late.

It is possible, by following the ridge to the south, to take an alternate route to the one described here. This route passes through Bhojpur, a large hill bazaar, famous for its excellent kukhris (the curved Nepali knife). There are flights from Bhojpur to both Kathmandu and Biratnagar (a total of five flights a week), or you can keep walking to the Arun, crossing it near Sati Ghat, and rejoin the trail described here in Day 10.

The trail to Hile descends through forests and past small herders' huts as it follows a spur separating the Irkhuwa Khola and the Sanu Khola. On this portion of the trail there is ample evidence of forest fires that occur in the dry season each spring due to fires in villages, careless smokers, lightning and shepherds burning the underbrush to allow new grass to grow. The trail continues through birch and rhododendron forests until it reaches a large stone overlooking the Irkhuwa Khola Valley, then drops almost vertically through bamboo forests into the Rai village of Phedi. There are many opportunities to get lost on the ridge; stay as high as possible and keep going east. Several trails drop off the ridge to the north and south; the trail to Phedi drops off the east end of the ridge. The best camp is below the village, at about 1680 metres, on the banks of the Irkhuwa Khola. This is one of the longest days and the longest downhill walk of the trek. The rakshi in Phedi is terrible.

Day 7: Phedi-Dhubidanda

The trek has now emerged into the fertile

rice-growing valley of the Arun River. The route follows the Irkhuwa Khola, a tributary of the Arun, crossing and recrossing the stream on a series of bamboo bridges, some quite substantial and some very flimsy, but all picturesque. After the continuous ups and downs of the last week, this is a particularly relaxing day. The trail loses elevation almost imperceptibly; yet by the end of the day, almost 900 metres of elevation have been lost. There are numerous pools large enough for swimming, and the water temperature – especially in comparison with streams higher up – is comfortable. A few hours below Phedi is Dotre Bazaar, which has the first real shops since Lukla. There is even a tailor shop that can outfit you with a new set of clothes while you wait.

Settlement in this part of the Arun basin is mixed; there are Rai villages, as well as those inhabited by Chhetris and Brahmins. Before the Gurkha conquest, which took place about 200 years ago, the entire middle hills region between the Dudh Kosi and Arun was populated almost entirely by Rais; but following in the wake of the conquest, when the Rais were defeated by the Gurkha army, considerable numbers of Hindus settled here, especially in the more fertile regions. The Rais and their neighbours on the other side of the Arun, the Limbus, are jointly known as the Kiranti. The Kiranti are the earliest-known population of Nepal's eastern hills and are believed to have settled here for at least 2000 years. Early Hindu epics such as the *Mahabharata* refer to the war-like Kirantis of the eastern Himalaya. This was the site of fierce fighting between Tibetan and Assamese warlords since the 7th century AD. The Kirantis joined the Gorkhali kingdom only in 1774.

There is a good camping place on the banks of the Irkhuwa Khola near the village of Dhubidanda at an elevation of about 760 metres.

Day 8: Dhubidanda-Chyawabesi

The trail makes a final crossing of the Irkhuwa Khola, this time on an excellent new bridge built by the local government. It soon begins to climb over a spur separating the Arun River from the Irkhuwa Khola. The trail is difficult to follow as it crosses fields, doubles back on itself and traverses small irrigation canals that supply water to rice fields. The main trail in this region climbs much higher and goes to the large village of Dingla at the top of the ridge. To avoid this long, unnecessary climb, the trail follows a circuitous route through the fields and back yards of a lower village.

Finally the mighty Arun River is seen to the north. This river, which has its headwaters in Tibet, is one of the major rivers flowing into the Ganges in India. The trail now turns south and descends to a small tributary of the Arun, the Chirkhuwa Khola, where there is a small shop and a fine swimming hole overlooked by a huge and noisy band of Rhesus monkeys. This village, called Balawa Besi, makes an excellent, though usually hot, spot to stop for lunch.

A short distance on, the route crosses the Arun River, here at an elevation of only 300 metres, on a large suspension bridge. There used to be a dugout-canoe ferry here, but in 1984 the bridge replaced this exciting ride. From the bridge at Kartike Ghat, the trail follows the east side of the river southward for about a half hour to a good camp at Chyawabesi, 280 metres elevation. Along the Arun Valley there are frequent bhattis, so finding food is no longer a problem here, though both the quality and sanitation are marginal.

Day 9: Chyawabesi-Khare

The trail follows the Arun as it flows south, sometimes climbing high above the river and sometimes traversing the sandy riverbed. The climate here is hot and tropical; the houses are built on stilts for ventilation and the people are more dark-skinned than those encountered so far on

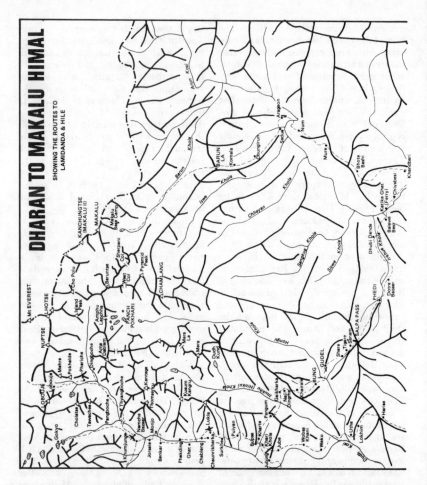

DHARAN TO MAKALU HIMAL

SHOWING THE ROUTES TO LAMIDANDA & HILE

the trek. You will probably want to change your schedule to do most of the walking in the very early morning to avoid the heat. Many of the settlements along the bottom of the Arun Valley are inhabited only during the planting and harvesting seasons by people who live higher in the hills above and own fertile farmlands in the valley.

It is a short uphill climb to a huge plateau that provides almost six km of completely level trail to Tumlingtar, a

small village with an airport served by regular RNAC flights. The 1984 schedule had flights three days a week to Kathmandu and three days a week to Biratnagar. The fare is US$35 from Tumlingtar to Kathmandu (the Biratnagar-Kathmandu fare is US$65 so you'll lose out if you take a flight to Biratnagar and then travel to Kathmandu). Many of the inhabitants of Tumlingtar are of the Kumal (potter) caste and earn their livelihood from the

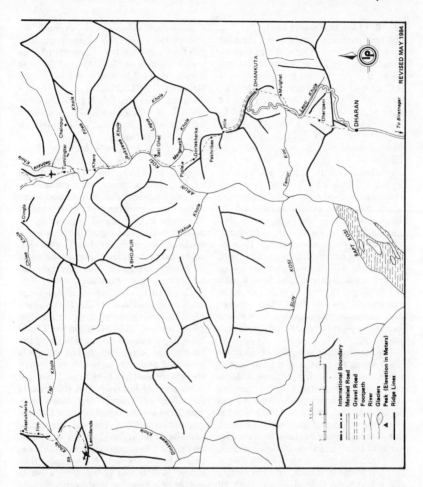

manufacture of earthenware pots from the red clay in this region. There is very little water on the plateau, so it is necessary to continue a long distance in the morning before lunch. A cup of tea, some oranges or bananas at the big shop under the Banyan tree in Tumlingtar will provide the refreshment to keep moving under the hot sun. The reward comes immediately after the short descent from the plateau when the trail crosses the Sabbhaya Khola, a tributary of the Arun. There is an excellent lunch spot beside a fine swimming hole in the warmest and most delightful stream along the entire trek route. You can avoid the Rs 1 toll on the bridge by swimming or wading across the river, though the riverbed is rocky and slippery. The afternoon is short, involving a climb of only a hundred metres over a ridge, then a descent to Khare, a tropical village on the banks of the Arun.

Day 10: Khare-Mangmaya Khola

The trail continues south along the east bank of the Arun. There are numerous porters on the trail from here to Dhankuta. These men carry goods from warehouses in Dhankuta to the bazaars of Bhojpur, Dingla and Chainpur; they often walk at night with small kerosene lamps tied to their dokos (the bamboo baskets in which they carry their loads). In another of his classic anecdotes, Tilman imagined these porters nose-to-doko along the trail as they often seemingly appear. Each porter carries a T-shaped stick that he places under his doko whenever (and wherever) he wishes to rest, usually as he stands in the middle of the trail. The entire trail then backs up, as each porter is forced to wait until the man ahead of him finishes his rest, thus halting a long line of porters. It presents a ludicrous picture, but a picture not totally removed from reality on this part of the trail. A short excursion into the villages here will often uncover such interesting items as papayas *mewa* (in Nepali), peanuts *badam* and pineapples *bhui katahar*.

The trail continues south, at no point climbing more than a hundred metres above the river, until it crosses under a cable that supports a river gauging station, just before a small village named Sati Ghat, the site of another dugout canoe ferry. Much of the vegetation along this part of the river has been devoured by herds of goats and sheep; these animals, more than humans, are responsible for the extensive deforestation of the entire country. After a short distance, the trail comes to a large pipal tree and chautaara overlooking a huge side valley of the Arun. At the foot of this valley flows the Mangmaya Khola; the grassy banks of this stream, at 200 metres elevation, afford an excellent campsite.

Day 11: Mamgmaya Khola-Hile

The trail crosses the broad valley, then climbs through hot tropical forests to the delightful village of Piple, two tea shops facing a small village square, at about 700 metres elevation. The upper portion of this town has a number of large shops. The trail continues to climb through villages inhabited by Limbus, relatives of the Rais, to Gorlekharka, at 1250 metres elevation. The trail finally gains the ridge and allows a fine view of Makalu (8463 metres) and Chamlang (7317 metres), almost 150 km away.

The route continues fairly level for some time to the British agricultural project at Pakhribas. This fantastic development presents a real contrast to the small gardens that surrounded every home throughout the trek. At Pakhribas there are huge rows of vegetables, all neatly labelled with signs; there are walls, roads and irrigation canals, all paved with stone and cement; and there are buildings of every description carefully labelled according to their function.

The trail then climbs a higher ridge crest to the roadhead at Hile. This is a very pleasant town situated high on a hill at 1850 metres; the elevation and cool breezes provide a welcome relief from the heat of the Arun Valley. The village is inhabited primarily by people of Tibetan stock who resettled here from Tibet and other parts of eastern Nepal, particularly the village of Walungchung, when trade with Tibet was disrupted after the Chinese occupation in 1959. There is often some genuine Tibetan jewellery for sale here, and many Chinese goods are available at prices below those in Kathmandu. The village is also well known for its ample supply of *tongba*, an 'instant beer' made from fermented millet and hot water which is sipped through a bamboo straw from fancy wooden and brass containers. There is a weekly market (hat) in Hile on Thursdays.

Day 12: Hile-Biratnagar-Kathmandu

The road descends down a spur to Dhankuta at 1220 metres. The 10-km stretch from Hile to Dhankuta is unpaved, so you might have to walk this part to get a

Top: The final climb from Muktinath to Thorung pass (SA)
Left: Starting out from Pokhara: Annapurna 2 and 4 in the background (SA)
Right: Thyangboche monastery after a rare winter snowstorm (SA)

Top: Machhapuchhare (elevation 6997 metres) from Hyangja (SA)
Bottom: Gurung houses near Pokhara (KS)

bus. From Dhankuta there are hourly buses to Dharan (about a 1½ hour ride to cover the 50 km) or you might find direct service to Biratnagar. Take whatever is available; bus service is frequent in this region, especially once you reach Dharan. The road does not pass through Dhankuta itself, but the town is worth a visit. It is a large, attractive, clean Limbu town, with whitewashed houses and winding streets paved with stone. This is the largest town on the entire trek route; there is a police station flanked by polished brass cannon, a hospital, a cold storage facility, bank, bakery, telegraph office and hundreds of shops. The region is famous for its wonderful oranges (suntala).

The road descends from Dhankuta and crosses the Tamur Kosi at Mulghat. The Tamur Kosi flows west to join the Arun at the same point where the Arun is joined by the Sun Kosi, which has made its long trip eastward across Nepal, having collected all the rivers that have flowed south into it. Together these rivers form the Sapt Kosi ('seven rivers') that flows to the Ganges containing the waters of the Sun Kosi, Bhote Kosi, Tamba Kosi, Dudh Kosi, Arun Kosi, Likhu Kosi and Tamur Kosi.

The road turns south up a side valley of the Tamur Kosi, following it until it is halted by the Siwalik Range (in Nepal called the Churia Hills) – the last range of hills before the plains. The road climbs to a pass at 1300 metres. From some places on this ridge, there are views of Kanchenjunga (8598 metres) and its prominent neighbour Jannu (7710 metres), on the eastern border of Nepal. Jannu's new name is Khumbhakarna Himal.

At the pass is a most dramatic sight – to the south is nothing but plains. After weeks in the hills, it is unusual to see country that is absolutely flat as far as the eye can see. The road descends to Dharan at 370 metres. Dharan used to be the major trading centre serving the eastern hills region but its role is changing now that the Dhankuta road has been built. Although located in the plains, most of

Dharan's population consists of hill people who have settled here. Dharan is also the site of a British Army recruiting centre for the Gurkha Brigade. In the old British Indian Army there were ten Gurkha rifle regiments; when India gained her independence in 1947, she took six of the regiments and Britain retained four. By agreement with His Majesty's Government of Nepal, Britain was allowed to establish two recruiting centres within Nepal; one at Dharan which recruits Rais and Limbus (for the most part) for the 7th and 20th GR, and one near Bhairawa, which recruits mostly Gurungs and Magars for the 2nd and 6th GR Recruits are accepted from other ethnic groups as well, but the bulk comes from these four groups in roughly equal numbers. The British camp development just to the west of Dharan is quite extensive and includes an excellent hospital.

An all-weather road links Dharan and Biratnagar, Nepal's second largest city and the kingdom's industrial centre. The largest factories here process jute into carpets, bags and rope. There are also many smaller factories making matches, cigarettes, tinned fruit, jam and other items. The road passes through cultivated fields and villages for most of the distance between the two cities. Originally this was all jungle and fine sal forest, but over the years it has been cut back drastically. There is little to remind one now of the extensive malarial jungle that once blanketed this region – although there are still glimpses of this jungle in Royal Chitwan National Park.

The return to Kathmandu may be made by bus directly, travelling south from Dharan to Itahari (it is not necessary to go all the way to Biratnagar), west on the east-west highway through Janakpur to Birganj, then up the Tribhuvan Rajpath or via Naranghat and Mugling to Kathmandu. An express bus service makes the long journey in a single day; the local buses, which are cheaper, take two days for the journey.

A more costly, but less tedious route is by bus to Biratnagar, then a flight back to Kathmandu. In contrast to Dharan, Biratnagar is a typical terai town, with noisy bazaars, inhabited mainly by plains people. There is nothing of interest in Biratnagar and the chaos of rickshaws and trucks makes it pointless to spend much time there as a tourist. The 45-km drive from Dharan to Biratnagar requires about an hour. Biratnagar airport, a bit north of town, is a fancy new facility built by a South Korean contractor. Unlike Lukla, the flights to Biratnagar are regular because there is rarely a weather problem, there are instrument landing facilities, the runway is paved, and the planes (44-passenger HS-748s) have enough capacity to meet the demands for flights. A flight to Kathmandu costs US$65 and takes 50 minutes; in clear weather it provides an excellent overview of the entire trek and good views of the Himalaya from Kanchenjunga to Langtang.

An alternative to the return to Kathmandu is to take a bus from Itahari to Kakarvita, cross into India and take a taxi to Siliguri. From Siliguri it is about a three hour drive by taxi (or a seven-hour train ride) to Darjeeling, one of the most pleasant of India's hill stations. It requires a special permit to cross this border, and you will be certainly refused entry to India if you do not have it. The permit can be obtained at an Indian Embassy, either in Kathmandu or overseas.

North of Kathmandu

Langtang is a narrow valley that lies just south of the Tibetan border, sandwiched between the main Himalayan range to the north and a slightly lower range of snowy peaks to the south. The valley is dominated by 7246-metre Langtang Lirung at the north, Gang Chhenpo (6388 metres) to the south and Dorje Lakpa (6975 metres) to the east.

This high and isolated region is inhabited by people of Tibetan origin who practice Buddhism. A visit to the Langtang Valley offers an opportunity to explore villages and monasteries as well as to visit glaciers at the head of the valley. According to legend, the valley was discovered by a Lama following a runaway yak, hence the name – 'lang' is Tibetan for yak and 'teng' (more correctly 'dhang') means to follow. Yaks still live in the valley, but are joined by numerous trekkers who make the 10 or 11-day roundtrip from Kathmandu. Because there are good opportunities for moderate climbing excursions here, you should allow a few extra days for exploration of the extensive glacier system.

A side trip to the holy lakes of Gosainkund at 4300 metres can be made from the trail to Langtang. The lakes are the destination of thousands of Hindu pilgrims during the month of August. The lake is also sacred to the Buddhists.

Helambu, about 75 km north of Kathmandu, may be reached directly from the capital, or from Langtang, either via Gosainkund or across the 5106-metre Ganja La Pass. In winter both of the high routes from Langtang are often snow covered and difficult, if not impossible. The seven or eight-day trek to Helambu is popular because it is short, stays below 3500 metres and is feasible all winter. It is the easiest trek to organise because the transportation from Kathmandu to Sundarijal, the starting point of the trek, is readily available and inexpensive. The major inhabitants of the Helambu Valley are Sherpas, but their culture and dress are different from that in the Solu Khumbu. The accessibility of Helambu has created an influx of tourists which contributes to begging, the sale of 'genuine antiques' aged over the family fireplace, and several incidents of thievery. You can combine both Langtang and Helambu into a single trek of 13 or 14 days to avoid back-tracking.

LANGTANG TREK

This section describes the four day approach to Langtang. From Langtang village or Kyanjin Gompa there are a number of alternatives for returning to Kathmandu. It is possible to make the trek back to Dhunche in only two days from Langtang village because much of it is downhill. An alternative route over the Ganja La is described in the following section. A third alternative is to trek as far back as Syabru from Langtang, then cross via Gosainkund into Helambu.

Day 1: Kathmandu-Trisuli-Dhunche

It is about a four-hour drive (six hours by local bus) on a paved highway twisting and climbing over ridges to the Trisuli Valley. Buses leave from Ghora Khute, which is near the intersection where the Balaju road enters Kathmandu, close to the Malla Hotel, at 7 am and 1 pm at a cost of Rs 13.50. Passing Balaju and Nagarjun, the road climbs over Kakani Pass (2145 metres), offering excellent views of Annapurna II, Manaslu and Ganesh Himal and descends into the broad Trisuli Valley. There is usually a tea stop at Rani Pauwa, the only large village on the route, at km 27. After the long descent, the road crosses the Tadi Khola at km 60 then climbs onto a plateau that separates the Tadi Khola and the Trisuli River and passes fields of corn and rice planted in

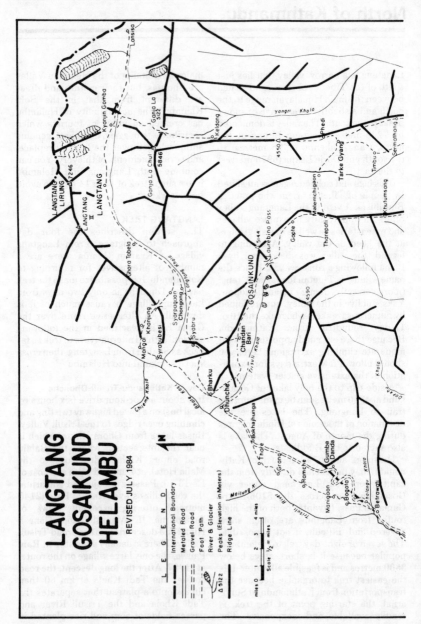

LANGTANG
GOSAIKUND
HELAMBU

REVISED JULY 1984

LEGEND

International Boundary
Metalled Road
Gravel Road
Foot Path
River & Glacier
Peaks (Elevation in Meters)
Ridge Line

△ 5122

Scale 1/2 = miles

miles 0   1   2   3   4 miles

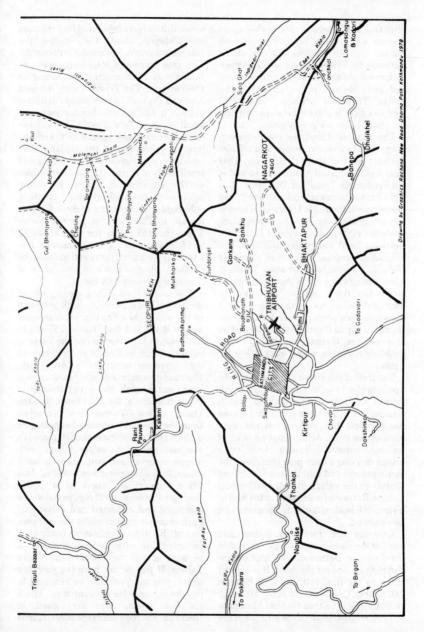

bright red soil. There is a police checkpost and an army camp just before Trisuli Bazaar at 548 metres, 72 km from Kathmandu. Trisuli Bazaar is a large town with many shops, and is the site of a dam and hydroelectric project built by the Indian Technical Mission. The hotel facilities here are extremely spartan and the restaurants are pretty grim.

The road to Langtang via Betrawati starts just before the bridge and follows the east bank of the Trisuli River. This road was completed in June, 1984 and is unpaved from Trisuli to Dhunche. It is eight km to Betrawati and another 42 km of steep switchbacks to Dhunche. There is sporadic minibus service as far as Kalikatan, elevation 1700 metres, about 14 km from Betrawati, and sometimes to Thare, Km 37, but no regular service as of spring 1985. It's a wild road; at some points it hangs onto a steep cliff a thousand metres above the river, and it is subject to continual landslides – especially when it rains – so even when bus service becomes regular, a trip to Dhunche will certainly be an adventure. If there is no bus, you can probably negotiate with a truck driver for a ride.

The trail, if you either can't get a ride or would prefer to walk, begins on the north side of the large bridge behind Trisuli Bazaar, and follows the canal that serves the hydroelectric project, on the west bank of the river. After about an hour of walking, cross the Trisuli River on a bridge carrying a huge pipe that feeds the hydro project and join the road, climbing slightly to the village of Betrawati at 620 metres. Betrawati is situated at the foot of a steep hill leading towards Langtang and Gosainkund.

Crossing the Phalangu Khola and passing the small hotels, shops, and police checkpost in Betrawati, the trail begins climbing on and off the road. It is a short climb to the first settlement of Bogota, 760 metres. Continuing to ascend through an oak forest, the trail reaches Manigaon at 1190 metres. Most of the villages at the lower altitudes are inhabited by Brahmins and Chhetris; above 1500 metres the villages are generally Tamang settlements. The trail continues its steep ascent to Ramche at 1790 metres and Grang at 1860 metres. The Trisuli Valley is broad here and the trail follows many circuitous detours in and out of side canyons where small streams flow down. The villages have become more spread out, and the intense cultivation of the lowland rice-growing country gives way to herding and small fields of corn, millet and vegetables as the elevation increases. Becoming more level, the trail contours, climbing only slightly through oak and rhododendron forests, to Thare at 1890 metres. Above Thare the trail meets the road at km 37 and follows it over a spur to Dhunche. It is a two-day walk from Betrawati to Dhunche on the trail; it is three to four hours of driving if you travel by road.

The motor road climbs steeply out of the Trisuli Valley, winding back and forth on the end of the ridge that separates the Trisuli River and the Phalangu Khola to Kalikatan at 1700 metres and the Tamang village of Gumbu Dando at 1970 metres then traverses north above the Trisuli. The road gets more and more exciting as it heads north, high above the trail. It is above Ramche at km 33, passes through Thare at km 37 and finally reaches Dhunche, the administrative headquarters of the region, at 1950 metres. Dhunche is a compact and picturesque village with narrow streets lined with stone houses, shops, inns and government offices. Just before the village there is a police checkpost where trekking permits are examined and endorsed and a National Park entrance station where the entrance fee of Rs 60 is collected from each foreigner. Be sure to keep the receipt because it will be checked at Ghora Tabela. If you do not have the entrance ticket, you will probably be required to pay the entrance fee a second time. There are five hotels, none very good, in Dhunche. The road will eventually continue

on from here towards Ganesh Himal where there is a lead and zinc deposit; there is some construction going on. The entire road is a Nepal Army project.

Day 2: Dhunche-Syabru

From Dhunche follow the road downhill to a U-turn and then divert onto the trail up the Trisuli Khola. The trail drops to a cantilever bridge at 1680 metres. The Trisuli Khola flows from Gosainkund where, according to legend, Lord Shiva released the waters of the holy lakes with his trident (*trisul*). The trail north, up the main valley, was once a major trade route with Tibet. The upper part of the river is called the Bhote Kosi ('river from Tibet'), as are most of the rivers that cross the Himalaya into Nepal. When it is joined by a Nepalese river, the Bhote Kosi assumes the name of its smaller tributary. Thus the Bhote Kosi becomes the Trisuli Khola below Dhunche.

From the bridge across the Trisuli, the trail climbs steeply up an almost vertical cleft in the rock beside a small stream for 250 metres. At the top of the steep climb is a bhatti at the intersection with the trail to Gosainkund, which follows the Trisuli Valley eastward. The trail to Langtang is the left-hand trail which follows around the forested ridge past small herders' huts to the village of Bharku, 1860 metres.

From Bharku there is a choice of trails. The new trail climbs over a ridge to Syabru, while the old trail continues north through Syabrubesi and Syarpagaon before turning eastward along the Langtang Khola. Because the new trail offers a saving of a day, and passes both interesting villages and deep forests, it is the best choice.

Climbing steeply from Bharku, the trail reaches a ridge crest at 2300 metres where the trail finally enters the Langtang Valley. There are views northward of the snow peaks in Tibet, west to Ganesh Himal and east to Langtang Lirung. The trail makes a short steep descent to Syabru at 2130 metres, a pleasant village strung out along a ridge. There are good hotels at the upper end of the village, just as the trail enters it.

Day 3: Syabru-Chongong

From Syabru, another trail leads to Gosainkund, climbing east out of the village. The trail to Langtang descends along the ridge, through the village, then continues the descent to the Langtang Khola through forests. The trail meets the river at about 1890 metres elevation, then follows it on its southern banks as the river gains elevation very steeply. For the rest of this day and the following morning there is almost no human habitation, but the forest is alive with birdlife. There is a teashop along this stretch and one at the bridge. The trail crosses to the north bank of the Langtang Khola at 2040 metres on a wooden bridge, then continues up its northern bank. The forest is less dense and drier on this side of the river, consisting mainly of scrub oak as opposed to the damp forests of large pines found on the shady southern bank, which receives almost no sunshine all day. The tiny settlement of Chongong at 2380 metres elevation offers both a camping spot and the *Lama Hotel*. There are also camping spots a short distance beyond in the forests and the *Riverside Lodge* about 1½ hours beyond.

Day 4: Chongong-Langtang Village

The trail climbs steeply above the river on the northern side of the Langtang Khola, in places so steep that the trail is on logs anchored to the valley wall. Tantalising glimpses of Langtang Lirung, 7245 metres, appear through the trees, until finally at Ghora Tabela the trail emerges into the open. Once a Tibetan resettlement project, Ghora Tabela, at 3000 metres, is now a Nepalese Army Post and has no permanent inhabitants but has an excellent lodge. There is another police checkpost here where another check is made to be sure that you paid the National Park entrance fee. If you somehow slipped past the

station at Dhunche, the fee of Rs 60 will be collected here. The trail ascends gradually, as the valley becomes wider and wider, through scattered Tamang villages until the large settlement of Langtang is reached at 3500 metres. This village is the headquarters for Langtang National Park; park administration buildings, minimal tourist facilities and yet another police checkpost are situated here. The houses of Langtang and the surrounding villages are of Tibetan style surrounded by stone walls enclosing fields of buckwheat, potatoes, wheat, turnips and barley. Herds of yaks and cattle are kept here and in the pastures above the village.

Day 5: Langtang Village-Kyanjin Gompa

The trail now climbs gradually through small villages and yak pastures as the valley becomes broader and broader. After crossing several small streams and moraines, the trail reaches the settlement of Kyanjin Gompa. Here there is a small monastery, a cheese factory and a large warm lodge. Tea has increased to Rs 4 per cup at this remote location, but the menu is varied and the food is good. The cheese factory was started in 1955 by the Swiss Association for Technical Assistance and produces many tons of cheese annually – all of it hauled by porters to the dairy in Kathmandu. It is easy to reach Kyanjin Gompa, at 3800 metres, by lunch time, allowing time to acclimatise and explore the surroundings.

Day 6: In Langtang Valley

A day hike may be made up the moraine to the north of Kyanjin Gompa to an elevation of 4300 metres or more. From the moraine there is a spectacular view of Langtang Lirung and the foot of one of its major glaciers.

For the more adventurous, a walk up the valley to Yala will provide outstanding views and an opportunity to climb a ridge to the north of the village. It is also possible to continue further up the Langtang Valley itself towards the peaks of Dorje Lakpa (6966 metres), Urkeinmang (6387 metres), and Loenpo Gang (6979 metres).

Return to Kathmandu

The return to Kathmandu may be made by the same route, or might be made by plane from the Pilatus Porter airstrip above Kyanjin Gompa at 3960 metres. This airstrip has no scheduled service. The charter flights are irregular, and in only four-passenger aircraft, so it is best not to count on finding a seat back to Kathmandu unless you have made prior arrangements. The airstrip is notorious for becoming snowbound in December, January and February for days at a time.

An alternative route to Kathmandu may be made either over Ganja La or via Gosainkund when there is no snow on these high altitude routes.

ACROSS GANJA LA

The route from Kyanjin Gompa in Langtang to Tarke Gyang in Helambu requires crossing the 5106-metre high Ganja La Pass. This pass is difficult and dangerous when covered by snow, so local inquiries about its condition, good equipment and some mountaineering experience are necessary for a safe crossing. The pass can generally be assumed to be open from April to November, though unusual weather can alter its condition at any time. A guide who knows the trail, a tent, food and fuel are imperative on a crossing of Ganja La.

Kathmandu to Kyanjin Gompa

As described in the preceeding section. An acclimatisation day in Langtang is necessary before beginning the crossing of Ganja La.

Day 1 Kathmandu-Dhunche
Day 2 Dhunche-Syabru
Day 3 Syabru-Chongong
Day 4 Chongong-Langtang village
Day 5 Langtang village-Kyanjin Gompa

Day 6 In the Langtang Valley
Day 7 Kyanjin Gompa-Ngegang

This is a short day from Kyanjin Gompa, but Ngegang is the last good place to camp before beginning the final ascent to the pass, and it is necessary to minimise the elevation gain in order to aid acclimatisation. Crossing the Langtang Khola below Kyanjin Gompa, the trail makes a steep climb up the ridge on the south side of the valley through a forest of rhododendron and juniper. Finally becoming less steep, the trail reaches the yak pasture of Ngegang at about 4000 metres elevation. There are goths here and on the other side of the pass, but they have no roofs during the winter months, so a tent is a useful item to have along on this trek. During the monsoon months, herders carry bamboo mats to provide roofs for the stone goths here and live the entire summer in high meadows with herds of yaks and goats.

Day 8: Ngegang-Keldang

The trail continues south, following streams and moraines, climbing steeply towards the pass. As the trail climbs higher and comes under the shadow of the 5800-metre peaks to the south, more and more snow is usually encountered. Turning south-west the trail makes the final steep ascent to the pass at 5106 metres; the last hundred metres of the ascent being a tricky balancing act on a snow slope above some steep rocks. The pass itself is flanked by gendarmes and topped by a large cairn of rocks and prayer flags. The views north from the pass of Langtang Lirung and snow peaks in Tibet are outstanding, and on a clear day there are views to the south of many ranges of hills.

The descent from the pass is steep and dangerous as it follows a loose scree slope for about 1200 metres before emerging onto a snow slope. Somehow the descent from Ganja La, like most mountain descents, seems more treacherous than the ascent – irrespective of which direction one crosses the pass. However, Ganja La is one of the steeper and more difficult of the major passes in Nepal. After the initial descent, the trail descends gradually in a huge basin surrounded by glaciated peaks. One peak, Ganja La Chuli, 5846 metres, is open to climbers upon prior application to the Nepal Mountaineering Association. A base camp in this region provides a good starting point for the reasonably easy climb.

The route descends in the large basin along an indistinct trail marked occasionally by rock cairns to a small stream. If you are proceeding from Helambu to Langtang, it will require a full day to reach this point, about 4400 metres elevation, from Keldang. Thus you should schedule two days from Keldang to the pass. From this campsite, the trail enters the steep Yangri Khola Valley and drops quickly down a rough scree slope to the stream. Following the stream for some distance through grassy meadows, the trail reaches a few goths (again without roofs) at Keldang, about 4270 metres elevation.

Day 9: Keldang-Dukpu

This is a long and tiring day as the trail descends along a ridge, making many ups and downs. In winter there is no water from Keldang to the bottom of the ridge, near Phedi, so it is important to plan food accordingly for this stretch of the trail. In October and November there is usually no water problem, because the monsoon rains leave an ample groundwater supply in several small springs.

The route descends the valley, but stays high above the river, finally meeting the ridge itself and following the ridge line throughout the day. The small summer settlement of Dukpu is reached at 4080 metres.

Day 10: Dukpu-Tarke Gyang

From Dukpu the trail descends further along the ridge before making a 180-metre climb to a pass at 4020 metres, offering a commanding view of the Himalaya from Dorje Lakpa east almost to Everest, and a panorama of the first part of the Everest trek from Lamosangu to Khumbu. Descending from the pass, the trail enters forests, descending through pines and rhododendrons, past tiny herders' settlements to a ridge high above Tarke Gyang. It is a steep descent to Gekye Gompa at 3020 metres, a small monastic community, and the first permanent habitation since Kyanjin Gompa. The trail continues its steep descent to Tarke Gyang, a large Sherpa village at 2560 metres.

Return to Kathmandu

For the route back to Kathmandu see the Helambu route description below:

Day 11 Kiul
Day 12 Pati Bhanjyang
Day 13 Kathmandu via Sundarijal

HELAMBU CIRCUIT

This is the description of a seven-day trek that makes a circuit of the Helambu region. The best starting point for this trek is Sundarijal because of its proximity to Kathmandu. The trek may be made in either direction, as it closes a loop from Pati Bhanjyang, the first night stop of the trek. The best route is as described here, visiting the high ridge to the west of Helambu Valley first, then going to Tarke Gyang and descending the Malemchi Khola before climbing back to Pati Bhanjyang. There are numerous other variations possible, including a direct route to Tarke Gyang from Pati Bhanjyang then down the ridge through Sermathang, ending at Panchkal on the Chinese Road.

The Helambu trek is an easy trek to organise after you have arrived in Kathmandu. The transportation to and from the starting point of the trek is fast and cheap, and the trek is at a low elevation so no fancy warm clothing is usually needed. There are fewer trekkers here than either the Everest or Annapurna regions.

Day 1: Kathmandu-Pati Bhanjyang

The trail to Helambu begins at Sundarijal, elevation 1265 metres, which is reached by an unpaved road from Bodhanath. You can take a bus, or even a taxi to Sundarijal, or you can begin the trek from Bodhanath, taking a few hours to walk to Sundarijal along the level roadway.

At Sundarijal there is a large water project that supplies much of Kathmandu's drinking water in a huge pipe. The trail begins on a set of concrete steps alongside the water pipe, then climbs continuously in forests beside the pipe and alongside a small stream to a dam. Crossing the dam, the trail leaves the water supply system and climbs steeply up to the top of the Seopuri ridge. The first village, Mulkharka, is situated at an elevation of 1895 metres, and offers a chance to rest in a small tea shop while enjoying a spectacular panoramic view of Kathmandu Valley. If the trek is made early in the morning, you will meet hundreds of people walking uphill to gather wood to be used as fuel in Kathmandu. The forests of Seopuri Ridge are densely forested with pine, oak and rhododendron.

Beyond the Tamang village of Mulkharka the trail becomes a bit less steep, but continues to climb steadily through the scattered settlement of Chaurabas at 2220 metres, to the top of the ridge at 2440 metres. Just below the ridge on the north side is the village of Borlang Bhanjyang. A night stop in one of the hotels in this village will afford excellent mountain views the following morning. The sunrise on the Himalaya, from Annapurna to Everest, is particularly outstanding from this point.

The route continues down the ridge through a forest of oak and rhododendron, then across meadows and fields to Pati Bhanjyang, situated on a saddle at the bottom of the ridge at 1770 metres elevation. This is a large Tamang village with a few shops and hotels, and a police check post.

Day 2: Pati Bhanjyang-Khutumsang

The trail climbs north out of Pati Bhanjyang and ascends the ridge through terraced fields, crosses a spur, descends and climbs again to Chipling at 2170 metres. Continuing on the ridge, through forests, the trail crosses a pass at 2470 metres, then descends and passes the Tamang village of Gul Bhanjyang, 2130 metres. The trail continues climbing up the ridge from Gul Bhanjyang to another pass at 2620 metres, then descends to Khutumsang, 2470 metres, situated in a saddle atop the ridge. Parts of the route are on slab rocks where the trail disappears. Be especially careful and watchful here – several trekkers have gotten off the route and falled off the ridge.

Day 3: Khutumsang-Tharepati

The route continues due north up the Yurin Danda ridge and affords views of the peaks above Langtang and of the Gosainkund peaks. The trail now enters fir and rhododendron forests where there are no permanent settlements. The small huts in the region are used by herders during the summer months. Continuing to climb, steeply at first, then more gradually, though there are some ups and downs, the trail finally reaches Tharepati, the site of a few goths, at 3490 metres. The trail to Gosainkund turns north-west from this point, but the trail to complete the Helambu circuit turns east just before the hamlet of Tharepati. There is no hotel, but there are a few stone huts here. A tent is useful, though it is possible to continue on to Malemchigaon for the night if you have no shelter. The region is now truly alpine with meadows and shrubs typical of high elevations.

Day 4: Tharepati-Tarke Gyang

The trail turns east and descends steeply down a ravine. The vegetation changes rapidly to large firs, then to oaks and rhododendrons as all the altitude gained during the last two days is rapidly lost. Crossing a stream, the trail reaches the

Sherpa village of Malemchigaon at 2530 metres. The Sherpas of Helambu are much different from their cousins in Solu Khumbu. Instead of the Tibetan-style black dress and colourful apron, the Sherpa women of Helambu wear a dress of red printed cotton. The language is also quite distinct from the Sherpa language of Solu Khumbu. Helambu women have a reputation for being very beautiful, and many Helambu Sherpa girls were employed in aristocratic Rana households in Kathmandu during the Rana regime.

From Malemchigaon, the trail descends further to the Malemchi Khola, crossing it on a bridge at 1890 metres, and immediately begins the ascent up the other side of the valley towards Tarke Gyang. It is a long climb to this pretty village, perched high on a shelf above the river.

Tarke Gyang is the largest village in Helambu and the destination for most trekkers in this region. There is a large new hotel at the southern end of the village. The gompa, with its impressive array of prayer flags, has recently been renovated. In 1949, Tilman described this gompa as in a sorry state of disrepair, but it is now well cared for, with new paintings and a huge brass prayer wheel. The stone houses of Tarke Gyang are closely spaced with narrow alleyways separating them. Inside, the homes are large, clean and often elaborately decorated and furnished, not only with traditional Tibetan carpets and brassware, but also with manufactured goods from Kathmandu and India. The people of Helambu do a lot of trading in India during the winter months. Many of the people are quite well-to-do, and own cultivated fields in the lower Malemchi Khola Valley. A special racket among the people of Helambu is the sale of antiques, usually purchased in Kathmandu and aged over smoky fires in the homes of Tarke Gyang – beware of any such bargain here. It is illegal to export any item over 100 years old from Nepal, so it is best to purchase well-made handicrafts in Kathmandu or Patan rather than attempt to beat the system by purchasing a phoney antique in the hills.

Day 5: Tarke Gyang-Kiul

From Tarke Gyang there is a choice of trails back to Kathmandu. The trail south along the ridge through Sermathang, down to the river at Malemchi, and down the road to Panchkal requires two days. The first part of the trail, along the ridge through forests and Sherpa villages, is quite delightful, but the later part of the route, on the dusty road along the Indrawati River is less interesting, though it may be possible to get a ride in one of the jeeps that ply this stretch of road. This route ends on the Chinese road at Panchkal (the name of the settlement where the trail meets the road is actually called Lamidanda), and it is a long ride back to Kathmandu by bus.

It is more worthwhile to take an extra day in the hills and walk back to Sundarijal, where it is easy, cheap and fast to catch transport back to Kathmandu.

The route to Sundarijal passes the hotel in Tarke Gyang, then begins the descent in a rhododendron forest, along a broad, well-travelled trail. Descending, the trail passes several chortens, mani walls (walk to the left) and kanis. Passing through the Sherpa village of Kakani at 2070 metres and Thimbu at 1580 metres, the trail enters the hot rice-growing country of the Malemchi and Indrawati valleys, and leaves the highland tribes for Brahmin, Chhetri and Newar people who inhabit the lower regions.

The steep descent continues to Kiul, 1280 metres, strung out along the terraces above the Malemchi Khola. The trail is now in semi-tropical banana and monkey country at an elevation below that of Kathmandu.

Day 6: Kiul-Pati Bhanjyang

From Kiul the trail follows the river, descending slightly, then crosses the river on a suspension bridge (do not take the first bridge the trail reaches, take the second one a bit further downstream), at 1190 metres elevation. A short distance beyond the bridge the trail reaches Mahenkal (1130 metres) and widens into a roadway. This was once a motorable road, but a monsoon flood washed away the crossing of the Taramarang Khola years ago, and this portion of the road has fallen into disrepair. It is being renovated and will go from Panchkal to Malemchigaon.

As the road descends the valley it passes through the village of Gheltum, the site of an imposing two-storey schoolhouse and a post office. Descending slightly, the trail cuts across some large switchbacks that the road follows, then descends into Taramarang, a pleasant village on the banks of the river at 940 metres. There are some small shops here, supplied by vehicles that come up the road and stop just across the Taramarang Khola.

Crossing the Taramarang Khola on a long, rather precarious, suspension bridge, the trail leaves the road and proceeds west up the south bank of the stream. From its good beginnings along rice terraces and fields, the trail deteriorates into a boulder-strewn route up the river valley. The same monsoon flood that destroyed the road at Taramarang also destroyed this portion of the trail and washed many fertile fields downstream in the process. After following the stream for a long distance, the trail begins a steep climb up towards the top of the ridge on a newly-widened well-constructed trail. From the uninhabited valley floor, the trail soon enters a densely populated region, passing through the village of Batache en route to the top of the ridge, which it reaches near the village of Thakani at 1890 metres. Following the ridge through meadows and terraced fields, the trail crosses over to its south side and descends to Pati Bhanjyang at 1770 metres, completing the circuit through Helambu.

Day 7: Pati Bhanjyang-Kathmandu

Retrace the route back to Sundarijal, as described on the first day of the trek.

GOSAINKUND

The trek through Gosainkund may be made in either direction combined with a trek to Helambu or Langtang. There is little dependable food or accommodation on the route and the National Park fuel restrictions are enforced here, so everything, including fuel and shelter, should be carried. The description here is from Dhunche to Helambu, but the trail is also accessible from Syabru, or the trek may be easily made in the opposite direction, starting from Helambu.

Day 1: Dhunche-Sing Gompa

From Dhunche at 1950 metres, the trail follows the route as described in Day 3 of the Langtang trek, crossing the Trisuli Khola and climbing up to the trail junction at 1920 metres. Leaving the main trail to Langtang, the Gosainkund trail follows the Trisuli Khola Valley uphill through a forest of oaks, and higher up to a forest of firs and rhododendrons. The trail climbs to a Buddhist monastery, Sing Gompa, and a small cheese factory at Chandan Bari, elevation about 3350 metres. If you are coming from Syabru the trail to Sing Gompa and Gosainkund is confusing and involves a lot of climbing – stay generally high and do not take the inviting-looking trail that descends steeply in a westerly direction, to an apple farm. Sing Gompa is south-east and is only a short descent (one hour) from the ridge – take the upper trail at all junctions.

Day 2: Sing Gompa-Gosainkund

The trail continues to climb steeply up the ridge, leaving the forests below. The only signs of habitation are herders' huts at the few points on the ridge where water is found. There are outstanding views across Langtang Valley to Langtang Lirung. To the west the view is even more dramatic with Himal Chuli (6893 metres), Ganesh Himal (7406 metres) and Manaslu (8156 metres) visible. On a clear day it is even possible to see all the way to the Annapurnas and Dhaulagiri.

Finally the trail descends from the ridge to the first of the lakes, Saraswati Kund, at 4100 metres. The second lake in the chain is named Bhairav Kund, and the third, Gosainkund, is located some distance beyond at an elevation of 4380 metres. There are three small stone shelters on the north side of the lake that are used by pilgrims who come here during the full moon festival each August. There is no food available here or at Gopte or Tharepati.

Gosainkund lake has a large white rock in the middle, said to be the remnants of an ancient shrine of Lord Shiva. According to legend, this high-altitude lake was created by Shiva himself when he pierced a glacier with his trident to obtain water to quench his thirst after consuming some poison. It is also said that the water from this lake disappears underground via a subterranean channel and surfaces in

Kumbeshwar pool, adjacent to the five-storey temple to Shiva in Patan, more than 60 km away.

Day 3: Gosainkund-Gopte
The trail leaves Gosainkund lake and climbs further through rugged country past four more small lakes to Lauribina Pass at 4610 metres, descends steeply alongside a stream, then ascends a ridge and enters forests. Gopte, at 3260 metres, has a cave that offers some shelter.

Day 4: Gopte-Tharepati
Descending along the ridge, the trail continues its steep descent through forests and past herders' huts to a stream at 3310 metres, then climbs to Tharepati at 3490 metres. Here the trail joins the Helambu route at Day 3 in the description, and you can travel on to Tarke Gyang or go directly down the ridge to Kathmandu via Pati Bhanjyang.

Central Nepal

Three major routes in this area are frequented by trekkers: Annapurna south face base camp, often called Annapurna Sanctuary (12 days round trip), Jomsom (14 days round trip) and a trek around Annapurna (17 days). The Annapurna base camp trek affords a fine opportunity to surround oneself with Himalayan peaks in a short period of time without having to contend with the extreme altitudes and flight problems of the Everest region. At an approximate elevation of 4000 metres you are well within the Annapurna Sanctuary and have a 360-degree view of Hinchuli, the Annapurna south face (climbed by the British in 1970), Annapurna III (7555 metres), Gangapurna (7454 metres) and Machhapuchhare (6997 metres). Campsites near the sanctuary are small and hotels are often crowded but the isolation of the high peaks quickly dispels any sense of constriction.

The trek to Jomsom is the best trek for those who elect the village inn approach to trekking. This is a major trade route, and you will share the trail with trains of burros and ponies travelling to Mustang and other areas closed to foreigners. Many villages have surprisingly well-equipped hotels operated by Thakalis, people of Tibetan origin who inhabit the Kali Gandaki Valley between Annapurna and Dhaulagiri. From the Kali Gandaki both the 1950 French Annapurna base camp and the base camp for Dhaulagiri may be reached by side trips. The views of the mountains are spectacular and the route actually crosses to the other side of the main Himalayan range for some unusual views of the northern flanks. The entire route remains below 3000 metres, an important consideration if you wish to avoid high altitudes, though the trek is still strenuous enough to be interesting.

Jomsom is the district headquarters for the Mustang region of Nepal. To many people, however, Mustang implies the area of Nepal that extends like a thumb into Tibet. This is the region described in Michel Piessel's book *Mustang* and includes the walled capital city of Mustang, Lo Monthang. This part of Mustang, however, is closed to foreigners, and despite the reassuring and optimistic brochures printed by many trekking agents, there are no signs that it will be opened soon. Parts of the Mustang district are open, but the area that most people refer to as Mustang is certainly not open (in 1984) to foreigners.

The area most recently opened to tourists is Manang, the area north of Annapurna. The opening of this region has made possible a complete circuit of the Annapurna Himal, involving the crossing of a single high pass, Thorung La, at 5416 metres. This trek is best started in Dumre and ended in Pokhara. There are hotels all along the route, but you should have warm clothing and a sleeping bag for the crossing of Thorung La.

JOMSOM TREK

The trek to Jomsom begins in Pokhara, known for its large lake, Phewa Tal, and its spectacular panorama of Nepal's central Himalaya: the Annapurnas, Machhapuchhare and Manaslu dominate the skyline. You can travel to Pokhara by bus for Rs 35 or by plane for US$40.

Accommodation in Pokhara includes the fashionable and peaceful *Fish Tail Lodge* located on the lake. The western-style *New Hotel Crystal*, the *Mount Annapurna Hotel* and the Tibetan-owned *Himalayan Hotel*, where you have a choice of setting up your own tent or using their simple bungalows (and eating their good food), are situated across from the airport. You can also find excellent accommodation among the many small hotels along the shore of Phewa Tal, or camp in the dirty and overcrowded campsite near the lake.

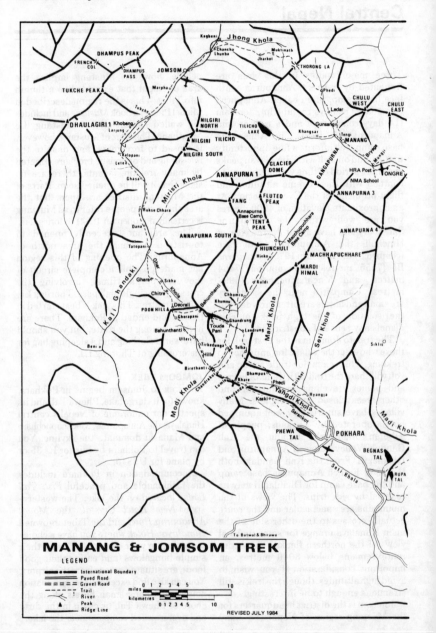

MANANG & JOMSOM TREK

LEGEND

- ●━●━● International Boundary
- ━━━━ Paved Road
- ═══ Gravel Road
- ─── Trail
- ∿ River
- ▲ Peak
- ━━ Ridge Line

miles 0 1 2 3 4 5   10
kilometres 0 1 2 3 4 5   10

REVISED JULY 1984

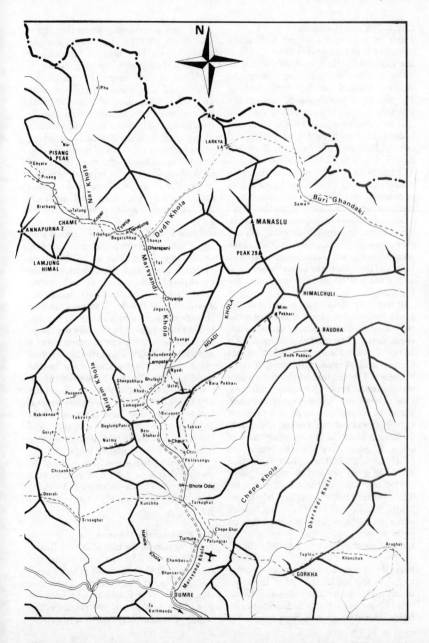

Day 1: Pokhara-Naudanda

From the lake or the airport in Pokhara you can either take a taxi (about Rs 20) or the city bus for Rs 1 to Bagar, elevation 1060 metres, the roadhead near the shining hospital at the north end of Pokhara. You can also walk through the Pokhara bazaar, but it's a long distance and all uphill on a paved road. There is a rudimentary road as far as Phedi and several Russian-built jeeps ply the route from Pokhara to Phedi a few times a day. The fare is Rs 13 per person plus Rs 5 for a rucksack and Rs 10 to 30 for larger pieces of baggage, and it's standing room only as the jeep lurches across bridges that don't exist and wallows in and out of mudholes. The service is unreliable, but if you are lucky enough to catch a ride, you can save some walking – although the drive takes an hour and the walk takes about three hours, so it's not worth waiting a very long time for a jeep.

If you walk, follow the road east on the south bank of the Yamdi Khola and cross the river above the dam that is under construction. The road climbs uphill a bit to the Tibetan Camp. There is a carpet factory and a monastery here; a large retinue of Tibetan traders sell their wares alongside the trail. The route continues, almost level, past many houses and small shops to Hyangja, a large and pleasant village spread out over several kilometres at 1070 metres. In the morning there is often a good view up the valley to Machhapuchhare. There is a trail junction at a large piple tree and chautaara; follow the left trail – the road with the tyre tracks. The right trail leads to the Seti Khola and Mardi Khola valleys. The road follows some irrigation canals, crossing them on wide stone slabs under huge shading trees, then emerges into a broad valley.

The road takes a long swing to the left here. If you are walking it is not necessary to follow the road; take one of the more direct routes across the valley to Suikhet at 1125 metres. One trail traverses rice fields, sometimes on a good track, but sometimes precariously across the tops of the dykes that provide water for the thirsty rice. The trail is particularly complex during rice growing season – early fall and late spring. In rice season, you should take a more circuitous route and follow a small canal near the north side of the valley along a trail that is usually drier. There are hotels and bhattis at Suikhet; it is an overnight stopping place for pony caravans. Beyond Suikhet the trail again follows the road, crossing a field of boulders and a small stream just before Phedi, where several bhattis greet you. This is the end of the road and there are already several derelict vehicles here.

From Phedi go uphill on a broad trail that climbs gently (for Nepal) to Naudanda, on the top of the ridge at 1430 metres. Naudanda is a large village with a police checkpost, school and several hotels varying from tiny bhattis to well developed, western-style hotels. Campers should consider the school yard or the ridge behind the village. The views of the entire Annapurna range in the morning make a night stop in Naudanda worth the sleepless night caused by barking dogs in the middle of the village. To the south, there are excellent views of Phewa Tal and the city lights of Pokhara. There are several hotels and another good campsite about 15 minutes above the village on the top of the ridge, but the local thieves work this area more than Naudanda itself.

The police checkpost here is insistent about trekking permits, so if you are on a day hike out of Pokhara without a trekking permit, this will probably be as far as you get.

Day 2: Naudanda-Tirkedungha

From Naudanda the trail climbs to Kaski, then further to Khare, a large strung-out village situated at the head of the Yamdi Khola Valley at 1710 metres. There is a signboard here in English that points the way to the British agricultural project in Lumle. The Jomsom route descends from

Khare on a muddy trail through deep forests, down a set of wide stone stairs below the British project, then continues to the village of Lumle. There are several hotels here (some advertise toilets and bathrooms) and there is even a medical hall among the slate-roofed houses of the village, elevation 1585 metres. The trail follows the village's flagstone-paved main street, exitting the village only a bit lower in elevation than where it entered it. If you find yourself heading steeply downhill, ask directions; this is the trail to Dhorpatan, Baglung and Beni, not the route to Jomsom. There are occasional trail signs erected by local people and by the Ministry of Tourism along this route, and all villagers know the way to Jomsom, so there is little chance of getting really lost on this trek.

Beyond Lumle the route continues along the side of the ridge, finally rounding a bend and descending to Chandrakot, perched on the end of a ridge at an elevation of 1550 metres. The views of Annapurna South and Machhapuchhare, the 'fish tail' mountain, are excellent from this point – except that it looks more like the Matterhorn than a fish tail from this angle. You must go into the Annapurna Sanctuary, several days to the north, to see the mountain in its proper perspective – but that's another trek. There are several hotels here with English signboards and menus – it's a good place for lunch.

From Chandrakot the trail descends a steep dusty (muddy when wet) trail that switchbacks down to the Modi Khola. Passing a few houses near the river, the route crosses a suspension bridge at 1065 metres. On the far side of the bridge is Birethanti, a large and prosperous town with a winding street paved with large stones, many well stocked shops, hotels and even sidewalk cafes. There is also a police checkpost here. A trail up the Modi Khola to Ghandrung begins at Birethanti just behind the first house of the village.

The hotels here are excellent, but if you

spend a night here it is a long 1700-metre climb the next day to Ghorapani. It's more comfortable to break the climb into two stages by continuing on to Hille or Tirkedungha for the night. If you are coming from Jomsom and are reading this backwards, then Ghorapani to Birethanti is an easy, though knee-cracking, descent and Birethanti makes a good stopping place. The trail follows the main street of Birethanti, passes through bamboo forests and past a large waterfall, then deteriorates where it was washed away by monsoon floods. It may have been repaired by the time you read this, so you'll just have to follow whatever looks best. The trail stays on the north bank of the Bhurungdi Khola (don't cross the inviting-looking large suspension bridge) to Baajgara, where a hotel with a river-view balcony has a signboard giving times from here to various destinations: Birethanti – one hour; Ghorapani – eight hours; Ulleri – three hours; Tirkedungha – 1½ hours and Hille 1¼ hours. These are a bit conservative and you can probably walk faster than these times. Beyond a pasture that is used by the pony caravans the trail becomes better and climbs steadily up the side of the valley, reaching Hille at 1495 metres. There are several hotels here and others in Tirkedungha, about 15 minutes (and 30 metres) above Hille. There is a large campsite just beyond Tirkedungha near two large bridges.

Day 3: Tirkedungha-Ghorapani
The trail crosses a stream near the campsite at Tirkedungha then crosses the Bhurungdi Khola itself on a large bridge. The trail climbs very steeply on a stone staircase, and the tops of Annapurna South (7273 metres) and Hiunchuli begin to emerge from behind the hills. The climb continues steeply to the large Magar village of Ulleri at 2070 metres, then more gently in pastures and cultivated fields above the village. The fields soon give way to deep forests as the trail climbs to Bahunthanti, a rustic settlement of seven

houses, most of which offer food, in a forest clearing at 2250 metres. The trail continues through magnificent oak and rhododendron forests, crossing two sparkling clear streams, finally crossing a small ridge and another stream before making a short final climb to Nayathanti, two hotels in a forest clearing at 2460 metres. 'Thanti' is a Gurung word meaning rest house or dharamsala; 'naya' is a Nepali word meaning new. In the winter the trail can be snow covered, and in many places it is sloppy mud, so all sorts of short detours are necessary along this stretch of trail. Ghorapani is about an hour past Nayathanti at 2775 metres elevation. The pass, Deorali (which means 'pass'), is at 2834 metres, about 10 minutes beyond the village. There is a large collection of hotels and shops and a camping place at Deorali; the Annapurna Hotel and the Snow View Hotel are the largest. It is worth staying at the pass to see the spectacular panorama of Dhaulagiri I, Tukche, Nilgiri, Annapurna I, Annapurna South, Hiunchuli and Glacier Dome. An early morning excursion may be made to Poon Hill (3193 metres), about an hour's climb, where a tower offers an even better unobstructed view of the high Himalaya. The best hotels are in Ghorapani itself, but there is no view from here. There is a hotel under construction at Poon Hill.

Ghorapani means 'horse water', and is no doubt a welcome watering stop for teams of horses, mules and ponies that carry loads between Pokhara and Jomsom. These picturesque caravans, with melodious bells that can be heard from great distances, and wonderous plumes and head-dresses on the lead horses, are reminiscent of ancient Tibet. Herded by Tibetan men who shout up and down the trail, they lend a unique touch to the Jomsom trek. The ponies also grind the trail into dust and slippery mud with their tiny sharp hooves and frighten trekkers into jumping into the bushes as they career downhill, but the colourful photographs and harmonious tinkle of bells

almost make it worth the trouble. On a typical day you will encounter 200 to 300 pack animals travelling in large trains of animals that range from huge mules to tiny burros which are about the size of a large dog.

Day 4: Ghorapani-Tatopani

From the pass at Deorali the trail makes a muddy steep descent through rhododendron and magnolia forests interspersed with a few shepherds' goths, bhattis and pastures to Chitre at 2390 metres, where there are some trekkers' lodges. The country opens up into a region of extensive terracing. At one point the trail crosses a huge landslide. Observe the way the slick mica soil has slid off the underlying rock. The trail descends towards Sikha, a large and prosperous Magar village at 1980 metres that has many shops and hotels; *Shanti's and someone's Bar and Grill* (the owner's name keeps changing) are near the top of the village above the British Army training centre. From Sikha the trail makes a gentle descent across another slide area to Ghara at 1705 metres, then climbs to the top of a rocky spur where a single house stands like a sentinel. There are some small bhattis here. The trail makes a steep descent of about 500 metres to the Ghar Khola, crossing it on a suspension bridge, then climbs a bit on a trail above the Kali Gandaki, crossing the river on a large suspension bridge at 1180 metres elevation. An older version of this bridge appeared on the cover of Toni Hagen's *Nepal, The Kingdom of the Himalayas*; the peak in the background is Nilgiri South (6839 metres). On the opposite side of the river the trail turns north; it is a short distance upstream to Tatopani.

Tatopani means 'hot water' in Nepali; the village gains its name from the hot springs near the river below the village. There is a choice of bathing spots, including a municipal bath with a cement-lined pool and a hotel at the southern end of the village. There are also several

Chortens-wayside shrines

springs among the rocks on the banks of the river. Tatopani also has many well-provisioned hotels, restaurants and shops, including a shop boasting a kerosene-powered refrigerator full of cold beer, cokes and orange soda. The *Dhaulagiri Hotel* and *Namaste Hotel* in the centre of Tatopani are both good. Most of the hotels and many homes have installed gobar gas generators to produce fuel for light and cooking; it is interesting to see these facilities in daily use – it is good progress in the alternate energy field. Many people who are making only a short trek come here from Pokhara and spend their time relaxing in the hot springs and enjoying the hospitality of this small village. There is a police checkpost here. This is citrus fruit country, so you can stock up on small mandarin oranges.

Day 5: Tatopani-Kalopani

The trail now heads up the Kali Gandaki gorge, said to be the deepest in the world (from the top of Annapurna I to the top of Dhaulagiri I, both above 8000 metres and only 38 km apart, the terrain drops to below 2200 metres). From Tatopani the route ascends gently, passing through a small tunnel carved out of the rocky hillside, to Dana, three separate settlements with elaborately carved windows and balconies, at 1400 metres. The hotels in Dana are near the post office on the south end of the village. Most of the people of Dana are Magars; there are also a few Brahmins and Thakalis. The large peak across the valley is Annapurna South (7273 metres); the large village high on the hillside across the valley is Nerchang.

From Dana a trail leads across the Kali Gandaki. After several days of rough climbing above the Miristi Khola in bamboo jungle this trail reaches the base camp used by Herzog's expedition in 1950 for the first ascent of Annapurna, at that time the highest mountain ever climbed. The base camp may also be reached by an equally difficult trail from Lete. Maurice Herzog's book *Annapurna* provides essential background reading for the trek up the Kali Gandaki.

Above Dana the trail continues to the hamlet of Rukse Chhara (1550 metres), situated at the foot of a high and spectacular waterfall that tumbles into a series of cataracts near the village. Beyond Rukse Chhara the trail crosses the river on a wooden bridge where the water rushes through a steep rocky canyon, then climbs on the east bank to Kopchepani where a signboard proclaims 'Welcome to Mustang'. This is the southern boundary of the Mustang district – you have not been magically transported to Lo Monthang. The trail then climbs over a ridge and descends again to the riverbank. The next stretch of trail is through the steepest and narrowest part of the canyon. The trail is cut through solid rock, and there is a short section that is a three-sided tunnel. Across the river there is a view of the old trail, now fallen into disrepair (though some people still use it), that has an even longer and more spectacular stretch of cliffhanging trail.

After descending to the riverbank, the trail climbs over a ridge, then crosses to the west side of the Kali Gandaki on a suspension bridge at 1935 metres. It is a short climb from the bridge to Ghasa, which has three settlements, at about 2000 metres elevation. This is the first Thakali village on the trek and the southernmost limit of Lama Buddhism in the valley. The best facilities are in middle Ghasa; these include the *Kali Gandaki*, the *Lekahli* and the *Mustang Guest Houses*. There are fine kanis in upper Ghasa and there is a large locally supported reforestation project behind the school. Here the vegetation changes from subtropical trees and shrubs, including stinging nettles and cannabis to mountain types, such as pine and birch. You might encounter grey Langur monkeys in this area.

The trail ascends steeply through forests to the Lete Khola. There are a few bhattis here, near the long suspension bridge. This bridge, as many in Nepal, has a steep ascent and descent on the approach, so there is an alternate trail that drops to the stream, crosses it on a log, and rejoins the trail on the opposite side. The trail then climbs through Lete itself (2470 metres), a spread-out town with three clusters of buildings. The *Namaste Fooding & Lodging* is the place to patronise here. From Lete it is about a 20-minute walk to Kalopani (2560 metres), another town that is prospering from the influx of trekkers. There is an enclosed campground among the whitewashed houses of the village; hotels include the *Kalopani Guest House*, the *Thak Lodge* and the *See You Lodge*, which has an extensive menu, including apple pie, and good rooms (with mountain views) upstairs. There is a 360° panorama of peaks here: Dhaulagiri, the three Nilgiris, Fang and Annapurna I.

Day 6: Kalopani-Jomsom

From Kalopani the trail goes up the east bank a short distance, then crosses to the west bank on a large bridge where the river races through a narrow cleft, climbs over a wooded ridge past some small lodges and bhattis, then descends to a new suspension bridge. Here there are two trails to choose from.

By crossing the suspension bridge, you can take the west bank trail that climbs to Sukung, then descends through pine, juniper and cypress forests to Larjung (2560 metres), an architecturally interesting town built with narrow alleyways and tunnels that connect houses with enclosed courtyards – a complex and picturesque system that provides protection from the winds of the Kali Gandaki gorge. A bit beyond Larjung is Khobang, also called Kanti, at 2560 metres elevation. This trail also provides access to the gompa just above Khobang. The best mountain views – of Dhaulagiri (8167 metres) and Nilgiri (7061 metres) – along the Kali Gandaki are to be had on this stretch of trail. There are three or four hotels at the south end of Larjung; on the roof of the northernmost house of the village are the remains of the hovercraft in which Michel Peissel travelled from Lete to Marpha in 1972.

A trail to the Dhaulagiri icefall begins just south of Khobang and climbs up the south bank of the Ghatte Khola. This route was explored by Herzog's expedition in 1950 and abandoned because it was too dangerous. In 1969, seven members of the American Dhaulagiri expedition were killed by an avalanche in this area. A side trip may be made to a meadow near the foot of the icefall at an elevation of about 4000 metres. It's a long long uphill climb on very steep grassy slopes, so it is wise to make an additional camp at Tal, a lake at about 3100 metres elevation above the village of Naurkot, and make a day trip to the icefall area, returning to Tal for the night.

The east bank trail makes a long, but easy, traverse along the gravel bars alongside the riverbed, then crosses the river on a series of temporary bridges just before Tukche. Here in its upper reaches, the Kali Gandaki is known as the Thak Khola, thus the name Thakali for those who live in this region.

The Kali Gandaki/Thak Khola Valley has been a major trade route for centuries. Until 1959, salt collected from salt lakes in Tibet was exchanged for rice and barley from the middle hills region of Nepal. Wool, livestock and butter were also traded for sugar, tea, spices, tobacco and manufactured goods from India, but the salt-grain trade dominated the economy. This trade has diminished not only because of the political and economic changes in Tibet, but also because Indian salt is now available through Nepal at a price much cheaper than Tibetan salt. Indian salt, from the sea, contains iodine. Many people in Nepal once suffered from goitres caused by the total absence of iodine in their diet. Indian aid programmes financially assisted the distribution of sea salt in a successful program to prevent goitres – but the Tibetan salt trade suffered because of the artificially low prices of Indian salt.

The Thakali people of the Kali Gandaki Valley had a monopoly on the salt trade of this region. They are now turning to agriculture, tourism and other forms of trade for their livelihood. They are traditionally excellent businessmen and hoteliers and have created hotels, inns and other businesses throughout Nepal. Their religion is a mixture of Buddhism, Hinduism and ancient shamanistic and anamistic cults, but they claim to be more Hindu than Buddhist. There are few mani walls or religious monuments along the Kali Gandaki, although there are large gompas in Tukche and Kobang. Despite their trade with Tibet, the Thakalis are not of Tibetan ancestry; they are related to the Tamangs, Gurungs and Magars.

Tukche, elevation 2590 metres, was once the most important Thakali village. Tukche ('Tuk' – grain and 'che' – flat place). It was the meeting place where traders coming from Tibet and the upper Thak Khola Valley with salt and wool bartered with traders carrying grain from the south. The hotels in Tukche are in beautiful old Thakali homes; the *Himali, Usha, Laxmi* and *Sunil* lodges are all good. At the north end of town the *Yak Hotel* advertises a 'real yak on display inside' – it's worth a look. The economic effect of the loss of the grain trade has not been entirely offset by tourism; many people have moved out of Tukche. A walk along the back streets of the village, particularly close to the river, will reveal many abandoned and crumbling buildings behind the prosperous facade of the main street.

As the trail proceeds north, it passes an agricultural project established in 1966 by His Majesty's Government to introduce new produce into the region. It may be possible to purchase fresh fruits, vegetables and almonds here. Local apple cider and fruit preserves are available in Marpha and Tukche, and so, of course, is excellent apple, apricot and peach rakshi.

Between the agricultural project and Marpha is *Om's Home*, a very clean hotel that has excellent food and facilities ranging from rooms with attached baths for Rs 30 to less fancy rooms for Rs 20 and Rs 10.

A dramatic change in the vegetation, from pine and conifer forests to dry, arid desert-like country takes place during this stretch of trail. The flow of air between the peaks of Annapurna and Dhaulagiri creates strong winds that howl up the valley. The breezes blow gently from the north during the early hours of the day, then shift to powerful guests from the south throughout the late morning and afternoon. From here to Jomsom these strong winds will be blowing dust and sand at your back after about 11 am.

From Tukche the trail follows the river valley northward to Marpha, a village huddled behind a ridge for protection from the wind and dust. This is a large Thakali village, at 2665 metres elevation, that exhibits the typical architecture of flat roofs and narrow paved alleys and passageways. The very limited rainfall in this region makes these flat roofs practical; they also serve as a drying place for grains and vegetables. In Marpha the Thakali inn system has reached its highest level of development – private rooms, menus, room service and indoor toilets; it is a clean and pleasant village. There is an extensive drainage system that flows under the flagstone-paved street, there are impressive kanis at both ends of Marpha and the gompa has recently been totally refurbished and painted. The *Dhaulagiri Lodge* and *Baba's Lodge* have elaborate carved windows, comfortable inner courtyards and good toilet facilities. *Bhakti's Lodge* can be identified by its plastic signboard.

Across the river from Marpha is the village of Chaira, a Tibetan settlement with a carpet factory. Traders from Chaira often sit along the trail near Marpha selling their wares. Pause a minute along this part of the trail and observe the scenery – high snow peaks, brown and yellow cliffs, splashes of bright green irrigated fields and flat-roofed mud houses clustered here and there. Except for the height of the peaks, this country is almost identical to central Afghanistan; it is eerie to find such similarity in a place so distant both physically and culturally.

Marpha may be a better choice than Jomsom for a night stop (or you can take it easy and spend a night at Tukche and then go on to Jomsom). It is a bit far, but not unreasonable to reach Muktinath in a single day from Marpha, though it would be more interesting to break the trip up with a stop at Kagbeni. From Marpha the trail continues along the side of the valley, climbing imperceptibly, to Jomsom.

Jomsom (or more correctly Dzongsam or 'new fort'), the administrative headquarters for the region, straddles the Kali Gandaki at an elevation of 2713 metres. It is inhabited by government officials and merchants engaged in the distribution of goods brought by plane and pony caravans. From Jomsom an easy side trip may be made to the gompa at Thini, about an hour from Jomsom on the east bank of the Kali Gandaki. Jomsom is in three separate parts: the section on the east bank of the river is the main part of the town, with dwellings, the *Nilgiri Lodge*, a bank and the post office; on the west bank are shops, bhattis, the telegraph office and a bakery; to the south, near the airport, are large hotels, restaurants and the RNAC office. The *Lali Guras*, the *Moonlight* and the *Alaka Hotels* are all situated here. Just north of the airport is an army post and the inevitable police checkpost. If you have come from Manang it is important to obtain the endorsement of this station on your trekking permit, because it will be required by all police posts to the south. There is a bit of incongruity to the power lines and electric lights and the military people jogging in the mornings in this remote location.

Flights to Jomsom are notoriously unreliable because the wind makes flying impossible after 10 or 11 am. Kathmandu is often fogbound until 10 am during the winter season, so flight departures are delayed. When the combination of unfavourable weather conditions at both Kathmandu and Jomsom makes flights impossible for several days, the crush of local people and trekkers waiting for planes in Jomsom can become intolerable. It is a far better choice to walk back to Pokhara than to rely on good weather allowing flights to maintain their schedule. With light porter loads and long days it is possible – though not particularly pleasant – to reach Pokhara in four days or less. Several times a week there are two flights a day from Jomsom to Pokhara. Because there is no fog problem in Pokhara these flights arrive early enough to beat the winds and are more reliable (and cheaper – US$40 instead of US$65) than a direct flight to Kathmandu.

Day 7: Jomsom-Muktinath

From Jomsom the trail follows the broad river valley, sometimes above the river, but mostly along the west bank of the river itself as it passes beneath vertical rock cliffs, then crosses the river and continues up the valley to Chhancha Lhumba, the site of the *Eklai Bhatti* ('alone hotel') at 2370 metres.

Unless you are in a tremendous rush, you should take a side trip to Kagbeni. From Chhancha Lhumba the trail follows the river to Kagbeni at 2810 metres, a green oasis at the junction of the Jhong Khola and the Kali Gandaki. Kagbeni looks like a town out of the mediaeval past, with closely packed mud houses, dark alleys, imposing chortens and a large ochre coloured gompa perched above. The people dress in typical Tibetan clothing, though the children have, even in this remote village, learned to beg, rather insistently, for candy. Kagbeni is the northernmost village that foreigners are allowed to visit in this valley; the police checkpost here prevents tourists from proceeding towards Lo Monthang, the

walled city of Mustang. The *New Annapurna Lodge* in the centre of the village has inexpensive dormitory accommodation, also apple pie, mustang coffee and a sun terrace.

From Kagbeni the trail makes a steep climb up the Jhong Khola Valley, climbing past hundreds of small piles of rocks made by pilgrims to honour their departed ancestors, joining the direct trail to Muktinath below Khingar.

The direct route to Muktinath climbs immediately upon leaving Chhancha Lhumba to a plateau above the Kali Gandaki and then turns east up the Jhong Khola Valley. The trail climbs to Khingar through country that is arid and desert-like, in the same geographical and climatic zone as Tibet. The striking yellows of the bare hillsides contrast dramatically with the blue sky, white peaks, and splashes of green where streams allow cultivation. The views of Dhaulagiri and Nilgiri are tremendous. The walk from Khingar (3200 metres) to Jharkot is a delightful walk amongst meadows, streams and poplar and fruit trees. There are often flocks of cranes in the area. The trail is now high above the Jhong Khola as it climbs to Jharkot, an impressive Tibetan village at 3500 metres. One of the hotels here offers solar-heated rooms. The village itself, with its picturesque kani is well worth exploring. There are some peach trees nearby; the seeds are ground up to make oil.

The trail then continues to climb to Muktinath at 3710 metres. The first part of Muktinath that you reach is called Ranipowa; here there is a large rest house for pilgrims and a host of hotels, bhattis and camping places. This area is often crowded with both pilgrims and foreign tourists. The Tibetan traders here are unrelenting in their efforts to convince you to buy their wares. One item that is unique in this region is black stones that, when broken open, reveal the fossilised remains of prehistoric ammonites, called *saligram*. They are overpriced, and you may be able to find some yourself between here and Jomsom, but you can always purchase them from these traders – and then curse yourself all the way back to Pokhara for carrying a rucksack full of rocks. Hindu pilgrims also purchase these ammonites because they represent the God Vishnu. They were formed about 130 million years ago.

The most colourful pilgrims to Muktinath are the ascetic *sadhus* whom you must have seen many times between Pokhara and here. They travel in various stages of undress, smear themselves with ash and often carry a three-pronged spear or *trisul*. A rupee or two donation to these holy men is not out of place. They are Shaivite mystics on a pilgrimage that, more often than not, began in the heat of southern India.

About 90 metres above Ranipowa are the temple and religious shrines of Muktinath. There are no hotels here and camping is not allowed. Muktinath is an important pilgrimage place for both Hindus and Buddhists. Situated in a grove of trees, the holy shrines at Muktinath include a Buddhist gompa and the pagoda-style temple of Jiwala Mayi, containing an image of Vishnu. This temple is surrounded by a wall from which 108 waterspouts cast in the shape of cows heads pour forth sacred water. Even more sacred is the water that issues from a rock inside an ancient temple situated a short distance below the pagoda. Inside this gompa behind a tattered curtain are small natural gas jets that produce a perpetual holy flame alongside a spring that is the source of the sacred water – an auspicious combination of earth, fire and water that is responsible for the religious importance of Muktinath. It is often possible to see Tibetan women with elaborate head-dresses embedded with priceless turquoise stones engaged in devotions at these shrines.

Perhaps the best description of Muktinath is the one on the signboard erected by the Ministry of Tourism at Jomsom:

> Muktinath is beautiful, calm and quiet, great and mysterious for pilgrims, decorated with god and goddess. Although you are kindly requested not to snap them.

ANNAPURNA SANCTUARY

The route to Annapurna Sanctuary (*Annapurna Deuthali* in Nepali), the site of the Annapurna South Face Base Camp is a spectacular short trek. Though it is not difficult, the route can become impassable because of snow and avalanches in winter. It is the only major trekking route in Nepal that has significant avalanche danger and it is imperative to inquire locally whether the trail is safe. Some trekkers have died, and others have been stranded in the sanctuary for days, because of avalanches. The route provides an interesting variety of terrain, from lowland villages where rice is grown to outstanding high mountain views. The trek from Pokhara to Annapurna base camp and back may be made in as few as 10 or 11 days, but it is best to allow two weeks for this trek to fully appreciate the high altitude scenery. A diversion from Ghandrung to Ghorapani on the return route provides a view of Dhaulagiri from Poon Hill.

Day 1: Pokhara-Dhampus

From Pokhara there are several choices of routes to Ghandrung. The first is to follow the trail towards Jomsom through Naud-anda to Chandrakot, then turn north up the Modi Khola Valley, descending and crossing the river on a small wooden bridge near the settlement of Sholebhati, then travelling north up the west bank of the Modi Khola, finally meeting the trail from Landrung and climbing up a stone staircase to Ghandrung. It takes 2½ to three days from Pokhara to Ghandrung.

The second option is to descend from Chandrakot to Birethanti, then proceed up the west bank of the Modi Khola all the way to Ghandrung. There is little to recommend this route over the first option, though there is better accommodation in Birethanti than most other places.

The third option, which is described here, requires two days to Ghandrung and is the most direct, though it involves more climbing than the other two choices. From Pokhara the trail begins near the Shining Hospital at the end of the paved road. See the first day of the Jomsom trek description for details of this portion. The trail to Dhampus leaves the Jomsom route at Phedi. To reach Dhampus, continue up the valley from Phedi; the trail leads off to the right. The valley is a maze of trails but you can spot the Dhampus trail coming down the hill and easily find it where it reaches the valley floor. Turning north, the trail climbs the ridge above the Yamdi Khola Valley. Starting in a forest that is so overgrazed that it looks like a manicured municipal park, the trail climbs steeply to the ridge at Dhampus, 1580 metres. From the ridge there are views of the mountains, and these continue to improve as you ascend along it. There are a few hotels at this end of Dhampus, including the Basanta Luxury Hotel, but it is a large village strung out over several km and there are other hotels about a half-hour walk from here at 1700 metres elevation.

Dhampus is the centre of the theft racket in this region and thieves often cut the tents of trekkers and remove valuable items during the night. It is best not to camp alone here; the trekking groups circle their tents like an old time wagon train and post a guard with a lighted lantern throughout the night. If you stay in a hotel, be sure that you know who is sharing the room with you and lock the door whenever you go out – even for a moment. The thieves do watch everyone in order to decide who has something worth taking or who is likely to be careless during the night. They will wait patiently all night to make their move if necessary.

Day 2: Dhampus-Ghandrung
From the grassy fields above Dhampus the trail climbs to Pothana, a bunch of

hotels that grew up around a new water pipe, then through forests to a clearing on top of the hill. Here, at a few deserted herders' huts at 2200 metres, there are great views of Annapurna South and Hiunchuli. The trail then makes a steep descent in forests alive with birds, ferns and orchids into a huge side canyon of the Modi Khola, finally reaching a single tea house at Bichok, then continuing the descent to the head of the canyon where the stream is crossed on a suspension bridge. The trail climbs gently out of the side canyon, passing another bhatti, emerging from the side canyon into the Modi Khola Valley where there are other bhattis. The trail crosses a dramatic slide area, a good example of the erosion that is resulting from the deforestation in Nepal, and descends further to Tolka, a small settlement with several bhattis at 1800 metres. In this region men hunt birds and wild goats with ancient muzzel-loading guns that look like leftovers from the American revolution. From Tolka the trail descends through forests, then fields, past some unusual oval-shaped houses, to the flagstone streets of Landrung, a Gurung village at 1650 metres. There are many hotels here, but most are small and a bit crummy. Along the trail and in the village it is likely that you will encounter people collecting money for schools. They will produce a ledger book showing the donations of other trekkers and enter your contribution into their records. They are legitimate, but it is an adult version of the creative begging that tourists have encouraged. From Landrung (some spell it Landruk) the trail descends steeply through fields of rice and millet to the river, crossing it at an elevation of 1370 metres on a suspension bridge. The trail then ascends steeply through cultivated fields and past a few scattered houses. The trail from Birethanti joins the route here; the climb continues on a seemingly endless set of stone stairs to Ghandrung, a huge Gurung village, at 2000 metres. This village is the second largest Gurung village in Nepal (the largest is Siklis), and is a confusing cluster of closely-spaced slate-roofed houses with neatly terraced fields situated both above and below the village. It is wonderfully easy to get lost in the maze of narrow alleyways while trying to get through the village. As you reach Ghandrung, stay to the left on the stone steps and you will find a set of signboards that describe the many facilities in town. There are hotels near here and a few inns below and to the north of the signboard, but the largest hotels are located near the top of the village – try taking the upper trail at every junction in the maze of narrow lanes. To find the trail to Annapurna Sanctuary, start from the signboard and descend to the school, then to the Shanti Hotel. Turn left along a lane in front of the hotel, take a right at the T intersection, and follow the stone pavement, neither climbing nor descending, as it leads out of town; it eventually becomes a trail that passes a few more houses outside of the main village of Ghandrung, then climbs around a large canyon.

Ghandrung has an extensive water supply system with tanks, pipes and taps throughout the village. There is a large handicraft factory at the top of Ghandrung, near the Himalayan Hotel. The views of Annapurna South (*Annapurna Dakshin*) from here are outstanding, and Machhapuchhare, seen from here in its fish tail aspect, peeps over a forested ridge. There is a way to get from Landrung directly to Chhomro, without climbing to Ghandrung, but the local people do not encourage its use because it avoids Ghandrung and Khumnu villages. It would be worth asking someone in Landrung about it if you want to take advantage of this short cut.

Day 3: Ghandrung-Chhomro

After winding its way through the village, the trail climbs towards a small creek, crosses it, and begins a climb among huge rocks to a pass north-west of the village. It crosses the pass (2220 metres), where a few houses and a tea shop offer refresh-ment, but no good accommodation. From the ridge, the trail descends very steeply to some stone lodges and a camping place beside the Khumnu Khola, crosses the stream at 1770 metres, then climbs on a stone staircase to the settlement of Khumnu (also called Kimrong) on the north side of the valley where there are two more lodges. A signboard here has the following times:

Kimrong-Chhomro 3 hours
Chhomro-Tibesa Danda 2½ hours
Tibesa Danda-Khuldi Ghar ¾ hours
Kuldi Ghar-doban 2 hours
Himalaya Hotel-Hinku ¾ hour
Hinku-Machhapuchhare base camp 3 hours

Climbing steeply, the trail regains the elevation lost from Ghandrung, then contours eastward out towards the Modi Khola, finally reaching a point about level with, and just north of, Ghandrung. This is the junction with the direct route from Landrung; there used to be a sign here. The trail to the Sanctuary turns north up the Modi Khola Valley and descends through light forests to Chhomro, a Gurung village at 1950 metres. This the highest permanent settlement in the valley, but herders take sheep and goats to high pastures in the valley during the summer. There is a tremendous view up the canyon to the north-west of Annapurna South, which seems to tower above the village, and there are good views of Machhapuchhare ('machha – fish and 'puchhare' – tail) across the valley. It is from this point and northwards that the reason for the name of this peak becomes apparent. Machhapuchhare was climbed to within 50 metres of its summit in 1957 by Wilfred Noyce and David Cox on one of the early expeditions in Nepal. The mountain is not now open to climbers, but a lower outlier to the south, Mardi Peak, elevation 5586 metres, is open to trekking parties. There is a huge hotel before the school; other hotels are down the stone staircase in the centre of the village. A Japanese man some years ago installed a miniature hydroelectric plant here and equipped the houses with tiny flashlight bulb lighting. The *Captain's Lodge* is Chhomro's most popular inn; all the hotels here have provision shops at which you can stock up on food for the trip into the sanctuary.

Day 4: Chhomro-Khuldi

Leaving Chhomro, the trail descends and crosses the Chhomro Khola on a new suspension bridge, then climbs out of the side valley in which Chhomro is situated. Climbing high above the Modi Khola on its west bank, the trail passes through forests of rhododendron and oak. In Sinwa is the *Maya Hotel*; the *Hotel High Cliff*, a branch of the Chhomro Captain's Lodge, is located in Tibesa Danda, also known as Naya Khuldi. It is a short distance to the British sheep breeding project at Khuldi (2380 metres) where the *Namaste Lodge* occupies a stone house. The bamboo forests beyond Khuldi are dense, though the trees are hacked down to make dokos, the woven baskets carried by porters, and mats for floors and roofs. In winter it is common to encounter snow anywhere from this point on. It is about a half hour down a muddy trail to the *Bamboo Hotel*. In early fall and late spring this part of the trail is crawling with leeches.

Day 5: Khuldi-Hinko

The trail climbs steeply through bamboo forests, then through rhododendron forest up the side of the canyon, occasionally dropping slightly to cross tributary streams, but generally climbing continuously. When there is snow, this stretch of trail is particularly difficult, because the bamboo lying hidden on the trail beneath the snow provides an excellent start to a slide downhill. At Doban, about two hours beyond Kuldi, there is a small bamboo hotel in a setting reminiscent of a Japanese watercolour painting. Beyond Doban the

trail climbs up and down across several avalanche chutes to the Himalaya Hotel, situated in a small clearing. It is then about a one-hour walk to Hinko, at 3020 metres. This is often called 'Hinko Cave' because a huge overhanging rock provides some protection above a small camping spot; there is no hotel here. There is no wood at Hinko or beyond, so fuel, whether wood, kerosene or gas, should be carried from below for the entire time that you plan to stay in this region.

Day 6: Hinko-Annapurna Sanctuary

The trail crosses a ravine just beyond Hinko, then climbs through large boulders as the valley widens and becomes less steep. The 'gates' to the sanctuary may be seen ahead, and they are soon passed at about 3570 metres. There are places to camp here, but it can be dangerous in winter and spring due to avalanches. Avalanches from Hiunchuli and Annapurna South, peaks which are above but unseen from this point, come crashing into the valley with unbelievable speed and frequency. More than one party has been forced to retreat from the approach to the sanctuary because of deep snows and continual avalanches.

As the trail continues into the sanctuary it crosses two wide avalanche tracks on a narrow trail that huddles up against the cliffs. The valley widens and reaches Deorali, a small bamboo shack that calls itself the *Hotel Mayalu Lodge* and a dirty campsite, then descends to meet the Modi Khola and follows it to Bagara, another bamboo hotel. The accommodation here is on the bamboo floor of one of the *Hotel Annapurna's* two rooms. The route then climbs across more avalanche paths to several inns at 'Machhapuchhare base camp'. These hotels may or may not be open, depending on whether the innkeeper – and his supplies – have been able to reach the hotel through the avalanche area. The food and accommodation in the sanctuary is primitive for this reason; it will mostly be *bhaat* and potatoes, not the fancy items served lower down. Most of the inns here close during the coldest winter months; they are all operated by people from Chhomro, so you can easily find out in advance which, if any, are open. An hour beyond here is another lodge and there are two more facilities with tarps for roofs at what is called Annapurna Base Camp, the base camp for the 1970 Annapurna South Face expedition. This climb, led by Chris Bonnington, was the most spectacular ascent of an 8000-metre peak, up the near-vertical south face of Annapurna that towers above the sanctuary to the north-west.

A number of peaks accessible from the sanctuary are open to trekking parties, *Tent Peak* (5500 metres) offers a commanding 360-degree view of the entire sanctuary, and its higher neighbour Fluted Peak (*Singu Chuli*, 6390 metres) offers a mountaineering challenge. *Hiunchuli* (6441 metres) to the south is also open to trekking parties that have made prior application to the Nepal Mountaineering Association and paid the appropriate fee. All three of these peaks are significant mountaineering challenges and require skill, equipment and advance planning. There are few birds in the sanctuary, but there are ghoral, Himalayan weasel and pika.

GHORAPANI TO GHANDRUNG

It is a long, though not difficult, day (except when the trail is covered by snow) from Ghorapani to Ghandrung. Local people almost never use this trail, but it is becoming an increasingly important trekking route and there has been overwhelming and uncontrolled development of the area in the past few years, including the chopping down of large parts of what used to be an unbroken stretch of rhododendron forest wilderness. From Ghorapani the trail climbs to the pass at Deorali, then turns south on a muddy trail through deep forests, finally emerging on a grassy knoll that offers good mountain views, including a view of Machhapuchhare, which is not visible from Ghorapani Pass, and a panorama all the way south to the plains of India. It is the same view as Poon Hill. The trail then descends along the ridge and drops into a canyon to two inns at a second place called Deorali. The trail follows a stream, and the mountains are hidden behind a ridge as the route makes a steep, sometimes treacherous, descent on a narrow trail alongside the stream, which has become a series of waterfalls. The steep descent becomes more gentle as the route reaches Bahunthanti, five recently constructed hotels in the lee of a huge rock face. The tables and benches outside the lodges here present a scene reminiscent of a ski lodge – especially when there is snow. (This is not the same Bahunthanti that is between Ulleri and Ghorapani.) The trail then leaves the moist high mountain forests and enters a field of cane, climbing to a vantage point that offers a brief view of the mountains, then descends again steeply to a stream before climbing again through forests to Tada Pani, four hotels with a spectacular view at 2530 metres.

From Tada Pani there is a trail to the left that descends through forests, then through terraced fields, to Khumnu Khola, providing a direct route to the Annapurna Sanctuary.

The Ghandrung trail descends steeply from Tada Pani through forests to a clearing with two hotels; this spot is yet a third Deorali. A short steep descent in rocks leads to a stream crossing, then the route continues less steeply past other streams, finally leading out on a ridge towards Ghandrung, entering the village near the tin-roofed handicraft factory, then descending on stone steps into the maze of the village itself. The first hotels that you encounter from this direction are the *Himalayan Hotel* and the *Gorkha Lodge*, both very heavy advertisers along the trail – you can't miss them. There are other hotels at the south end of the village where the trail to Landrung begins.

TREK AROUND ANNAPURNA

It takes a minimum of 18 days to trek around the entire Annapurna massif, visiting the Tibet-like country on the north slopes of the Himalaya and the dramatic Kali Gandaki gorge. The route to Manang was opened for the first time to trekkers in April 1977 although a few expeditions and scientific parties visited the region in the 1950s.

The last seven days of this trek are the popular Jomsom Trek from Pokhara. This is described from Pokhara to Jomsom in another section; you will have to read that part backwards when you get there.

It is best to cross Thorung Pass, 5416 metres, from *east to west*, as shown in this route description. Here's why: there are no camping spots or water sources on the west side of the pass from a meadow above

Muktinath at 4100 metres, to a spot two to three hours beyond the pass on the Manang side at 4510 metres, if you travel in the *reverse* direction. This means that you have to make a 1300-metre climb plus at least a 900-metre descent in a single day – an impossibility for many people, especially if they are unacclimatised. From Manang to Muktinath the pass is not difficult, but you should be aware of the possibility of returning to Dumre if it is impossible or dangerous to cross Thorung La because of snow or altitude sickness. There are years where the weather is unusual but Thorung La should be considered snowbound and closed from mid-December to mid-April.

Clothing and equipment for porters must be a prime consideration if you are taking them over the Thorung La. Many

lowland porters from Dumre have suffered frostbite or snowblindness on this pass because trekkers (and their sherpas) have not provided the proper footgear, clothing and – most important – sunglasses for the pass. Porters from near-tropical villages like Dumre have no idea what to expect on a snow-covered pass and join a trekking party clad only in cotton clothing. If you employ porters for a crossing of Thorung La you incur both a moral and legal obligation for their safety and well being.

Day 1: Kathmandu-Turture (by road maybe)
The trek begins with a 135-km drive (that takes about five hours on the narrow road) from Kathmandu to Dumre. Leaving the Kathmandu Valley, the road descends from the Chandragiri Pass on a wild series of steep switch-backs along the narrow Indian-built Tribhuvan Rajpath. It then continues south through cultivated fields to Naubise, 26 km from Kathmandu. At Naubise the Ariniko Rajpath, completed in 1971 with Chinese assistance begins. The Tribhuvan Rajpath continues south from this point and winds its way to the Indian border at Birganj. The Chinese road heads east along the Mahesh Khola to its confluence with the Trisuli River. It then follows the Trisuli Valley to Mugling, elevation 220 metres, at the confluence of the Trisuli and Marsyandi rivers 110 km from Kathmandu.

The large river thus formed flows south to become the Narayani River, one of the major sources of the Ganges. Most rafting in Nepal is done on this stretch of river, finally emerging at one of the game parks in Royal Chitwan National Park. A new road follows the Narayani Valley south from Mugling to join the East-West highway at Narayanghat in the terai. Twenty-five km beyond Mugling, on the banks of the Marsyandi River, is Dumre, a new village that was settled by Newars from the nearby town of Bandipur after the completion of the Kathmandu-Pokhara road.

At an elevation of 440 metres, Dumre exists because it used to be at the beginning of trails that lead both to Gorkha, a day's walk away, and to the Marsyandi Valley and Manang. Most of the village consists of warehouses, shops and bhattis serving porters who carry loads from the roadhead to remote villages; there are also a few hotels catering to trekkers. A 41-km-long motor road is under construction from Dumre to Besi Sahar (sometimes called Lamjung), the headquarters of the Lamjung District. In 1984 the road had reached Besi Sahar, but was unpaved and therefore impassable. The only transport available on the first part of the road was a single four-wheel-drive truck and a few farm tractors and these could usually travel only as far as Turture, 18 km from Dumre. Besi Sahar is said to be two hours' drive from Turture, but this is probably overstated because of poor road conditions. When you read this, the road may have been completed, but construction of this road is proceeding very slowly, so it will probably remain a rough mud track for several years. If it is passable, you should be able to take a jeep or bus to Besi Sahar and save a day of walking. If not, the following section describes the route and suggests an alternative route on the other side of the river starting from Philesangu that avoids the hot, dusty and boring road.

After crossing the Nahala Khola, the trail begins in level country, passing through terraced rice fields and small villages inhabited by Newars, Brahmins and Chhetris. There is a gradual ascent to Bhansar (530 metres), then the trail continues to ascend gradually to the top of a ridge. From here there is a good view of the Marsyandi and Chyanglitar valleys, a large flat expanse of rice fields and sub-tropical forests. The trail then makes a short, steep descent to the west bank of the Marsyandi at 460 metres and follows the river upstream through a region dotted with chautaaras, resting places under the shade of huge banyan and pipal trees. These trees, planted centuries ago,

Top: Makalu (8463 metres) and Chamlang from Gorlekharka (SA)
Left: The chain bridge over the Tamba Kosi near Bigute (SA)
Right: Ama Dablam (elevation 6856 metres) (SA)

Top: A sherpa cook packing provisions for a group trek (SA)
Left: Porters often carry more than food and equipment (Christine Kolisch)
Right: Porters en route from Pheriche to Phalang Karpo (SA)

have broad leaves and branches that extend outwards for a long distance in mushroom fashion, offering welcome shade to travellers. It was under a banyan tree (also called a bodi tree) that Buddha attained enlightenment in India, over 2000 years ago. The banyan, a related species to the pipal tree, can be differentiated from the latter by the long roots that droop down from the limbs, a peculiarity of the banyan. Around the huge shade trees have been built walls and chautaaras, stone benches, for porters to rest their loads upon as they pause during the hot steep climbs. Many people build a chautaara in the name of a deceased relative.

A short distance on, from the town of Chambas, at 500 metres elevation, there are good views of the high Himalaya, especially Baudha (6672 metres) and Himalchuli (7893 metres). A short descent and another climb brings the trail to Turture (530 metres), a small boom town that has developed to serve trekkers on the Manang route and to provide facilities for construction workers on the Besi Sahar road. The *Hotel Beauty* is the best facility in town. The village is above the river, overlooking Palangtar, the airport that is called Gorkha. Gorkha is the major town in the central hills region and is the site of the ancient palace of King Prithvi Narayan Shah, the founder of modern Nepal. Palangtar airport is no longer served by scheduled flights because the new roads in this region have made flying unnecessary. It is about a two-day walk from Palangtar to Gorkha.

Day 2: Turture-Besi Sahar

Descending to the banks of the Marsyandi River and following it upstream, the trail reaches a large suspension bridge near Tarkughat, a fair-sized bazaar on the east bank at 490 metres elevation. The route to Manang does not cross the bridge, but stays on the west bank of the river, following the motor road upstream through fairly level country, crossing the Paundi

Khola, elevation 505 metres, at an excellent spot for swimming. There is now a long, straight and hot stretch of road that passes through Shurebas before reaching the small village of Bhote Odar at 550 metres. The *Hotel Marsyandi* has rooms for Rs 15 per night and has good cement toilet and bath facilities. The road deteriorates here as it climbs over a ridge, passing Udipu at 730 metres and descends to the Thakali bazaar of Philesangu at 670 metres.

At Philesangu there is a bridge perched high above a narrow wooded gorge. By crossing the Marsyandi on this bridge a side trip to Bara Pokhari may be made. Bara Pokhari is a high-altitude lake (elevation 3100 metres) offering outstanding views of Manaslu, Himalchuli and Baudha. The trip requires a long steep climb, but it may be made in as few as three days, departing from the main trail at Phalesangu and rejoining the trail to Manang below Usta on Day 2.

The bridge at Phalesangu also provides access to an alternative route that avoids the motor road. From the east side of the bridge at Phalesangu a trail climbs to Chiti, then follows the river valley north through sal forests and rice terraces to Chaur, elevation 760 metres, where the route enters a sugar cane-growing region. From Chaur (also called Simbachaur) the trail stays near the river, crosses the Bhachok Khola, and climbs through Baragaon, elevation 910 metres, and over a ridge before descending to Bhulbule where it joins the route described below.

From Philesangu the motor road makes a few small ascents and descents and fords a lot of small streams before reaching Besi Sahar, situated on a plateau at 790 metres. Here is the first of many police checkposts, radio and watch repair facilities, shops selling Chinese and Japanese goods, and some trekkers' hotels. Above Besi Sahar to the west is Gaonsahar (elevation 1370 metres), where there are the remains of an old fortress and palace. From the 15th to 18th centuries this region was a collection of independent kingdoms that continually waged war on each other. Lamjung, the principality ruled from this palace, was finally absorbed into the kingdom of Gorkha in 1782.

Day 3: Besi Sahar-Lampata

From Besi Sahar the trail makes a steep descent of about 150 metres followed by an equally steep climb through the deep river gorge. It is a long walk with several ups and downs through rice fields, subtropical forests and small hamlets to Khudi, 790 metres elevation, a mixture of tin and thatch roofed houses clustered around the anchors of a long sagging suspension bridge. Take the old bridge; the new one is a long way upstream. There are a few rudimentary bhattis and shops here but in 1983 there was no trekkers' hotel. The best camp is at the school, 10 minutes beyond the village.

Khudi is a Gurung village, the first to be encountered on the trek. Most of the wide river valley below Khudi is inhabited by Brahmins and Chhetris, although Gurung villages are found in the side valleys and slopes above the river. Gurungs are known largely for their service as soldiers in the Gurkha regiments of both the British and Indian Armies, as well as the Royal Nepal Army and police. It is not unusual to encounter ex-soldiers on the trail who have served in Malaysia, Singapore, Hong Kong and Britain; the stories of their exploits – in excellent English – provide fascinating trailside conversations. An important source of income in most Gurung villages is the salaries and pensions of those in military service. The remaining income is from herding – particularly sheep – and from agriculture – rice, wheat, corn, millet and potatoes.

Gurungs are Mongoloid in their features, and the men are easily recognised by their traditional dress of a short blouse tied across the front and a short skirt of white cotton material, or often a towel, wrapped around their waist and held by a wide belt.

The Gurung funeral traditions and dance performances (the latter staged at the slightest excuse) are particularly interesting, and it is often possible to witness such aspects of Gurung life during a trek in this region – with a running commentary by an elderly English-speaking ex-Gurkha Captain who will explain the rituals and regale trekkers with long, involved stories of his World War I and II campaigns in France, Germany, Italy and North Africa.

The trail continues northward up the Marsyandi Valley, with Himalchuli and Peak 29 (also known as Manaslu II and now renamed Ngadi Chuli, 7879 metres) dominating the horizon, then crosses the river on a suspension bridge at Bhulbule, elevation 825 metres. The *Hotel Arjun*, which looks like a Spanish hacienda, is just across the bridge on the right; the other major hotel here is the *Hotel Manang*. There are shops and even a tailor near the bridge. The trail now travels up the east bank of the river, past a beautiful waterfall 60 metres high surrounded by pandanus or screwpine, a tropical tree, then through small villages scattered amongst extensive rice terraces. Beyond Bhulbule there are good views of Manaslu (8162 metres) and Peak 29. At the small stone settlement of Ngadi there are several hotels run by Manangis; this used to be only a winter settlement before trekkers came to the region. Beyond Ngadi the trail crosses the Ngadi Khola on a long new suspension bridge at 880 metres elevation. It is amazing to see the extensive public works programme in the hills of Nepal – the steel cables and towers for this bridge, for example, had to be carried for several days. There are thousands of bridges throughout the country in unbelievably remote locations that have required huge expenditures of time and money for their construction. It is all too easy to see only the undeveloped aspect of Nepal and ignore the progress that has been made in the last 30 years to develop an extensive network of trails and bridges.

Above the Ngadi Khola is the village of Usta; the trail from Bara Pokhari rejoins the route to Manang here. After the bridge there is a trail junction; there is a pipal tree on the left and a stone dharamsala or rest house on the right. Just beyond these landmarks take the trail to the left; the right trail goes up the Ngadi Khola, not to Manang. Climbing steadily through scrub forests, the trail finally enters a horseshoe-shaped village. This is Lampata, elevation 1135 metres, a Mamangi village with Tibetan-style prayer flags. There are better hotels here than in Bahundanda. The flocks of birds in the ricefields are slaty-headed parakeets.

Day 4: Bahundanda-Chyanje

It isn't far from Lampata to Bahundanda, a picturesque village situated at 1310 metres in a saddle on a long ridge. The school here is nestled in a grove of bamboo; there are a few shops and bhattis and a Brahmin hotel. Bahundanda ('Hill of the Brahmins') is the northernmost Brahmin settlement in the valley. If you are camping, this may be a better choice than Lampata.

The trail descends steeply past amphitheatre-shaped rice terraces, across a stream and across a large slide area to Khane, 1180 metres, high above the river. Continuing in and out of side canyons, the trail drops to a long suspension bridge at 1070 metres. There are shops and two hotels, the *Sonam* and *Karma*, in the village of Syange on the west bank of the river. Beyond Syange the trail climbs high above the river on a somewhat terrifying trail carved into near-vertical cliffs forested with rhododendron and pine and festooned with healthy crops of stinging nettles and marijuana. Because of the steep terrain, the villages in this region are small and infrequent. In 1950, when Tilman visited Manang, this portion of the trail did not exist. Instead, the route followed a series of wooden galleries tied to the face of the rock cliffs alongside the river. At 1070 metres is the village of Jagat, which is

inhabited, as are most villages in this region, by people of Tibetan stock. There are shops and hotels in Jagat but they are small, dirty and depressing; the stone village has a mediaeval atmosphere. From Jagat the trail climbs through forests to Chyamje, 1400 metres. The *Tibetan Hotel* in Chyamje has bins of roasted soybeans, *chiuraa*, and popcorn – a good place to load up on trail snacks. There is a place to camp just across the suspension bridge on the west side of the river at Sattale, 1430 metres elevation.

Day 5: Chyanje-Bagarchhap

The path is rough and rocky in this portion and passes under a huge boulder that forms a tunnel over the trail. There are lots of lizards in this region as well as more stinging nettles. Following the east bank of the Marsyandi the trail climbs gradually except where it is necessary to cross steep ridges, but it is a long uphill climb. The valley suddenly opens into a large plateau. In this picturesque setting, at the foot of a large waterfall, is the village of Tal, 1675 metres elevation. There are three or four Manangi hotels here arranged so that they look like an old American pony express outpost. The trek has now entered the Manang district. The village is the southernmost in Manang and is in a region called Gyasumdo, one of three distinct divisions within Manang. Gyasumdo was once highly dependent on trade with Tibet. Since the disruption of this trade in 1959, herding and agriculture have assumed greater importance. Corn, barley, wheat, buckwheat and potatoes are grown in this region, which has enough warm weather and rainfall to produce two crops a year. The people of Gyasumdo used to hunt musk deer, and the sale of musk was once an important source of income and trade. Although they are Buddhists, the people throughout Manang slaughter animals and hunt in the nearby hills, unlike other Buddhists who have strict taboos against the taking of life.

The trail crosses the broad flat valley

that was once a lake (Tal means 'lake'), through fields of corn, barley and potatoes, then climbs steeply on a stone staircase high above the river, finally cresting on a spur at 1860 metres and descending on a staircase-like trail to Orad. The trail then makes some significant ups and downs before descending to a suspension bridge at 1850 metres. Just before the bridge is a tiny hot spring that flows from a fissure near the trail; you can take a bath if you have a cup. The forests in this steep valley are mostly blue pine. The trail climbs from the bridge to an unpainted stone archway, or kani, that marks the entrance to Dharapani, elevation 1890 metres. All the old villages from here to Kagbeni have these entrance chortens at both ends of the village; the kanis get more elaborate and picturesque as the Tibetan influence becomes stronger in each successive village. There is a police checkpost here and there are hotels in the village; the large *Dharapani Hotel* is about 10 minutes beyond. From Dharapani the trail passes a school and climbs over a spur before descending to Bagarchhap. The villagers in this region recently made extensive trail renovations, and the route to Manang was graded and widened to allow horse and mule caravans to transport supplies to these remote villages – though you may not believe this as you walk the rough trails. The catch, of course, is that the Tal-to-Dharapani trail is still too steep and narrow for horses. Across the Marsyandi, just beyond Dharapani, is a long covered bridge. This leads to Thonje, an important village at the junction of the Marsyandi and the Dudh Khola. It is not necessary to go to Thonje en route to Manang. There is a police checkpost in Thonje controlling the route up the valley that leads to the Larkya La.

The trail turns into the east-west Manang Valley in a forest of blue pine, spruce, hemlock, maple and oak. The jay-like bird that you see is the nutcracker; it eats the seeds from the blue pine cones. Bagarchhap, at 2160 metres, is the first village on the trek with typical Tibetan architecture – closely-spaced stone houses with flat roofs piled high with firewood. The village is in a transition zone between the dry upper Marsyandi and the wet regions of the lower valley, so there are also a large number of sloping wooden shingle roofs. Higher in the Marsyandi and Kali Gandaki valleys where there is little rainfall, the shingle roofs disappear, the houses are packed even closer together, and all have flat roofs. The well-maintained whitewashed Diki Gompa in Bagarchhap contains many Tibetan Buddhist paintings and statues and the *Pearly Gates* hotel offers 'heavenly food and lodging'. From here the trail travels west up the Manang Valley with the high Himalayan peaks to the south; there are occasional glimpses of Lamjung and Annapurna II (7937 metres) through the trees. To the east, Manaslu provides a dramatic backdrop to the tree-filled valley.

Day 6: Bagarchhap-Chame

Much of the Manang Valley is virgin forest of pine and fir, but construction of new houses and the constant requirements of firewood are encouraging people to cut down many of these fine trees. On the trail to Manang there is much evidence of this cutting: huge piles of firewood are stacked alongside the path and great timbers are being hauled to homesites.

The trail climbs along the new mule track through forests to Danejung (also called Syal Khola, 'the river of jackals', and sometimes called Tibang Phedi, 'lower Tibang'), a new settlement (elevation 2290 metres) inhabited by people from Bagarchhap. The Gurung Furniture Factory is located here. From this village a trail leads to Tibang, 2600 metres, and climbs over Namun bhanjyang (5784 metres) en route to Ghanpokhara in the south. This was the old route to Manang; it is now rarely used except by herders. Namun bhanjyang is a difficult route because there is no food or shelter for four days.

Climbing further, the trail continues to

be rough and rocky. Suddenly a broad level stretch of trail appears. There is a fine wooden bridge near a waterfall and the trail is supported by outstanding stonework for about 100 metres, then it degenerates again to a rock-strewn path. Construction projects, including trail construction, are allocated to local contractors; it is interesting to note the obvious difference in workmanship amongst contractors, even in such a remote locale. Climbing further, the route reaches Tyanja, also called Nattamarang, elevation 2360 metres. There is a small and dirty bhatti here. There is a tiny hot spring across the river, but it is hard to get to.

The track stays near the river in forests of oak and maple, climbing and descending amongst river-worn boulders, then crosses a large stream before reaching Kopar (2590 metres), situated in a meadow surrounded by huge pine and spruce trees. This is a police checkpost controlling access to the Nar-phu Valley to the north. That remote Valley, populated by only 850 people, is one of the three regions of Manang. It has a heritage and traditions different from that of other parts of the district. The region is closed to foreigners. Kopar is the site of the *Mustang Lodge*, which has a disco and a dancing girl (who is 10 years old).

The next village is Chame (2685 metres), the administrative headquarters for the Manang district. Here there is a wireless station, school, several shops, a health post, post office, police checkpost and bank amongst the closely-spaced stone dwellings. The incongruity of a shotgun-toting guard in front of the bank is almost worth a picture. The *Kamala Lodge* is the most popular trekkers' hotel; there are also several others to choose from. Across the river there are two small hot springs; they are not big enough for swimming, however. Throughout the day there are views of Lamjung Himal (6986 metres), Annapurna II (7937 metres) and Annapurna IV (7525 metres).

From Chame the trail crosses a side stream, and then the Marsyandi itself on a cantilevered wooden bridge, passes by a few houses and the Kesang Lodge and Chhiring Lodge on the north side of the river, and proceeds through fields of barley to Talung (2775 metres). After passing a huge new apple orchard surrounded by a high wooden fence (apples are available everywhere in the region), the trail descends to a bridge at 2840 metres. The village just above this bridge, Brathang, used to be a Khampa settlement, although it is now largely abandoned. The Khampas had installed a gate on the bridge, thus controlling the traffic up and down the Manang Valley; you can still see the remnants of the gate. In Brathang, there is a small carved stone that is a memorial to a Japanese climber who died in an avalanche while trekking across the Thorung La – a grisly reminder to wait several days after any heavy snowstorm before attempting the pass.

Day 7: Chame-Pisang

The valley is steep and narrow here and the trail is in deep forests. It crosses the river on an extremely long cantilevered bridge at 2910 metres, then climbs steeply through forests of birch and juniper on the river's north bank to another bridge at 3040 metres. Here there is the first view of the dramatic Paungda Danda rock face, a tremendous curved slab of rock rising more than 1500 metres from the river. There are also views of Annapurna II to the south and Pisang peak to the north-east. Continuing, climbing over a ridge, the trail continues the steep ascent to the upper Marsyandi Valley. The lower portion of Pisang, a cluster of houses near the bridge, is at an elevation of 3200 metres. Note the wooden canals for water to drive the two mills in this village. There are many hotels here; the *Tourist Cottage*, the first hotel on the right, is the nicest. A long new mani wall has been erected here. The main village of Pisang is across the bridge and 100 metres uphill. There are excellent camping places in the forest on the south bank of the river.

Day 8: Pisang-Manang

The trek is now in the region known as Nyesyang, the upper portion of the Manang district, comprising about 5000 inhabitants in six major villages. The region is much drier than the Gyasumdo region down the valley. There is only a small amount of rainfall here during the monsoon because the Annapurna range to the south alters the climate significantly from that of the rest of Nepal, south of the Himalaya. The people of Nyesyang raise wheat, barley, buckwheat, potatoes and beans, but the cold, almost arid, climate limits them to single crop annually. They keep herds of yaks, goats, cows and horses. Horses are an important means of transportation in the relatively flat upper portion of Manang Valley and are often used as pack animals and by riders as high as 5416 metres, over the Thorung La between Manang and Jomsom.

An interesting situation exists in Nyesyang as a result of special trading privileges the people enjoy through a decree of King Rana Bahadur Shah in the year 1784. These facilities included passports and import and export concessions not available to the general population of Nepal. Beginning long ago with the export of live dogs, goat and sheep skins, yaks tails, herbs, and musk, the trade has now expanded into the large scale import of electronic goods, cameras, watches, silk, clothing gems and other high-value items in exchange for gold, silver, turquoise and other resources available in Manang. The trade network of the Manang people extends throughout South-East Asia and as far away as Korea; it is not uncommon to see large groups of Manang people jetting to Bangkok, Singapore and Hong Kong. Many people in Nyesyang villages speak fluent English and dress in trendy western clothing purchased during overseas trading excursions, presenting an incongruous picture

as they herd yaks and plow the fields of these remote villages. This exposure also makes them shrewd and eager businessmen, so the traders and shops of Manang are all expensive. There are few bargains to be had here. If you travelled from Hong Kong or Bangkok, perhaps you saw Tibetan-looking people all dressed in identical jogging suits and carrying identical luggage; these people were Manangi's returning from a shopping expedition.

A short distance beyond Pisang the trail climbs a steep ridge that extends across the valley. At the top of this spur is an excellent view of Manang Valley with Tilicho peak (7132 metres) at its head and a view back to Pisang peak, one of the peaks open for climbing under the 'trekking peak' regulations. After a short descent from the ridge, the broad forested valley floor is reached at an elevation of 3350 metres. Most of the valley is grazing land for sheep, goats, horses and yaks. Across the river, high on the opposite bank, is the village of Ghyaru. It is possible to take an alternate route from upper Pisang and stay on the north bank of the river, passing through Ghyaru and rejoining the main trail at Mungji. A side trip may be made to Ser Gompa, located on a plateau high above the river on the north side.

The southern trail avoids all this climbing and follows the valley past the airstrip at Ongre, elevation 3325 metres. There is a police checkpost here, the last in the valley; a few bhattis and small hotels have grown up around the airport. The infrequent flights to Manang are usually charter flights arranged by rich Manangis en route to and from trading excursions, so there is almost no chance of obtaining a seat either to or from Kathmandu. The trail passes through Karma Phunjo; a half hour beyond the airport there is a huge valley with Annapurna III and IV at the head. Just south of the trail, in this spectacular setting, is the building that houses the mountaineering school funded by the Yugoslav Mountaineering Federation, and operated since 1980 by Nepal

Mountaineering Association in cooperation with UIAA, the Union of International Alpine Associations. There is a six-week course offered to climbers from Nepal and neighbouring countries during August each year. The Himalayan Rescue Association uses this building as a clinic, and a doctor is in attendance during the trekking season. The doctor often visits the hotels of Manang, but there should always be someone here to assist you if you need it.

The trail crosses the Marsyandi again near Mungji at 3360 metres, then traverses to Bryaga, 3475 metres. The largest part of this picturesque village of about 200 houses is hidden behind a large rock outcrop. The houses are stacked one atop another, each with an open veranda formed by a neighbour's rooftop. The gompa perched on a high crag overlooking the village is the largest in the district and has an outstanding display of statues, *thankas* (ornate Tibetan paintings) and manuscripts estimated to be 400 to 500 years old. The kanis over the trail that mark the entrance and exit from Bryaga are particularly impressive. There is a good place to camp in the meadow below the village. The hotels here are all in homes; the better hotels are a half hour away in Manang.

The country is now very arid, dominated by wierd cliffs of yellow rock eroded into dramatic pillars alongside the trail and by the towering heights of the Himalaya across the valley to the south. It is only a short walk past mani walls, across a stream where several mills are operating, to the plateau upon which Manang village is built at 3535 metres elevation. The *Annapurna Himal Hotel* adjoins the entrance kani to Manang village and has Tibetan gloves, hats and sweaters for sale as well as food and lodging. The walls are decorated with pictures from Chinese and Hindi film magazines. There are other hotels before the main part of Manang; the *Karma Hotel*, in the centre of the village, is the most popular facility.

Day 9: Manang

The day should be spent in Manang village and the vicinity to acclimatise for the higher elevations to be encountered towards Thorung La. There are many opportunities for interesting day-excursions from Manang. It is possible to climb the ridge to north of the village for excellent views of Annapurna IV, Annapurna II, and Glacier Dome (now named Tarke Kang), 7193 metres, or to descend from the village to the glacial lake at the foot of the huge icefall that drops from the northern slopes of Gangapurna, 7454 metres. It is interesting to walk to the village of Khangsar, the last village in the valley en route to Tilicho Lake. There are splendid views of the 'Great Barrier', a name given by Herzog to the high ridge between Roc Noir and Nilgiri North, from Khangsar. Another choice would be a walk to visit the Bhojo Gompa, the red edifice perched on the ridge between Bryaga and Manang. This is the most active monastery in the region.

Before Manang was opened to trekkers in 1977, the region saw few outsiders. The only traders were the people of Manang themselves, and the population was generally intolerant of outsiders. Therefore, there was little need of inns and other facilities here. In 1950, Maurice Herzog came to Manang village in a futile search for food for his party, only to return nearly starving from his camp at Tilicho Lake. With the advent of tourism, however, there has been extensive hotel construction, and tourists – particularly those with lots of rupees – are now warmly welcomed by the Manangis. The resourceful Manangbhot people have been quick to adapt to this new source of income, selling semi-precious stones, (from Tibet, they claim, but more likely from Bangkok), foodstuffs, Tibetan jewellery and other items of interest to tourists. An alternative to a day hike is a bargaining session with these skilful traders.

The village itself is a compact collection of 500 flat-roofed houses; the entrances are reached from narrow alleyways by ascending a steep log notched with steps. The setting of the village is most dramatic, with the summits of the Annapurna and Gangapurna less than eight km away, and a huge icefall rumbling and crashing on the flanks of the peaks.

Day 10: Manang-Phedi

The trek now begins the 1980-metre ascent to Thorung La. From Manang village the trail crosses a stream, climbs to Tengi, 120 metres above Manang, then continues to climb out of the Marsyandi Valley, turning north-west up the valley of the Jarsang Khola. The trail follows this valley north, passing a few herders' huts as it steadily gains elevation. The large trees have been left below, and the vegetation consists of scrub juniper and alpine grasses.

The trail passes near the small village of Gunsang, a cluster of flat mud roofs just below the trail at 3960 metres. The *Marsyandi Hotel and Lodge*, alongside the trail, has great Tibetan bread (and chhang). The route is now through meadows where horses and yaks graze and sparse forests of juniper, rose and barberry. After crossing a large stream that flows from Chulu Peak and Gundang, the trail passes an ancient mani wall in a pleasant meadow at 4000 metres. Villagers from Manang collect firewood from the slopes above. An hour further on is a single two-storey house, now rapidly falling apart – the stone walls are falling down and the biscuit-tin roof is both rusting and blowing away – at 4250 metres. This is Ledar, the next-to-last shelter before the pass and is a good spot for lunch. A very westernised young Manangi operates *Jimmy's Home* here where you can get almost anything – granola, chocolate, beer. Less popular is the *Lathair Guest House*.

From Ledar (some spell it Lathar) the trail continues to climb along the east bank of the Jarsang Khola, then descends and crosses the river on a covered bridge at 4310 metres. After a short ascent on a good trail built in connection with the bridge, the route follows a narrow trail across an unstable scree slope high above the river, then descends to Phedi, a dirty rock-strewn meadow surrounded by vertical cliffs at 4420 metres. This is the best campsite on this side of the pass, although camping is possible on a shelf about 10 minutes above, and another small flat spot about an hour beyond that. Local traders ride horses from Manang to Muktinath in a single day, but the great elevation gain, the need for acclimatisation, and the high altitudes involved all make it imperative to take at least two days for the trip on foot. The hotels at Phedi are on the first shelf, about 10 minutes above the valley; they can be very very crowded, especially if there is snow. Nights are made even more miserable by the 3 am departure that many people schedule; it really isn't necessary to start that early, and in fact it can be dangerous because it is quite cold until the sun rises; this can lead to hypothermia. The operator of one of the hotels at Phedi has a horse that you can ride over the pass for an exhorbitant price if you are not well. Blue sheep often appear magically in this valley; the crow-like birds are choughs and the large birds that circle overhead are lammergeiers and Himalayan griffons, not eagles. Be sure to boil or treat water here; the sanitation in Phedi and Ledar is terrible and giardia is rampant.

Day 11: Phedi-Muktinath

Phedi, which means 'foot of the hill' is a common Nepali name for any settlement at the bottom of a long climb. The trail becomes steep immediately after leaving the Phedi, switchbacking up moraines and following rocky ridges as it ascends to the pass. This trail has been used for hundreds of years by local people travelling on horseback and bringing huge herds of sheep and yaks in and out of Manang. Thus the trail, while often steep, is well defined and easy to follow. The only complications to the crossing are the high elevation and the possibility of snow. When the pass is blocked by snow, usually in late December and January, the crossing becomes difficult – often impossible. It then becomes necessary to retreat back to Dumre or wait until the snow has consolidated and local people have forged a trail. The only shelter between here and Muktinath are the tiny facilities at 4100 metres, far down the other side of the pass. An overnight stop in the snow, unless well planned in advance, can be dangerous, especially for porters.

The trail climbs and climbs, traversing in and out of many canyons formed by interminable moraines. It is a reasonably good trail unless there is snow, in which case the route may traverse scree slopes and ascend steep snow. It is only about four hours from Phedi to the pass, but the many false summits make the climb seem to go on forever. The pass, with its traditional chorten, prayer flags and stone cairn built by travellers, is reached at 5416 metres. The views from the trail and from the pass itself are outstanding high Himalayan scenes: the entire Great Divide with the Annapurnas and Gangapurna to the south, the barren Kali Gandaki Valley far below to the west, the rock peak of Thorungtse (6482 metres) to the north and a heavily glaciated peak (6484 metres) to the south. Well-acclimatised, technically proficient and well equipped trekkers have climbed high on this peak during a crossing of the pass.

The descent is steep and rough on the knees – a loss of more than 1600 metres in less than three hours. The descent often begins in snow which soon gives way to switchbacks down another series of moraines. During the descent there are excellent views of Dhaulagiri (8167 metres) standing alone in the distance across the valley. Eventually the moraines yield to grassy slopes and the final descent to Muktinath is a pleasant walk along the upper part of the Jhong Khola Valley. There are three or more bhattis at 4100 metres elevation where the grassy slopes begin that offer drinks, food and even souvenirs in this remote location. They are better relied upon for refreshment than for accommodation, though you could stay here if you were crossing the pass in the opposite direction. It is also possible to camp here if the tiny stream nearby is flowing. The trail crosses meadows, drops into a ravine that is the start of the Jhong Khola, climbs out of the ravine and enters Muktinath near the temple at 3800 metres. There is a police checkpost near the temple. There is no accommodation here, but it is only a five to 10-minute walk to Ranipowa where there is a large choice of accommodation. The *Muktinath Hotel* here is the best, charging Rs 25 for a room with twin beds and hot baths from a bucket. The young couple who run the hotel serve good food (and good apple rakshi).

Day 12-18: Muktinath-Pokhara

The route to Pokhara follows the Jomsom trek described here, but you must read this part backwards. Kagbeni is worth a visit, as is the Dhaulagiri icefall above Larjung, so an extra three days on this route is well spent.

Western Nepal

Western Nepal is often described as 'unexplored', but westerners have a bad habit of assuming that what is unknown to them is unknown to everyone. Western Nepal is densely populated by both Hindus and Buddhists and the countryside is criss-crossed by trails in all directions. It is remote and unknown from the western viewpoint because of its relative inaccessibility and distance from Kathmandu. Regular flights to Jumla and several other airstrips in the west greatly reduce this remoteness but add considerably to the cost and logistic nightmares. A flight from Kathmandu to Jumla costs US$110 each way if you are a foreigner. The flight operates twice a week and is heavily booked by local people who pay a lower fare. You could consider flying to Nepalganj, a hot terai town, and trying for space on one of the frequent shuttle flights to Jumla. You could also plan a trek that walks from the roadhead at Surkhet.

Another factor that discourages trekkers in western Nepal is that many of the culturally and scenically interesting regions are closed to foreigners. Many of the trails in the west continue to the north side of the Himalayan ranges of Nampa, Saipal and Kanjiroba, making it possible for trekkers to zip up easy trails along river valleys into Tibet – a practice that both the Nepalese and Chinese would like to discourage. Dolpo and Phoksumdo Lake to the east of Jumla are closed. Humla to the north-west of Jumla is restricted, as is the Mugu Karnali Valley north of Mugu village. The map on the following pages show the regions of western Nepal closed to foreigners as of mid-1984.

JUMLA TO RARA LAKE

Rara Lake, elevation 2980 metres, is the focal point of Lake Rara National Park and is a major destination for treks in western Nepal. The trek to Rara Lake is the most interesting trek that is currently open to foreign trekkers in the west. The route is very much 'off the beaten track' and affords glimpses of cultures and scenery much different from that in the rest of Nepal. Rara Lake itself is a clear high-altitude lake ringed with pine, spruce and juniper forests and snow-capped Himalayan peaks. In the winter there is often snow on the ridges surrounding the lake. There are no people living at the lake; all the people of Rara and Chapra villages were moved out when the area was declared a National Park.

The trek to Rara is somewhat strenuous and tends to be expensive because both food and labour are scarce and overpriced in this part of Nepal. For those seeking an opportunity to experience solitude in the wilderness and who are able to overcome the logistical complications of the region, this trek may be the best choice. It is visited by less than 10 trekkers a year. The following information was provided by Terence Walker, who has spent a lot of time in the region.

Day 1: Jumla-Uthagaon

It is a two-hour flight by Twin Otter aircraft from Kathmandu to Jumla. If you manage to obtain a seat you still may not be able to take all your baggage, even if you agree to pay for the excess, because of the weight limitations of the aircraft. The alternatives are to try to find a seat on a charter flight arranged by a trekking company or by the National Parks office.

Jumla, elevation 2434 metres, is a large bazaar situated above the Tila River. There is a chronic food shortage in this region – most of the Nepalganj-Jumla shuttle flights are cargo flights that carry rice and other staples – so it is usually impossible to purchase enough food for a trek in Jumla bazaar. It is better to carry all your food from Kathmandu – if you can get it onto the plane. There are a few porters available in Jumla, but they are expensive, do not speak English, and are not particularly eager to leave their homes. The people throughout the region are Thakuris, a Chhetri caste that has the highest social, political and ritual status. Westerners, being considered low-caste by high-caste Hindus, are traditionally not welcome in Thakuri homes, so a trek in the Jumla region cannot be arranged as a village inn trek.

From Jumla the trail to Rara follows the north bank of the Tila River, then turns north up the Chaudhabise River. The Jumla Valley soon disappears behind a ridge as the trail follows the river, keeping fairly level, passing through fields and pine forests. This is a major trade route into Jumla bazaar and it is not uncommon to meet traders not only carrying goods, but also packing goods on horses and even goats. The first village to be encountered is Uthugaon, elevation 2531 metres; there is a good campsite near the school, across the river from the village.

Day 2: Uthagaon-Sinja Khola

From Uthugaon the trail begins an ascent up the Ghurseni Khola Valley, beginning gently, but becoming steep as the climb continues. The canyon becomes very narrow with vertical cliffs on both sides as the trail ascends through a deep forest of pines, spruces and firs. At about 2900 metres elevation the large Chhetri town of Padmora, the last village in the valley, is reached. Above Padmora the logistics of the trek become more complex because of the limited water supply high on the ridge. Therefore, the day is a long one, continuing over the pass at 3400 metres and down to the Sinja Khola on the opposite side.

Near the pass is a small shepherd's camp where water may usually be found in the fall; this offers an alternative camp and makes a shorter day if water is available here. From the pass there are views of Patrasi Himal (6860 metres) and Jagdula Himal (5785 metres) to the east.

The area near the pass is a rhododendron and birch forest where it is usually possible to spot the Danfay or Impeyan pheasant, the colourful national bird of Nepal. From the pass the descent is steep to the Sinja Khola, where a camp may be made at an elevation of 2700 metres near a log bridge that spans the river.

Day 3: Sinja Khola-Chautha

The day begins with a casual walk along the river valley through forests and occasional fields of wheat and corn. The trail then crosses a stream and ascends very steeply for about 1½ hours to the village of Bumra, 2850 metres. From Bumra the trail meanders high above the river, then descends to a tributary stream, the Chautha Khola. Just across this stream is a small hotel in the tiny village of Chautha – but food and supplies may or may not be available here. In order to make the following day easier, it is best to continue an hour or more up the valley and make a camp in the forest alongside the stream.

Day 4: Chautha-Rara Lake

The climb up the Chautha Khola Valley continues on through beautiful forests to a high meadow, then on to the Ghurchi Lagna Pass at 3450 metres. From the pass there are spectacular views of the Mugu Karnali River and snow peaks bordering on Tibet. There is a choice of trails from the pass. The easiest trail is the trade route that descends steeply from the pass to the village of Pina, 2400 metres. From Pina the trail contours above the village of Jhari, then climbs a 3000-metre-high ridge above Rara Lake. It is a short descent to the lake where there is an abundance of excellent camping spots among the grassy meadows and juniper groves along the south shore of the lake.

The more scenic, but difficult, trail along the ridge begins from the Ghurchi Lagna Pass, then traverses the ridge to the west. It climbs gradually through high meadows and forests, then becomes

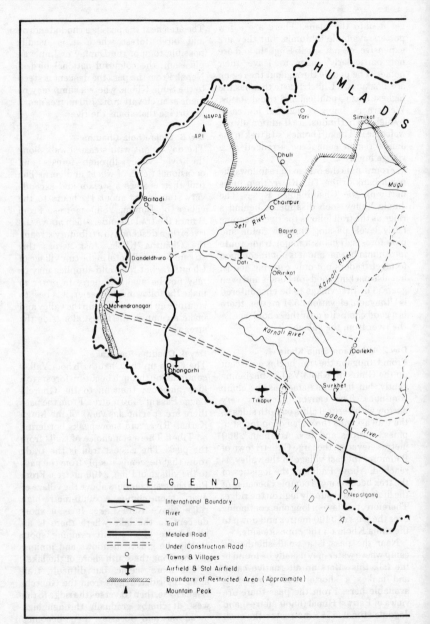

L E G E N D

	International Boundary
	River
	Trail
	Metaled Road
	Under Construction Road
	Towns & Villages
	Airfield & Stol Airfield
	Boundary of Restricted Area (Approximate)
	Mountain Peak

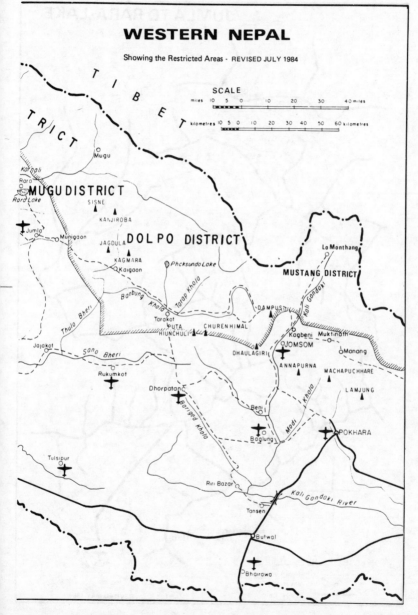

WESTERN NEPAL

Showing the Restricted Areas - REVISED JULY 1984

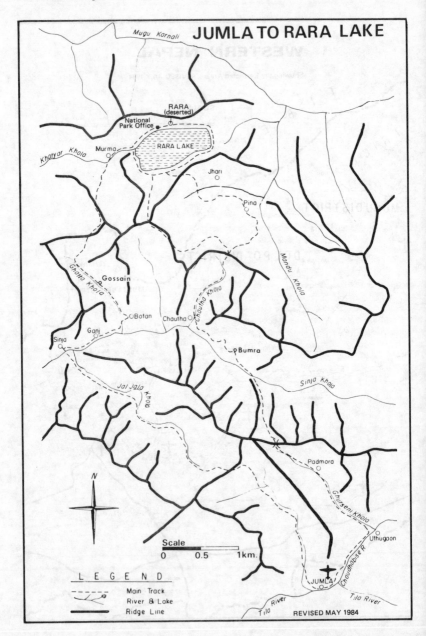

JUMLA TO RARA LAKE

REVISED MAY 1984

Scale
0   0.5   1km.

L E G E N D
- - - - Main Track
River & Lake
Ridge Line

steeper as it heads towards the top of the ridge at an elevation of more than 4000 metres. From this ridge, Rara Lake appears like a giant crater with a high Himalayan backdrop. Continuing along the top of the ridge for 1½ hours, the trail finally reaches a large rock chorten, then drops towards Rara Lake through heavy pine and spruce forests until it reaches the grassy meadows on the shores of the lake. This is a difficult route and can be blocked by snow in the winter. The trail is not always obvious; a local guide is an asset on this route.

Day 5: Rara Lake

Rara Lake, at 3062 metres elevation, is the largest lake in Nepal. It is almost 13 km around the lake, and a day devoted to making this circuit is well spent. Designated a National Park in 1975, the region offers a remoteness and wilderness experience unlike any other in Nepal. An entrance fee of Rs 60 is charged by the National Park office. There are a few park wardens' houses and the remnants of the now deserted villages of Rara and Chapra are on the north side of the lake, but otherwise it is an isolated region where birds, flowers and wildlife thrive. Among the mammals in the region are Himalayan bear, Himalayan tahr, serow, goral, musk deer, red panda and both Rhesus and Langur monkeys. The 170-metre-deep lake has otters and fish and is also an important resting place for migrating water fowl.

Day 6: Rara Lake-Gossain

It is possible to return to Jumla via the same route, but it is more interesting to make a circuit via a different trail. The first day from Rara Lake is long because, again, there are few water sources along the route. An early start is essential in order to reach Gossain in a single day.

From the west end of Rara Lake the trail follows the Khatyar Khola (called the Nisa Khola in its upper reaches) south-west to the village of Murma. The trail crosses the river on a log bridge below the village, then climbs steeply to 3300 metres up the ridge at the south end of the lake. If the weather is clear, there is an excellent view of the western Himalaya from the top of this ridge. The trail stays high, then descends through forests to reach the Ghatta Khola and follows this stream towards Gossain at 3100 metres elevation. There are several excellent camping places along the stream both above and below Gossain.

Day 7: Gossain-Sinja

Today is a short walk (needed after yesterday's long day) down the Sinja Khola to the village of Sinja. Descending the Ghatta Khola past Botan, the trail turns west along the Sinja Khola, then follows the fertile valley through a very heavily populated region. This a Brahmin and Chhetri area that was the capital of Malla Kingdom in 1300 AD. The ruins of the old palace can be seen across the river from Sinja, 2400 metres elevation.

Day 8: Sinja-Jumla

It is possible to reach Jumla in a single day from Sinja, though there are camping places before Jumla that would allow a more leisurely two-day trip. From Sinja the trail goes back into uninhabited wilderness, meeting very few people. The deep forests along the way are very lush and abound in wildlife. The trail climbs gradually, but continually, passing a large meadow en route to the pass at 3500 metres. The long descent from the pass to Jumla is through a forest of mystical-appearing birch trees draped in Spanish moss. There are many good campsites along this stretch of trail if there is no rush to reach Jumla.

Other Destinations

As interesting, culturally enriching and historic as the major treks may be, the possibility of visiting other regions should not be neglected. Although there are restrictions involved with the issuance of trekking permits, and some areas are still closed to foreigners, there are many places in Nepal that are both fascinating and accessible. Many trekkers make the mistake of varying their route by attempting a high pass (5500 to 6000 metres) only to discover that they, their equipment, or other members of the party are totally unfit for the cold, high elevation and the technical problems that the pass presents. Often they are forced to turn back, severely altering their schedule, so that they fail to reach their primary objectives. High passes are best attempted only after the major goal of the trek has been achieved – usually on the return to Kathmandu.

It is not necessary to go to a particularly remote region in order to escape heavily travelled trails. The major trade routes are the shortest way to a particular destination but if you allow another few days it is possible to follow less direct, often parallel, routes through villages not even on the maps in areas less westernised than the primary trails.

In 1984 I visited an area less than a day's walk from an important trekking route where the local people insisted that I was the first trekker who had ever been there. Other foreigners had visited the region, of course, as engineers, doctors and teachers, but no foreigner had previously come there simply to trek. There must be thousands of similar places in Nepal. In such places a guide is helpful, and it is almost imperative to carry your own food and the means with which to cook it. In areas that are frequented by neither trekkers nor local porters there are no bhattis and the time and effort necessary to scrounge out food and accommodation in homes would make progress almost impossible.

Some other possible trekking destinations are:

Kathmandu-Pokhara

Before the Pokhara road was completed in 1971, the only way to reach Pokhara from Kathmandu was to fly or to walk. The trek from Kathmandu to Pokhara may be made as an easy nine or 10-day trek from Trisuli Bazaar to Begnas Tal, just outside of Pokhara. This is the easiest trek in Nepal and has few uphill climbs of any significance. There is an opportunity to visit Gorkha, to make side trips to Bara Pokhari, a high-altitude lake overlooking Manaslu, and to visit Siklis, the largest Gurung village in Nepal. The views of the Himalaya are good on this trek, but the route never actually gets into the high mountains.

A lot of the interest and remoteness of this trek has vanished because the new road to Gorkha has totally changed the trading habits and culture of the region. Local people hardly ever walk this route now, so the facilities for food and accommodation have degenerated.

Between Kathmandu and Pokhara there are three major groups of peaks: Ganesh Himal, Manaslu and Himalchuli, and the large Annapurna Himal. A trek from Kathmandu to Pokhara starts from Trisuli Bazar, 65 km from Kathmandu, on the same road that leads to the start of the Langtang trek. Trekking west there are many alternatives: a northern route presents a trek close to the mountains – Manaslu (7945 metres), Himalchuli, Baudha (6674 metres) and a side trip to Bara Pokhari, a fine high-altitude lake. The more direct southern route to Pokhara allows a visit to the ancient town of Gorkha with its large bazaar and fort. This route has the attraction of lower altitudes and avoids the extreme elevation gains and losses common to other treks in Nepal. Treks in this region can be almost any length; nine days is sufficient from Trisuli Bazaar to Pokhara. A round trip to Pokhara without backtracking is possible – or you can fly to Pokhara and walk back to Kathmandu, gaining a preview of the route from the plane. The southern routes are often travelled by westerners, but many parts of the northern regions are still virgin.

Rolwaling (restricted)

Rolwaling is the east-west valley below Gauri Shankar (7145 metres), just south of the Tibetan border. This region is isolated and interesting but most treks conclude their visit to Rolwaling by crossing the Tesi Lapcha Pass (5755 metres) into Khumbu. A crossing of Tesi Lapcha is best made from Khumbu into Rolwaling, not by visiting Rolwaling first. There are two reasons for this: well-equipped, willing porters are easier to get in Khumbu and in Rolwaling and in the event of altitude sickness there are better facilities for help if you make your retreat on the Khumbu side than if you make a retreat back to the isolated villages of Beding or Na in Rolwaling. A second way to visit this region would be to forgo Tesi Lapcha and go as far as Na, then retrace the route back to Kathmandu. Tesi Lapcha is particularly dangerous because of frequent rockfalls on its west side, and the route through the icefall is becoming technically more and more difficult due to the movements of the glacier. The Rolwaling porters operate a Mafia-like system and will not allow outside porters to approach the pass from Rolwaling, forcing parties to accept people from Beding and Na as porters. The local porters then either get frightened of the rockfall and return without notice or demand exorbitant pay after the party is halfway up the pass. There are no facilities whatsoever between Na and Thami; Tesi Lapcha is a true mountaineering project.

Rolwaling and Tesi Lapcha are (in 1984) closed to foreigners; it seems to be different interpretations of the same rules rather than new regulations that determines whether you will be issued a trekking permit or not.

Makalu Base Camp

An outstanding trek in eastern Nepal may be made from either Hile or Tumlingtar by walking north up the Arun River to Sedua and Num, then crossing Barun La (4110 metres) into the upper Barun Khola Valley for a close look at Makalu (8463 metres) and Chamlang (7317 metres). The route is not particularly difficult but it becomes a long trek because of the great distance up the Arun that must be covered. An even wilder trek may be put together by crossing Sherpani Col and West Col into the upper Hongu Basin. This trek has been attempted a few times and has proved itself a most difficult and potentially dangerous trek. Better to travel from Lukla if you want to go into the upper Hongu Basin and the five lakes, Panch Pokhari, situated there.

Tilicho Lake

There is another pass south of Thorong La between Manang and Jomsom. From Manang, the trail goes on to the village of Khangsar, then becomes a goat trail scrambling over moraines to Tilicho Lake (4120 metres), at the foot of Tilicho Peak (7132 metres). Tilicho Lake is usually frozen (except when you decide to trust the ice and walk on it) and is depicted on Herzog's maps as the 'great ice lake'. From the lake, there are several alternative routes, including Meso Kanto Pass (5330 metres) and another alternate pass a little further north. The trail is difficult and hard to find. One very experienced trekker described the trail as only a figment of someone's imagination – he claimed there was no trail at all. Thorong La is a good safe route between Manang and Jomsom; better to make a side trip to Tilicho Lake from Manang and not take all your equipment and porters on the Tilicho Lake trail. Often there are army training exercises in the valley east of Jomsom and the route to Tilicho Lake may be closed at this point. Inquire in Kathmandu and again in Manang before you make your plans. You might cross the pass only to be turned back to Manang an hour before Jomsom.

Jugal Himal

To the east of Kathmandu is a chain of peaks called Jugal Himal, which includes Dorje Lakpa (6966 metres), Madiya (6257 metres) and Phurbi Chhyachu (6637 metres). From the south it is an easily-accessible region, although it requires a long uphill climb. From Dolalghat on the Kodari road there is a jeepable road to the large bazaar of Chautara (1410 metres). A trail from Chautara descends to the Balephi Khola, then follows a ridge to Bhairav Kund, a holy lake at 3500 metres elevation. A return may be made from here to Tatopani on the Kodari road, or a circuit may be made around the head of the Balephi Khola Valley to Panch Pokhari, five lakes at an elevation of 3600 metres. From Panch Pokhari, trails lead to Tarke Gyang in Helambu, or back down the ridge to Panchkal on the Kodari road. This is a remote and unfrequented region, despite its proximity to Kathmandu. Treks in this area involve a lot of climbing on narrow trails. The 'Himalayan Hash' brought 185 trekkers here in 1983.

Kanchenjunga (restricted)

The Kanchenjunga base camp is still a restricted area (in 1984) despite assurances that it will be one of the next areas opened to trekking. It can be approached from the roadheads at Hile or Ilam or from the airstrips at Tumlingtar or Taplejung. There is also a 138-km-long road under construction from Ilam to Taplejung that may sometime make access to this region easier. You can get some distance towards Kanchenjunga without entering the closed area, so a good three or four-week trek can now be arranged here. When the Kanchenjunga area is opened, treks to the north face base camp via Walunchung Ghola and to the south base camp will both be possible. Kanchenjunga is on the Indian border, so a circuit of the mountain is impossible.

Manaslu & Larkya La (restricted)

The other area that may open soon is the Larkya La (5105 metres), the pass between the Buri Gandaki and the Marsyandi valleys. This would allow a circuit of Manaslu (8162 metres) and Himalchuli (7893 metres) that will require three weeks. The trail that approaches the Larkya La is narrow, steep and slippery on the east side and there is no food or shelter available near the pass. Trekkers have slipped through the bureaucratic net and made this trek in the past, but you will probably be stopped by the police if you try it. The Rupina La (4663 metres), a pass to the south, offers an alternative; it is a steep snow-covered route with little to recommend it.

Phoksumdo Lake (restricted)

The high route from Pokhara to Jumla via Phoksumdo Lake (3600 metres) takes 25 days and the high passes are closed in the winter. Peter Matthisen's book, *The Snow Leopard*, describes much of this route. Because it travels through the Dolpo region, it is yet another trek that is not allowed with the current definition of restricted areas, but it will be an interesting trek when the regulations are finally relaxed.

Further Information

MOUNTAINEERING IN NEPAL

Although this is a book about trekking, a short discussion of mountaineering in Nepal is appropriate. The first trekkers in Nepal were, of course, mountaineers who were either on their way to climb peaks, or were exploring routes up unclimbed peaks. There was furious mountaineering activity in Nepal from 1950 to the 1960s; all the 8000-metre peaks were climbed during this time.

By the early 1970s the emphasis had shifted to impossible feats like the south face of Annapurna and finally Everest South-West Face, both climbed by expeditions led by Chris Bonnington. The expeditions in the '60s and '70s were often well-equipped and sometimes lavish as governments, foundations, magazines, newspapers, film-makers, television producers and even private companies sponsored expeditions to higher and more spectacular peaks. Expeditions have become big business and climbers now approach the job with the appropriate degree of seriousness and dedication. It is not uncommon for trekkers to be refused admission into expedition base camps. The team members do not have time or energy to entertain tourists and there have also been incidents of trekkers pinching souvenirs from among the expensive and essential items that often lay around such camps.

In 1978 the Nepalese mountaineering regulations were changed in a manner that is consistent with current trends in mountaineering to allow small scale attempts on 18 peaks. No longer is it necessary to go through a long application process and organise a huge assault on a major peak in order to try Himalayan mountaineering. The 18 peaks provide a great range of difficulty and are spread throughout Nepal. Any well-qualified climber can attempt them.

There are three seasons for mountaineering in Nepal. The pre-monsoon season from April to early June was once the only season during which major peaks were attempted. In the '50s all the attempts were in the 'lull before the storm' period that occurs between the end of the winter winds and the beginning of the monsoon snow. The Swiss attempt on Mount Everest in 1952 was driven back by the terrific cold and high winds when they made an expedition in the fall season. It was not until 1973 that Everest was successfully climbed in the fall, though the fall, or post-monsoon, season of September and October is now a period of many successful expeditions. In 1979 the Ministry of Tourism established a season for winter mountaineering. It is bitterly cold at high elevations from November to February, but recent advances in equipment technology have allowed several teams to accomplish what was thought before to be impossible – a winter ascent of a Himalayan peak. Climbing during the monsoon, from June to August, is not practical.

Many individuals and trekking agents have organised private expeditions to both large and small peaks in Nepal, and the ascent of a small peak (if a peak higher than any in North America can be presumed to be 'small') is often included as part of a trek. Because the regulations for climbing a small peak require an established liaison in Kathmandu (usually a trekking company), it is easiest to get in touch with a trekking agent in order to organise a climb, rather than try to do the whole project on your own – though it is possible to organise a climb without any assistance if you have a good idea of what you need and where you are going. Before you consider climbing a 'trekking peak', reread some books on Himalayan expeditions. The weather is often bad, and you may be forced to sit in your tent for days at a time. Usually a well-equipped base camp is necessary, and the ascent of a peak requires one or more high camps that must be established and stocked. Most of the trekking peaks require a minimum of four days and it can take as much as three weeks for an ascent.

Small Peaks

Climbing in Nepal is administered by two organisations. The Ministry of Tourism is responsible for major expeditions, and the Nepal Mountaineering Association issues permits for the small peaks open to trekking groups. The type of climbing that is interesting to most trekkers is encompassed by the regulations for small peaks. There is a minimum of formality, requiring only the payment of a fee and the preparation of a simple application. The fee is US$200 for peaks above 6100 metres and US$100 for peaks less than 6100 metres. The permit is valid for a period of one month and a group of up to 10 persons. An extra US$5 per person is charged if the group exceeds 10 climbers.

The peaks available under the trekking peak regulations are:

Everest Region

Island Peak 6153 metres (20,188 feet). One steep and exposed 100-metre ice or snow climb, otherwise a non-technical snow climb. Its new name is Imja Tse Himal.

Kwangde 6194 metres (20,323 feet). Difficult north face (seen from Namche). South side is a moderately technical climb (allow two-three weeks) from Lumding Kharka.

Kusum Kangru 6369 metres (20,897 feet). Most difficult of trekking peaks.

Lobuje East 6119 metres (20,076 feet). Top is exposed and often rotten snow. Exposed knife ridge and some crevasses. Not a trivial peak.

Mehra Peak 5820 metres (19,095 feet). Rock and ice climb; not difficult from either the Imja Valley or Lobuje. Now named Khongma Tse.

Mera Peak 6431 metres (21,100 feet). Easy snow climb from the Mera La, but sometimes crevasses complicate the route. No food at all on the approach from Lukla; requires two weeks.

Pokhalde 5806 metres (19,050 feet). A short steep snow climb from the Kongma La.

Rolwaling Region

Pharchamo 6282 metres (20,611 feet). Steep snow climb subject to avalanches; approached from Tesi Lapcha.

Ramdung 6021 metres (19,755 feet). Long approach through Rolwaling valley; Rolwaling is now closed, so the climb must be made from the south.

Manang Region

Chulu East 6200 metres (20,342 feet). Long approach from Manang; needs one or two high camps.

Chulu West 6630 metres (21,753 feet). Needs two high camps; the route circles Gusang Peak to climb Chulu West from the north.

Pisang 6091 metres (19,985 feet). Long snow slog above Pisang village. Steep snow at the top.

Langtang Region

Ganga La Chuli 5846 metres (19,180 feet). Snow and rock climb from a base camp either north or south of Ganja La.

Annapurna Region

Fluted Peak 6390 metres (20,966 feet). New name *Singu Chuli*; in Annapurna Sanctuary. Its name comes from the steep ice slopes that make it difficult to climb.

Hiunchuli 6337 metres (20,792 feet). Snow, ice and rock. Not easy.

Mardi Himal 5555 metres (18,226 feet). Five day slog up the Mardi Khola to approach the peak.

Tent Peak 5500 metres (18,045 feet). Glaciers and crevasses; new name Tharpu Chuli. Most people climb the easier 'Rakshi Peak' to the south.

Ganesh Himal

Paldor Peak 5894 metres (19,338 feet). 10 day trek to base camp from Trisuli Bazaar.

The peaks range from simple, but long, walk-ups like Mera Peak to reasonably difficult and dangerous peaks like Kusum Kangru. There is no comprehensive guidebook to these peaks, though a search of old Himalayan Journals and expedition books will turn up a lot of information.

To get a climbing permit, go to the Nepal Mountaineering Association (NMA) office on Ram Shah Path (also called Putali Sadak). Payment must be in foreign currency cash or travellers' cheques. You must employ a sardar who is currently registered with the NMA, and if any Nepalese are to climb above base camp, they must be insured and you must supply them with climbing equipment. A climbing permit does not replace a trekking permit; you must have both. NMA's telephone number is 211596.

Climbing gear can be bought or rented in Kathmandu, saving the expense of airfreighting ironmongery around the world. Good mountain tents, stoves, sleeping bags, down clothing and most other expedition necessities can be rented. As with trekking gear, the items that might be in short supply are socks, clothing, large size boots and freeze dried food.

Mountaineering Expeditions

The rules for mountaineering on major peaks require a minimum of six months advance application to the Ministry of Tourism, a liaison officer, a royalty of US$1000 to $5000 depending on the elevation of the peak, and endorsement from the government or the national alpine club of the country organising the expedition. There are 87 peaks open for foreign expeditions and another 17 peaks open for joint Nepalese-foreign expeditions. Some peaks, such as Everest, are booked many years in advance, while others have very few expeditions. Further information is usually available through alpine clubs in your own country. Even the most budget-conscious expedition under these regulations would cost US$10,000 or more because of liaison officer salary, insurance and equipment, peak fees, sherpa insurance, sherpa equipment and other compulsory expenses. If you want an inexpensive climb in Nepal it is far more reasonable to set your sights on one of the trekking peaks.

Climbs on Everest

Mountaineering and trekking in Nepal has relied heavily on the progress and inspiration developed by various expeditions to Everest. Much of the attraction of Nepal in the early days resulted from the discovery that the highest peak in the world lay within the forbidden and isolated kingdom. Though it was named Mount Everest by the Survey of India in 1856 after Sir George Everest, retired Surveyor-General of India, the peak had been known by other names long before. The Nepalese call it Sagarmatha and the Sherpas call it Chomolungma. The Chinese now call it Qomolangma Feng. The history of attempts and success on the mountain is one of the classics of mountaineering history. By 1984 there had been 168 ascents of Everest, including several persons who climbed it two or three times.

1921 – British

The first expedition was a reconnaissance through Tibet from Darjeeling led by Lt Col C K Howard Bury. They spent months mapping and exploring the Everest region and gave the first climbing school for Sherpas on the slopes leading to the North Col. Though it was not an actual attempt on the peak, they reached the North Col at a height of 7000 metres.

1922 – British
The first attempt on the mountain was led by Brig Gen C G Bruce. The expedition, as were all attempts until 1950, was made from the north after a long approach march across the plains of Tibet. The highest point reached was 8320 metres. Seven Sherpas were killed in an avalanche below the North Col.

1924 – British
Again Bruce led a team of British gentlemen in their tweed suits to Everest. They didn't have crampons and had a furious argument about whether the use of oxygen was 'sporting'. On this expedition George Leigh Mallory and Andrew Irvine climbed high on the mountain and never returned. Lt Col E F Norton reached 8565 metres without oxygen.

1933 – British
This expedition, under the leadership of Hugh Ruttledge reached a height of 8570 metres, just 275 metres short of the summit. Frank Smythe's book *Camp Six* is an excellent personal account of this expedition.

1934 – a solo attempt
Maurice Wilson flew alone in a small plane from England to India, then crossed Tibet to make a solo attempt on Everest. While usually dismissed as a crank, Wilson did accomplish a lot before he pushed himself too far and froze to death on the slopes below the North Col.

1935 – British
A name to become associated with Everest first came into prominence when Eric Shipton led a small expedition as far as the North Col.

1936 – British
Another British expedition led by Ruttledge reached a point only slightly above the North Col.

1938 – British
Another famous name associated with Everest came to the forefront when H W Tilman led a small expedition in which Eric Shipton reached almost 8300 metres.

1947 – a solo attempt
Earl Denman, a Canadian, disguised himself as a Tibetan monk, travelled to Everest and tried a solo attempt. He quit below the North Col and returned immediately to Darjeeling.

1950 – British/American
After the war, Tibet was closed, but Nepal had begun to open her borders. Tilman made a peripatetic trip all over Nepal, including a trek from Dharan to Namche Bazar. This was the first party of westerners to visit the Everest region. They made the first 'ascent' of Kala Pattar and walked to the foot of the Khumbu Icefall.

1951 – solo from Nepal
K Becker-Larson, a Dane, followed the same route as the Tilman party, then crossed into Tibet, reaching the North Col before returning.

1951 – British
Eric Shipton led another reconnaissance, reached the Western Cwm at the top of the Khumbu Icefall, and proved that Everest could be climbed from the south.

1952 – Swiss
Leader Dr Wyss-Durant organised an effort in which Raymond Lambert and Tenzing Norgay reached a height of almost 8600 metres.

1952 – Swiss
Rushing to beat the British, the Swiss tried again in the fall of 1952 but cold and high winds drove them back from a point just above the South Col.

1953 – British success
The huge British expedition, led by John Hunt, was successful in placing Edmund Hillary and Tenzing Norgay on the summit on 29 May 1953.

1956 – Swiss
Albert Eggler led an expedition that placed four climbers on the summit of Everest and also made the first ascent of Lhotse.

1960 – Indian
The first Indian expedition reached a height of 8625 metres but was forced to retreat because of bad weather.

1960 – Chinese
The first ascent from the north; three members of this team reached the summit in the night.

1962 – Indian
The second Indian expedition also was unsuccessful, though they reached a height of 8700 metres.

1962 – an illegal attempt
Woodrow Wilson Sayre and three others obtained permission to climb Gyachung Kang, then crossed into Tibet and tried to climb Everest. They reached a point above the North Col before they returned.

1963 – American
The American Mount Everest Expedition, led by Norman Dyhrenfurth, was successful in placing six persons on the summit, including two by the unclimbed West Ridge.

1965 – Indian
Captain M S Kohli lead an Indian team that placed nine climbers on the summit of Everest.

1966-1968
Nepal closed to mountaineers.

1969 – Japanese
The Japanese made a reconnaissance to look for a new route up the South-West Face of Everest.

1970 – Japanese
A 38-member Japanese team placed four climbers on the summit. This was the expedition that included the famous 'ski descent' of Everest. Six Sherpas were killed in the Khumbu Icefall.

1971 – International
Norman Dhyrenfurth led an ambitious expedition with climbers from 13 nations attempting both the South-West Face and the West Ridge, finally retreating from a height of 8488 metres on the face route.

1971 – Argentine
An unsuccessful attempt led by H C Tolosa.

1972 – Europeans
K M Herligkoffer led a team that attempted the South-West Face, reaching a height of 8300 metres.

1972 – British South Face
An attempt on the South Face was led by Chris Bonnington.

1973 – Italian
The largest Everest expedition ever, under the leadership of Guido Monzino, placed eight climbers on the summit.

1973 – Japanese
Two members of a team led by Micheo Yuasa, reached the summit in the first successful ascent in the fall season. The ascent was via the traditional South Col route after the team made no progress on the South-West face.

1974 – Spanish
Financed by a Spanish battery company, the Spanish expedition was unsuccessful.

1974 – French
This expedition ended in disaster when an avalanche killed the leader and five sherpas.

1975 – Japanese
The Japanese Women's Everest Expedition was successful when Mrs Junko Tabei and Sherpa Ang Tsering reached the summit.

1975 – Chinese
A few days after the Japanese success, a Chinese team placed nine persons, including a women, on the summit. The large survey tripod they erected is still on the top of Everest.

1975 – British South Face
Bonnington led, and Barclays Bank financed, an expedition that successfully climbed the difficult South-West Face of Everest.

1976 – British-Nepal Army
Two British members of a joint British-Nepal Army expedition reached the summit in the spring.

1976 – American
The American Bicentennial Everest Expedition, led by Phil Trimble, placed two members on the summit during the fall.

1977 – New Zealand
A New Zealand expedition in the spring was stopped by bad weather and heavy snow.

1977 – South Korean
The fall attempt of the South Koreans, in which two climbers reached the summit, was the earliest fall success ever.

1978 – Austrian
In three separate teams, nine climbers reached the summit of Everest. Reinhold Messner and Peter Habler made the first ascent of the mountain without using oxygen.

1978 – German/French
Led by Dr Herligkoffer and Pierre Mazeaud, this gigantic expedition placed 16 climbers on the summit via the South Col and a live radio broadcast from the 'roof of the world'.

1979 – Yugoslav
Five climbers reached the summit via a new route – the West Ridge all the way from the Lho La. Ang Phu Sherpa fell and was killed during the descent.

1979 – Swabian
Another international group placed 13 climbers on the summit under the leadership of Gerhard Schmatz. Mrs Schmatz and Ray Genet died during an overnight bivouac on the descent.

1980 – Polish winter expedition
The first winter ascent was made via the South Col after a long struggle. Two climbers reached the summit.

1980 – Polish
Another Polish expedition in the spring, with many of the same climbers as the winter expedition, pioneered a new route via the South Pillar, to the right of the British South Face route. The summit was reached by two climbers.

1980 – Basque
For the first time, two teams were allowed on the mountain simultaneously, and two climbers reached the summit via the traditional South Col route.

1980 – Japanese – from the North
After being closed for more than 40 years, Tibet was once again accessible to mountaineers. A large and expensive expedition reached the summit by two different routes from Tibet. One climber reached the summit via the North-East Ridge and two climbers via the North Face.

1980 – Reinhold Messner – Solg
On August 20, Reinhold Messner made his second oxygenless ascent of Everest, this time from the Tibet side – and alone.

1980 – Nepal/Italian
A post-monsoon joint expedition of the Nepal Mountaineering Association and Club Alpino Italiano was forced back from the summit because of weather and logistic complications.

1981 – Japanese
A winter expedition was led by 1970 Everest summiter Naomi Uemura. It ended without success after reaching the South Col.

1981 – British
At the same time as the Japanese winter attempt, a British team led by Allan Rouse attempted the West Ridge, but was not successful.

1981 – Japanese
Meiji University sponsored a spring attempt on the West Ridge led by Sinichi Nakajimi.

1981 – American
The first attempt on the Kangshung Face in Tibet was led by Richard Blum.

1981 – American
Three Americans and two Sherpas reached the summit via the South-East ridge during the American Medical Research Expedition.

1982 – Canadian
Two Canadians and four Sherpas reached the summit in a huge expedition that included live television transmissions from the mountain.

1982 – British
During an attempt on the North-East Ridge from Tibet, Joe Tasker and Peter Boardman were killed.

1982 – Soviet
Eleven climbers reached the summit via the South-West Face.

1982 – French
A French Army expedition led by J C Marmier was unsuccessful.

1982 – Spanish
An attempt from Nepal led by L Belvis was unsuccessful.

1982 – American
An attempt from Tibet led by Lou Whittaker.

1982 – Dutch
An attempt from Tibet.

1982 – French
A winter attempt from Nepal was unsuccessful.

1982 – Japanese
Yasuo Kato made a solo winter ascent (his third ascent of Everest) and perished during the descent.

1982 – Belgian
A winter attempt via the West Ridge; one member fell into Tibet and eventually made his way back to Kathmandu by bus.

1983 – Japanese
Three Japanese climbers reached the summit via the South col in the fall.

1983 – American
Six Americans climbed the difficult Kangshung face from Tibet on the same day that the Japanese climbed the peak from Nepal.

1983 – Japanese
Three Japanese climbers reached the summit via the South-East Ridge.

1983 – German-American
Gerard Lenser led an expedition that placed six Americans and two Sherpas on the summit via the South Col.

1983 – Chilean
From Tibet

1983 – American
An attempt from Tibet led by Robert Craig.

1983 – Japanese
A winter ascent by three Japanese and a Sherpa from the South Col.

1984 – Indian
The first Indian woman and four other climbers reached the summit via the South Col.

1984 – Bulgarian
Five Bulgarians reached the summit via the West Ridge; four climbers made a traverse and descended via the South-East Ridge.

SUGGESTED READING

There are hundreds of books about Nepal, Tibet and Himalaya, some dating back to the 1800s. A trip to your local library will provide you with an armload of fascinating books. The following list includes publications that are historically important and interesting; most are recent enough to be available in large libraries. Many of these books, and others not available in the west, can be purchased in Kathmandu.

Another good source of material about Nepal is the (American) National Geographic Magazine. There have been about 10 issues over the years that have had some material about Nepal and the Himalaya. Also look up copies of the Himalayan Journal, an annual publication of the Himalayan Club in Bombay, India.

Nepal

Nepal – the Kingdom in the Himalayas Toni Hagen (Kummerly & Frey, Bern, 1980) – a definitive documentation of the geology and people of Nepal; contains many fine photos.

Mount Everest, the Formation, Population & Exploration of the Everest Region Toni Hagen, G O Dyhrenfurth, C Von Furer Haimendorf and Erwin Schneider (Oxford University Press, London, 1963) – a shortened version of material in Hagen's book (above) combined with other works describing in detail the Solu Khumbu region. Contains good maps.

The Sherpas of Nepal C Von Furer Haimendorf (John Murray, London, 1964) – a rather dry anthropological study of the Sherpas of the Solu Khumbu region. A revised edition is to be released soon.

Himalayan Traders C Von Furer Haimendorf, (John Murray, London, 1975) – the sequel to Sherpas of Nepal, but more readable. A fascinating study of the change in trading patterns and culture among Himalayan peoples throughout Nepal.

Mustang - a Lost Tibetan Kingdom Michel Peissel (Collins & Harvill Press, London, 1968) – a description of the restricted Mustang region north of Jomsom.

Nepal Himalaya H W Tilman (Cambridge University Press, London, 1952) – a delightful book filled with Tilman's dry wit. It describes the first treks in Nepal in 1949 and 1950. The book is out of print and very hard to find; try a large library, it's impossible to buy a copy anywhere. It has been reprinted by the Seattle Mountaineers in a Tilman anthology.

People of Nepal Dor Bahadur Bista (Ratna Pustak Bhandar, Kathmandu, 1967) – an excellent overview of the various ethnic groups in Nepal, written by a Nepalese anthropologist.

The Festivals of Nepal Mary M Anderson (George Allen & Unwin, London, 1971) – describes the important festivals of Nepal; contains a lot of background information about the Hindu religion.

High in the Thin Cold Air Edmund Hillary & Desmond Doig (Doubleday, New York, 1962) – describes many of the projects undertaken by the Himalayan trust; also contains the story of the scientific examination of the Khumjung yeti skull.

Schoolhouse in the Clouds Edmund Hillary (Penguin, London, 1968) – describes the construction of Khumjung school and other projects in Khumbu. Good background on where all those bridges, hospitals and schools came from.

The Kulunge Rai Charles McDougal (Ratna Pustak Bhandar, Kathmandu, 1979) – anthropological studies of the Rais in the Hongu Valley, especially the village of Bung.

Vignettes of Nepal Harka Gurung (Sajha Prakashan, Kathmandu, 1980) – personal accounts of treks throughout Nepal. Good historical and geological background is included. Many maps.

Mani Rimdu, Nepal Mario Fantini (Toppan Co, Singapore, 1976) – colour photos and descriptions of the dances of the Mani Rimdu festival at Thyangboche monastery.

Natural History

Birds of Nepal Robert L Fleming Sr, Robert L Fleming Jr & Lain Bangdel, published by the authors, Kathmandu, 1976 – the definitive work on the hundreds of species of birds in Nepal. Contains many outstanding colour paintings of birds.

Discovering Trees in Nepal Adrian and Jimmie Storrs (Sahayogi Press, Kathmandu, 1984) – good information about the trees of Nepal, including their economic and cultural significance.

Flowers of the Himalaya Oleg Polunin and Adam Stainton (Oxford University Press, London, 1984) – highly technical and very detailed information.

The Arun Edward W Cronin, Jr (Houghton Mifflin Company, Boston, 1979) – a natural history of the Arun River Valley.

Stones of Silence George B Schaller (Viking Press, New York, 1980) – a naturalist's travels in Dolpo.

Himalayan Flowers & Trees Dorothy Mierow & Tirtha Bahadur Shrestha (Sahayogi Press, Kathmandu, 1978) – the best available field guide to the plants of Nepal.

Mountaineering Expeditions

Americans on Everest James Ramsey Ullman (J B Lippincott, Philadelphia, 1964) – the official account of the 1963 American expedition.

The Moated Mountain Showell Styles (Hurt & Blackett, London, 1955) – a very readable book about an expedition to Baudha Peak; Styles makes fascinating cultural observations as he treks to the mountain.

Forerunners to Everest Rene Dittert, Gabriel Chevalley & Raymond Lambert, translated by Malcolm Barnes (Harper & Row, York, 1954) – a description of the two Swiss expeditions to Everest in 1952; includes a fine description of the old expedition approach march.

Annapurna Maurice Herzog (Jonathan Cape, London, 1952) – a mountaineering classic that describes the first conquest of an 8000-metre peak. Contains a good description of the

Annapurna region, including Manang, and a visit to Kathmandu in 1950.

Annapurna South Face Christian Bonnington (Cassell, London, 1971) – the beginning of a new standard of mountaineering in Nepal and an excellent description of the problems of organising an expedition.

Faces of Everest Major H P S Ahluwalia (Vikas, New Delhi, 1977) – an illustrated history of Everest by a summiter of the 1965 Indian expedition.

Everest Walt Unsworth (Allen Lane, London, 1981) – a detailed history of mountaineering on Everest.

The Ascent of Rum Doodle W E Bowman (Dark Peak, Sheffield, 1979) – a classic spoof of mountaineering books; good diversion after you have read a few expedition accounts that take themselves too seriously.

Nepali Language
Nepal Phrasebook (Lonely Planet, Melbourne, 1984) – a handy phrasebook for Nepalese with a particular emphasis on trekking.

Basic Gurkhali Grammar M Meerendonk (Singapore, 1964) – one of the best introductory texts on Nepali, which the British Army calls Gurkhali. Written for the army, so it teaches a slightly weird military vocabulary.

Basic Gurkhali Dictionary M Meerendonk (Singapore, 1960) – a handy pocket sized dictionary of the Nepali language. Quite useful once you understand the rudiments of the grammar.

Trekkers Pocket Pal Summer Institute of Linguistics (Avalok, Kathmandu, 1977) – a handy phrase book for trekkers.

Tibet
Tibet Thubten Jigme Norbu & Colin Turnbull – an excellent account of the culture and religion of Tibet by the brother of the Dalai Lama.

The Secret War in Tibet Michel Peissel – a one-sided description of the resistance of Khampa warriors against the Chinese in Tibet; published in England as *Cavaliers of Kham.*

Seven Years in Tibet Heinrich Harrer – the best-selling book describing Harrer's adventures in Tibet before the Chinese occupation; also contains commentary on Harrer's discussions with the Dalai Lama.

Nepal Guidebooks
Kathmandu & the Kingdom of Nepal Prakash A Raj (Lonely Planet, Melbourne, 1985) – a complete guidebook to Nepal, written by an American-educated Nepali, resident in Kathmandu.

Nepal Namaste Robert Rieffel (Sahayogi Press, Kathmandu, 1978) – a good general guidebook written by a long-term resident of Kathmandu.

A Guide to Trekking in Nepal Stephen Bezruchka (The Mountaineers, Seattle, 1981) – detailed information about how to organise a backpacking or village inn trek; many route descriptions.

The Trekkers Guide to the Himalaya & Karakoram Hugh Swift, (London, Hodder & Stoughton, 1982) – route descriptions are not as detailed, but it covers a larger area than other books.

Treks on the Kathmandu Valley Rim Alton C Byers III (Sahayogi Press, Kathmandu, 1982) – one-day and overnight treks near Kathmandu.

Nepal Trekking Guidebooks John L Hayes (Avalok, Kathmandu, 1976) – a series of three guidebooks describing trekking routes in Nepal.

Nepal Trekking Christian Kleinert (Bergverlag Rudolf Rother, Munich, 1975) – a set of route descriptions in a fancy plastic cover that you can carry with you on your trek. Describes some very ambitious routes and schedules.

Other Guidebooks
Trekking in the Indian Himalaya Garry Weare (Lonely Planet, Melbourne 1985) – many treks in and around the famous hill stations and mountains beyond. Written by a professional trekking guide.

Kashmir, Ladakh & Zanskar – a travel survival kit Margaret & Rolf Schettler (Lonely Planet,

Melbourne 1985) – around India's beautiful north-west Vale of Kashmir; several treks included.

China – a travel survival kit Alan Samagalski & Michael Buckley (Lonely Planet, Melbourne 1985) – for those interested in venturing into recently-opened Tibet the 'back way'.

Medicine

Medicine for Mountaineering James A Wilkerson (The Mountaineers, Seattle, 1975) – an outstanding reference book for the layman. Describes many of the medical problems typically encountered in Nepal. One copy should accompany every trekking party.

Mountain Medicine Michael Ward (Crosby, Lockwood, Staples, London, 1975) – good background reading on cold and high altitude problems.

Where There is No Doctor David Werner (The Hesperian Foundation, Palo Alto, Calif, 1977) – a good layperson's guide with lots of application to Nepal.

Altitude Sickness Peter Hackett (American Alpine Club, New York, 1979) – required reading for anyone who treks above 4000 metres.

NEPAL TREKKING COMPANIES

There are more than 30 trekking companies in Nepal. The following are the names and addresses of those that are likely to reply to correspondence from overseas. To make this list I sent a letter and questionaire to every trekking company in Nepal; the list includes those that replied. If a company could not get it together to provide their name and address for this guidebook, it is unlikely that they would do very well in answering your letters. Not surprisingly, the list includes the biggest and best trekking companies, those that have office staff and can deal with correspondence. A complete list of trekking companies is available from the Department of Tourism, and a walk through the bazaars of Kathmandu will uncover a lot of offices that are not included in this list, or even in the list prepared by the Department

of Tourism. Many of these are reliable and easy to deal with in person once you arrive in Nepal even if they do not have a real office capable of handling inquiries by mail. Those companies that will arrange a sherpa are shown with an (S), those that will arrange a porter (or many porters) are shown with a (P) and those that will rent equipment are shown with an (E).

Ama Dablam Trekking (S) (P)
Thamel, PO Box 3035, Kathmandu
Tel: 216211
Cable AMADABLAM
Annapurna Mountaineering & Trekking
Durbar Marg, PO Box 76, Kathmandu
Tel: 212736, 211234, 211754, 212329, 211739
Telex: 2204 YETI, 2303 AMXREP
Cable: AMTREK
Express Trekking (S)(P)(E)
Naxal, Bhagabati Bahal, PO Box 339, Kathmandu
Tel: 213017
Cable: GREATREK
Himalayan Explorers (S)(P)(E)
Jyatha Tole, PO Box 1737, Kathmandu
Tel: 216142
Telex: 2268 PAGODA
Cable: HIMEXPLORE
Himalayan Journeys
Kantipath, PO Box 989, Kathmandu
Tel: 215855, 214626
Telex: 2344 HJTREK
Cable: JOURNEYS
International Trekkers (E)
Durbar Marg, PO Box 1273, Kathmandu
Tel: 215594
Telex: 2353 INTREK
Cable: INTREK
Journeys Mountaineering & Trekking (S)
Kantipath, PO Box 2034, Kathmandu
Tel: 213533, 414243
Telex: 2375 PEACE
Cable: JOMTREK
Lama Excursions (S)(P)(E)
Durbar Marg, PO Box 2485, Kathmandu
Tel: 211786, 215840
Telex: 2237
Manaslu Trekking (S)(P)
Durbar Marg, PO Box 1519, Kathmandu
Tel: 212422
Telex: 2205 AAPU
Cable: MANASTREK

Mountain Travel
 PO Box 170, Kathmandu
 Tel: 212808
 Telex: 2216 TIGTOP
 Cable: TREKKER
Natraj Trekking
 Kantipath, PO Box 606, Kathmandu
 Tel: 216644
 Telex: 2270 NATRAJ
 Cable: NATOURS
Nepal Treks & Natural History Expeditions
(S)(P)
 Ganga Path, PO Box 459, Kathmandu
 Tel: 212511
 Telex: 2239
 Cable: NEPTREK
Sherpa Co-operative Trekking (S)(P)
 Lake House, Kamal Pokhari, PO Box 1338,
 Kathmandu
 Tel: 215887
 Cable: SHERPAHUT
Sherpa Society (P)(E)
 Chabahil, Chuchepati, PO Box 1566,
 Kathmandu
 Tel: 216361
 Cable: SSTREK
Sherpa Trekking Service (S)(E)
 Kamaladi, PO Box 500, Kathmandu
 Tel: 216243, 212489
 Telex: 2205 AAPU
 Cable: SHERPTREK
Trans Himalayan Trekking
 Durbar Marg, PO Box 283, Kathmandu
 Tel: 213854, 213871
 Telex: 2233 THT
 Cable: TRANSEVIEW
Yeti Mountaineering & Trekking (S)(P)(E)
 Ramshah Path, Kathmandu
 Tel: 216841
 Telex: 2268 PAGODA

TREKKING AGENTS

It becomes difficult to prepare an up-to-date list of all trekking agents throughout the world because new agents spring up (and sometimes disappear) every season. This list gives the addresses of most agents who specialise in trekking. It includes overseas offices of Nepalese companies, tour operators who form entire groups to Nepal, and agents who sell space on treks organised by others. The huge number of agents now selling trekking makes it difficult to make any

judgment about the quality of service you may expect. From each of these agents you should be able to obtain any additional information you need about Nepal and trekking – most have staff who have trekked in Nepal. The list also concentrates on agents that have been organising treks in Nepal for several years – an indication that they know the details necessary to organise your trek properly and that they are financially stable. All these agents offer a variety of treks and several choices of dates; most of them can also arrange your plane tickets to and from Nepal if you wish. Most will also allow you to book your trek and flights through your own travel agent.

Australia & New Zealand
Adventure Travel Centre
 First Floor, 28 Market St, Sydney, NSW 2000.
Adventure Travel, New Zealand
 PO Box 6044, Napier, New Zealand.
Australian Himalayan Expeditions
 28-34 O'Connell St, Sydney, NSW 2000.
Ausventure
 860 Military Rd, PO Box 54, Mosman, NSW 2088.
AREA
 PO Box 4692, Sydney, NSW 2001.
Mandala Expedition
 168 Stirling Highway, Nedlands West 6009.
Peregrine Expeditions
 Suite 710, 343 Little Collins St, Melbourne, Vic 3000.
Venture Treks
 71 Evwlyn Rd, Howick, Aukland, New Zealand.
Travel Administration
 5th floor, 58 Pitt St, Sydney (tel 02 241 1136)

USA & Canada
Adventure Centre
 5540 College Ave, Oakland, California 94618.
Folkways International Trekking
 14903 SE Linden Lane, Milwaukie, Oregon 97222.
Himalayan Rover Trek
 PO Box 24382, Seattle, Washington 98124.
Himalayan Travel
 PO Box 481, Greenwich, Connecticut 06830.

Inner Asia
2627 Lombard St, San Francisco, California 94123.
Journeys International
PO Box 7545, Ann Arbor, Michigan 48107.
Mountain Travel
1398 Solano Ave, Albany, California 94706.
Mountain Travel Canada
737 Burley Drive, West Vancouver, BC V7T 1Z7.
Nature Expeditions International
PO Box 11496, Eugene, Oregon 97440.
Sobek Expeditions
PO Box 7007, Angels Camp, California 95222.
Wilderness Travel
1760 Solano Ave, Berkeley, California 94707.

United Kingdom
Exodus Expeditions
All Saints Passage, 100 Wandsworth High St, London SW18 4LE.
ExplorAsia
Blenheim House, Burnsall St, London SW3 5XS.
Himalayan Journeys
185 Streatham High Road, Streatham, London SW16 4EG.
Sherpa Expeditions
131A Heston Road, Hounslow, Middlesex, TW5 0RD.
WEXAS International
45 Brompton Road, Knightsbridge, London SW3 1DE.

France
Club Mediterranee
Place de la Bourse, 75088 Paris.
Delta Voyages
54 Rue des Ecoles, 75005 Paris.
Explorator
16 Place de la Madeleine, 75008 Paris.
Jean Louis Georges, Guides haute montagne
Herbeys, 38320.
Nouvelles Frontieres
37 rue Violet, 75015 Paris.

Germany
Dav Berg-und-Skischule
Furstenfelder Strasse 7, D 8000 Muenchen 2.
Hauser Exkursionen
Neuhauser Strasse 1, 8000 Muenchen 2.
Sporthaus Schuster
Rosenstrasse, 8000 Muenchen 2.

Other European Countries
Ulf Prytz Adventure Travel
PO Box 7573, Skillebaek, Oslo 2, Norway.
Norsk Rejsebureau
Frederiksberggade 10, 1459 Copenhagen, K. Denmark.
Arca Tour
Gartenstrasse 2, CH-6301 Zug, Switzerland.
ARTOU
8 rue de Rive, CH-1204 Geneve, Switzerland.
Intertrek
Lehnstrasse, CH-9050 Apenzell.
Trekking International
Via Giafrancesco Re, 78-10146 Torino, Italy.

Asia
Alpine Tour Service
7F Kawashima Hoshin Bldg, 2-2, 2-chome, Shimbashi, Monato-ku, Tokyo.
Saiyu Riyoko, 1-1-17 Kouraku Bunkiyoku, Tokyo.

Other
Holland International
Far East Shopping Centre, 545 Orchard Road No.06-01, Singapore 0923.
Mera Travel
Room 1308 Argyle Centre Phase 1, 688 Nathan Road, Kowloon, Hong Kong.
Peggy Craig Travel
Room 1002 Sea Bird House, 22-28 Wyndham St, Hong Kong

The Nepali Language

Nepali is the working tongue of Nepal and is understood by almost everyone in the country. Many ethnic groups have their own language which they speak amongst themselves and use Nepali outside their own region. The Sherpas speak Sherpa, Nepali and some Tibetan. Nepali is the mother tongue of the Brahmins, Chhetris and Thakurs – the highest castes in Nepal. It belongs to the Indo-Aryan or Sanskrit family of languages. Its nearest relative today is Kumaoni (spoken in a region of north-west India). Nepali has much in common with Hindi, the official language of India, which has the same origins. It has also taken many words from Persian, through Hindustani.

Some useful words and phrases are listed below. Since Nepali, like Hindi, uses the Devangari script, transliteration to Roman script is necessary. The transliteration system used here is from Meerendonk's book. To make it easier to see the difference in pronunciation, a double 'a' is used here where Meerendonk used an 'a' with a macron over it (ā).

Pronunciation

a	as in	balloon
aa	as in	father
e	as in	cafe
i	as in	rim
o	as in	go
u	as in	cuckoo
ai	as in	chaise

A big key to the correct pronounciation of Nepali is the 'a' and 'aa' sound. They sound like either the Australian a or the American a in 'mate' or 'take', both do not occur very frequently in Nepali. The Australian a is transliterated here as ai, as in *paisa* (money) and the American a is best represented by an e as in *tel* (oil) or *Nepaal*. The sound represented here by a single a is like the u sound in 'up' and the

sound of aa is a true 'a' sound as in 'car' or 'far'. *Chhang*, for example, sounds more like 'bung' or 'rung,' than 'clang' or 'bang'.

Another difficulty is the 'h' sound. In Nepali the h almost vanishes in pronunciation, particularly when it follows a consonant. Ask a Nepali to pronounce *dhungaa* (stone) and *dungaa* (boat); they will probably sound the same to you, as will *ghari* (wristwatch) and *gaari* (automobile). *Mahango* (expensive) sounds to a westerner like 'mungo', but a Nepali would include (and hear) the h sound. In the transliteration used here the true h sound is represented by hh (as in *chha*, to have, which is pronounced as in 'gotcha').

R's are rolled, and are pronounced almost like 'dr'; in fact some transliteration systems replace the r with a d or dr. Why is it not written as it sounds? Because each of these sounds is a different letter or character in the Devanagari script used to write Nepali, and in Nepali they are distinct letters and sounds – even if they sound the same to westerners. Nepali has more vowels than English, so English letters must be combined to represent these sounds.

Phrases

In Nepali the verb is placed at the end of a sentence. Grammatically, questions are identical to statements. The differentiation is made by the inflection of one's voice.

What is your name?
Timro naam ke ho?
My name is . . .
Mero naam . . . ho
Is the trail steep?
Baato ukaalo chha?
How are you?
Tapailai kasto chha?
Which trail goes to . . .?
Kun baato . . . jaanchha?

Where is my tent?
Mero tent kahaan chha?
The food is good?
Khaana mitho chha?
This river is cold
Yo kholaa chiso chha
What time is it (now)?
(aile) Kati bajyo?
It is 5 o'clock
Paanch bajyo
What is this?
Yo ke ho?
It is cold today
Aaja jaaro chha
It is raining
Paani parchha
That is OK
Thik chha
What is the name of this village?
Yo gaaunko naam ke ho?
Where is a shop?
Pasal kahaan chha?
Please give me a cup of tea
Ek cup chiyaa dinuhos
It is enough
Pugchha
I don't know
Thaahaa chhaina

25	*pachchis*
30	*tis*
40	*chaalis*
50	*pachaas*
60	*saathi*
70	*sattari*
80	*ashi*
90	*nabbe*
100	*ek say*
1000	*ek hajaar*

Vocabulary

hello, goodbye	*namaste*
thank you	*dhanyabaad*
bird	*charo*
chicken	*kukhoro*
cow	*gaai*
dog	*kukur*
horse	*ghoraa*
pig	*sungur*
water-buffalo	*bhainsi*
beer (local)	*chhang* or *jaanr*
whisky (local)	*rakshi*
tea	*chiyaa*
water	*paani*
hot water	*taato paani*
cold water	*chiso paani*
boiled water	*umaleko pani*
meat	*maasu*
bread	*roti*
egg	*phul*
food	*khaanaa*
vegetable	*saag*
cooked vegetable	*tarkaari*
rice (cooked)	*bhaat*
rice (uncooked)	*chaamal*
hot	*taato*
hot (spicy)	*piro*
tasty	*mitho*
mountain	*pqrbat*
river (small)	*kholaa*
river (large)	*nadi, kosi*
trail	*baato*
house	*ghar*
shop	*pasal*
latrine	*charpi*
steep (uphill)	*ukaalo*
steep (downhill)	*oraalo*
cold (weather)	*jaaro*
warm (weather)	*garam*

Numbers

1	*ek*
2	*dui*
3	*tin*
4	*chaar*
5	*paanch*
6	*chha* (some people say *chhe*)
7	*saat*
8	*aath*
9	*nau*
10	*das*
11	*eghaara*
12	*baahra*
13	*tehra*
14	*chaudha*
15	*pandhra*
16	*sohra*
17	*satra*
18	*athaara*
19	*unnaais*
20	*bis*

mother	*aamaa*	yes (it is ...)	*ho*
father	*baabu*	no (it is not ...)	*hoina*
son	*chhoro*	this	*yo*
daughter	*chhori*	that	*tyo*
younger sister	*bahini*	mine	*mero*
younger brother	*bhaai*	yours	*timro*
elder sister	*didi*	expensive	*mahango*
elder brother	*daai*	cheap	*sasto*
friend	*saathi*	big	*thulo*
day	*din*	small	*sano*
morning	*bihaana*	maybe	*hola*
night	*aat*	good	*ramro*
today	*aaja*	not good	*naraamro*
yesterday	*hijo*	clean	*saaph* or *saphaa*
tomorrow	*bholi*	dirty	*mailo*
day-after-tomorrow	*parsi*	heavy	*gahrungo*
sometime	*bholi-parsi*	his, hers	*unko*
happy	*khushi*	here	*yahaan*
left	*baayaan*	there	*tyahaan*
right	*daahine*	which	*kun*
tired	*thaakyo*	where	*kahaan*
enough	*pugyo*		

Index of Treks

Temperature

To convert °C to °F multiply by 1.8 and add 32

To convert °F to °C subtract 32 and multiply by ·55

Length, Distance & Area

	multiply by
inches to centimetres	2.54
centimetres to inches	0.39
feet to metres	0.30
metres to feet	3.28
yards to metres	0.91
metres to yards	1.09
miles to kilometres	1.61
kilometres to miles	0.62
acres to hectares	0.40
hectares to acres	2.47

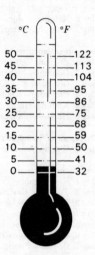

Weight

	multiply by
ounces to grams	28.35
grams to ounces	0.035
pounds to kilograms	0.45
kilograms to pounds	2.21
British tons to kilograms	1016
US tons to kilograms	907

A British ton is 2240 lbs, a US ton is 2000 lbs

Volume

	multiply by
Imperial gallons to litres	4.55
litres to imperial gallons	0.22
US gallons to litres	3.79
litres to US gallons	0.26

5 imperial gallons equals 6 US gallons
a litre is slightly more than a US quart, slightly less
than a British one

Guides to West Asia

India – a travel survival kit
An award-winning guidebook that is recognised as the outstanding contemporary guide to the subcontinent. Looking for a houseboat in Kashmir? Trying to post a parcel? This definitive guidebook has all the facts.

Kashmir, Ladakh & Zanskar – a travel survival kit
This book contains detailed information on three contrasting Himalayan regions in the Indian state of Jammu and Kashmir – the narrow valley of Zanskar, reclusive Ladakh, and the beautiful Vale of Kashmir.

Kathmandu & the Kingdom of Nepal – a travel survival kit
Few travellers can resist the lure of magical Kathmandu and its surrounding mountains. This guidebook takes you round the temples, to the foothills of the Himalaya, and to the Terai.

Pakistan – a travel survival kit
Pakistan has been called 'the unknown land of the Indus' and many people don't realise the great variety of experiences it offers – from bustling Karachi, to ancient cities and tranquil mountain valleys.

Trekking in the Indian Himalaya
The Indian Himalaya offers some of the world's most exciting treks. This book has advice on planning and equipping a trek, plus detailed route descriptions.

Trekking in Turkey
Western travellers have discovered Turkey's coastline, but few people are aware that just inland there are mountains with walks that rival those found in Nepal. This book, the first trekking guide to Turkey, gives details on treks that are destined to become classics.

Also Available:
Hindi/Urdu phrasebook, *Nepali phrasebook* and *Sri Lanka phrasebook*

Lonely Planet Guidebooks

Lonely Planet guidebooks cover virtually every accessible part of Asia as well as Australia, the Pacific, Central and South America, Africa, the Middle East and parts of North America. There are four main series: 'travel survival kits', covering a single country for a range of budgets; 'shoestring' guides with compact information for low-budget travel in a major region; trekking guides; and 'phrasebooks'.

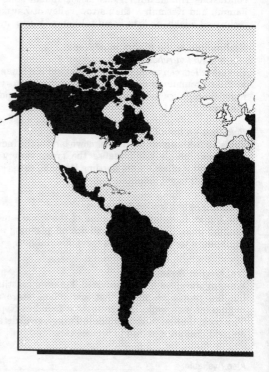

Mail Order

Lonely Planet guidebooks are distributed worldwide and are sold by good bookshops everywhere. They are also available by mail order from Lonely Planet, so if you have difficulty finding a title please write to us. US and Canadian residents should write to Embarcadero West, 112 Linden St, Oakland CA 94607, USA and residents of other countries to PO Box 617, Hawthorn, Victoria 3122, Australia.

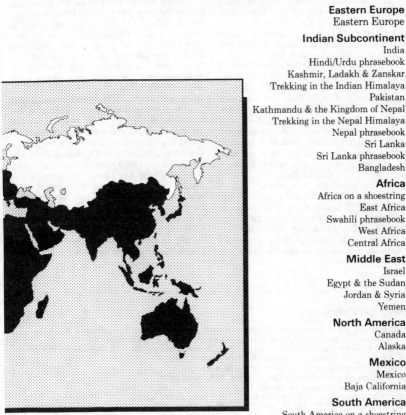

Lonely Planet

Lonely Planet published its first book in 1973. Tony and Maureen Wheeler had made a lengthy overland trip from England to Australia and, in response to numerous 'how do you do it?' questions, Tony wrote and they published *Across Asia on the Cheap*. It became an instant local best-seller and inspired thoughts of a second travel guide. A year and a half in South-East Asia resulted in their second book, *South-East Asia on a Shoestring*, which they put together in a backstreet Chinese hotel in Singapore in 1975. The 'yellow book', as it quickly became known, soon became *the* guide to the region and has gone through five editions, always with its familiar yellow cover.

Soon other writers came to them with ideas for similar books – books that went off the beaten track with an adventurous approach to travel, books that 'assumed you knew how to get your luggage off the carousel,' as one reviewer put it. Lonely Planet grew from a kitchen table operation to a spare room and then to its own office. It's international reputation began to grow as the Lonely Planet logo began to appear in more and more countries. In 1982 *India – a travel survival kit* won the Thomas Cook award for the best guidebook of the year.

These days there are over 70 Lonely Planet titles. Over 40 people work at our office in Melbourne, Australia and another half dozen at our US office in Oakland, California.

At first Lonely Planet specialised in the Asia region but these days we are also developing major ranges of guidebooks to the Pacific region, to South America and to Africa. The list of walking guides is growing and Lonely Planet now has a unique series of phrasebooks to 'unusual' languages. The emphasis continues to be on travel for travellers and Tony and Maureen still manage to fit in a number of trips each year and play a very active part in the writing and updating of Lonely Planet's guides.

Keeping guidebooks up to date is a constant battle which requires an ear to the ground and lots of walking, but technology also plays its part. All Lonely Planet guidebooks are now stored and updated on computer, and some authors even take lap-top computers into the field. Lonely Planet is also using computers to draw maps and eventually many of the maps will be stored on disk.

The people at Lonely Planet strongly feel that travellers can make a positive contribution to the countries they visit both by better appreciation of cultures and by the money they spend. In addition the company tries to make a direct contribution to the countries and regions it covers. Since 1986 a percentage of the income from each book has gone to aid groups and associations. This has included donations to famine relief in Africa, to aid projects in India, to agricultural projects in Nicaragua and other Central American countries and to Greenpeace's efforts to halt French nuclear testing in the Pacific. In 1988 over $40,000 was donated by Lonely Planet to these projects.

Lonely Planet Distributors

Australia & Papua New Guinea Lonely Planet Publications, PO Box 617, Hawthorn, Victoria 3122.
Canada Raincoast Books, 112 East 3rd Avenue, Vancouver, British Columbia V5T 1C8.
Denmark, Finland & Norway Scanvik Books aps, Store Kongensgade 59 A, DK-1264 Copenhagen K.
India & Nepal UBS Distributors, 5 Ansari Rd, New Delhi – 110002
Israel Geographical Tours Ltd, 8 Tverya St, Tel Aviv 63144.
Japan Intercontinental Marketing Corp, IPO Box 5056, Tokyo 100-31.
Netherlands Nilsson & Lamm bv, Postbus 195, Pampuslaan 212, 1380 AD Weesp.
New Zealand Transworld Publishers, PO Box 83-094, Edmonton PO, Auckland.
Singapore & Malaysia MPH Distributors, 601 Sims Drive, #03-21, Singapore 1438.
Spain Altair, Balmes 69, 08007 Barcelona.
Sweden Esselte Kartcentrum AB, Vasagatan 16, S-111 20 Stockholm.
Thailand Chalermnit, 108 Sukhumvit 53, Bangkok 10110.
Turkey Yab-Yay Dagitim, Alay Koshu Caddesi 12/A, Kat 4 no. 11-12, Cagaloglu, Istanbul.
UK Roger Lascelles, 47 York Rd, Brentford, Middlesex, TW8 0QP
USA Lonely Planet Publications, PO Box 2001A, Berkeley, CA 94702.
West Germany Buchvertrieb Gerda Schettler, Postfach 64, D3415 Hattorf a H.
All Other Countries refer to Australia address.